Palgrave Macmillan Transnational History Series

Titles include:

Palgrave Macmillan Transnational History Series
Series Standing Order ISBN 978–0–230–50746–3 Hardback
978–0–230–50747–0 Paperback
(*outside North America only*)

You can receive future titles in this series as they are published by placing a standing order. Please contact your bookseller or, in case of difficulty, write to us at the address below with your name and address, the title of the series and the ISBN quoted above.

Customer Services Department, Macmillan Distribution Ltd, Houndmills, Basingstoke, Hampshire RG21 6XS, England

Cold War Rivalry and the Perception of the American West

Pawel Goral

Department of History, University of Texas at Arlington, USA

First published 2014 by
PALGRAVE MACMILLAN

Palgrave Macmillan in the UK is an imprint of Macmillan Publishers Limited, registered in England, company number 785998, of Houndmills, Basingstoke, Hampshire RG21 6XS.

Palgrave Macmillan in the US is a division of St Martin's Press LLC, 175 Fifth Avenue, New York, NY 10010.

Palgrave Macmillan is the global academic imprint of the above companies and has companies and representatives throughout the world.

Palgrave® and Macmillan® are registered trademarks in the United States, the United Kingdom, Europe and other countries.

ISBN 978–1–137–36429–6

This book is printed on paper suitable for recycling and made from fully managed and sustained forest sources. Logging, pulping and manufacturing processes are expected to conform to the environmental regulations of the country of origin.

A catalogue record for this book is available from the British Library.

A catalog record for this book is available from the Library of Congress.

To my parents, Barbara and Bogdan Goral

Contents

Illustrations

Series Editors' Preface

A fascinating subject of study in the broad field of transnational history is the question of what may be termed "transnational memory," that is, how various nations seek to understand the past, not just their own but also that of other people. It may be as much transnational imagination as transnational memory in that imagination and memory are frequently interlocked, one influencing the other. Works of art, from literature and paintings to music and dramas, contribute to and reinforce historical memory and imagination.

In a book published in the Palgrave Macmillan Transnational History series, *Europeanization in the Twentieth Century* (edited by Martin Conway and Kiran Klaus Patel), the editors speak of the European Union as "a community of shared memory." Europeans have endeavored to understand their collective history as a shared experience. To the extent that they have succeeded, they have been able to imagine a past in which they and their forebears have all taken part. One may wonder if other regions of the world have developed, or will be able to develop, similar communities of shared memory.

A trans-Atlantic search for transnational memory is presented in this book. It describes a fascinating story of how Germans after the Second World War sought to relate the history of the American West to their own recent past. Having experienced the devastating war and now become divided into West Germany and East Germany, respectively tied to the United States and the Soviet Union during the Cold War, postwar Germans incorporated what they understood of the American experiences in "the wild west" to their own recent history. And they did so through movies, "German Westerns." The stories of the "wild west," in particular the relationship between American Indians and white frontiers and cowboys held a fascination for Germans at many levels: the frontier experience, the heroism – or the brutality – of the frontiersmen, their relationship with native Americans, race prejudice as well as efforts to overcome it, interracial cohabitation and miscegenation, and many others.

How the two Germanys incorporated their understanding of American history into their own self-definition makes fascinating history. As the author shows, selective themes from the story of the

American west – from frontier heroism to the extermination of an alien race – had obvious relevance to Germany's own recent past, so that such phenomena as Nazism and the Holocaust could be seen not as uniquely German but rather as transnational. As the author notes, German Westerns were "transnational products that created transnational heroes in which both West Germans and East Germans found superheroes with whom they could identify." Of course, not only superheroes but super villains abounded both in the American west and in Nazi Germany, so one could find "good Germans" and "bad Germans" to identify with among the American frontiersmen and American Indians. In so doing, the makers and viewers of "German Westerns" were blending, at times even equating, the experiences of the two nations.

This may have been a rather unusual instance of transnational imagination and memory sharing, but we may place it in the context of what goes on daily in the contemporary world. We relate ourselves to worldwide occurrences, whether domestic upheavals, natural disasters, or struggles for the rights of women and minorities, in terms of personal and local agendas. In so doing, we may collectively be searching for a shared understanding of the past. That may be one important consequence of a transnationally shared history; global, national, and personal identities become blurred, "blended" in the author's term, so that rather than emphasizing our differences from one another, eventually we shall come to see all humans as interrelated.

Acknowledgments

Inspiration for this project came during my numerous meetings with Thomas Adam – my dissertation chair and mentor. Thomas inspired me to write my dissertation, and then this book, reminding me of how as a boy I used to dream of the Wild West created by my favorite author, Karl May, and his heroes, Old Shatterhand and Winnetou, who showed how good always defeated evil.

I would like to thank other scholars who assisted me in the course of my research and writing. I am especially indebted to Joyce Goldberg, Sam W. Haynes, Meredith McClain, and Steven Reinhardt.

I would also like to thank other scholars, librarians, archivists, and friends whom I would like to recognize for their support: Kim Breuer; Elisabeth Cawthon; Stephanie Cole; William Dulaney; Robert Fairbanks; John Garrigus; Stephen Maizlish; Christopher Morris; Stanley Palmer, the University of Texas at Arlington; Ute Klawitter, Bundesarchiv-Filmarchiv, Berlin; Wiebke Witzel, Archiv der Berlin-Brandenburgischen Akademie der Wissenschaften; Judith Leitz, Bibliothek und Textarchiv des Deutschen Filminstituts, Frankfurt am Mein; Andreas Barth; Wanda Brooks; Grace Darling; Robin Deeslie; and the most helpful staff at the Central Library at the University of Texas at Arlington. Last but not least, I would like to thank the reviewers who commented on my manuscript, the editors at Palgrave Macmillan, as well as the editorial board of the Transnational History Series.

I also thank my parents, Barbara and Bogdan Goral, and my wife, Andrea, without whose support this project would never have happened.

Introduction

Many American movie viewers might find it amazing to see Western films and hear "the white-Stetsoned cowman growl 'Hände Hoch!' while his lips are forming the English words, 'Better put up your hands.'" It might further bewilder them to realize that they are not watching American actors whose voices were dubbed by their German counterparts, but German-written films in which German actors play cowboys and Indians. "Only then will some Americans," as Richard Cracroft pointed out, "experience an intellectual epiphany, a realization that Europeans (along with Asians, South Americans, Australians, and nearly everyone else) have distinctive, indigenous, deep-seated literary and cultural traditions regarding life in the American West..." Indeed, there is a longstanding Wild West literary tradition in most European literatures which, in some cases, equates to, or even transcends in significance that of the United States.[1] Moreover, a distinct Western cinematic tradition developed in Europe as well. It started in West Germany with the production of the first Karl May film in 1962 and shortly after enveloped other parts of the Old World. Following the arrival of American actors Clint Eastwood and Yul Brynner, Italy became a second Hollywood. The Yugoslavian film company Jadran, which coproduced all Karl May Westerns, became the favorite site for American filmmakers, coproducing *Navarone* and *War and Remembrance*, among others.[2]

This book demonstrates how the two adversaries of the Cold War, West Germany and East Germany, endeavored to create two distinct and unique German identities. This proved to be a complicated process whereby two newly created German states chose myths from another country located in another hemisphere to come to terms with their own recent past and articulate a vision for a better future. In their endeavor to claim legitimacy, the German cinematic representation

1

of the American West became an important cultural weapon of mass dissemination during the Cold War. Additionally, while attempting to portray what it meant to be German, the competition between the two German states resulted in the creation of transnational productions, with transnational heroes, in a transnational setting, eagerly embraced on both sides of the Iron Curtain as their own.

The most influential of all German novelists was a little-known failed schoolteacher in Saxony who had never visited the United States before writing his famous *Winnetou* novels. More than 100 million copies of his books were sold worldwide and his novels were translated into over 30 languages. Despite the popularity of his works, Karl May remains virtually unknown in the United States, even though his works first appeared there in 1899 and his best-known novels concern the myth of the American West. While May's novels do not appeal to American readers, it is essential for American cultural historians to study them since these novels have influenced readers around the world for more than a century and created an image of the United States that still has a powerful grip on people's imagination. It does not matter that this image was not based upon first-hand experience and is more fiction than reality. It is a powerful image that cannot be ignored.[3]

May's novels had a tremendous impact upon the creation of German identities and the European perception of the United States. Karl May Westerns, based on the novels of May and produced during the 1960s, proved to be the most successful film series in postwar West German history. Amid the Cold War rivalry and in facing the troubling Nazi past, Karl May Westerns became the quintessence of the German Western tradition and provided essential understanding of German–Indian relations.

Furthermore, the production of Karl May films instantaneously triggered the production of Westerns in East Germany which proved tremendously popular as well. Perhaps as many as 10 million people viewed the first East German Western, *The Sons of Great Mother Bear*. This is truly an astounding number considering that the population of East Germany amounted to only 16 million. Indians were presented as a vanishing people who left open territory for European settlers. While West German movies presented the genocide of Native Americans from the perspective of white settlers, East German movies depicted it from the perspective of Native Americans.

Because May's works had been favored by Adolf Hitler, they could be published only in West Germany.[4] Therefore, East Germany's film company (DEFA) labeled its own Westerns *Indianerfilme* to distinguish them from their West German counterparts. Threatened by the popularity of Karl May films, which were easily accessible to nearly all East Germans since access to West German television stations was assured by West German technology, the East German government charged DEFA (East Germany's state-owned film studio) with producing a version of the myth of the American West that would counteract the popularity of Karl May films. DEFA hired Liselotte Welskopf-Henrich, a history professor at Humboldt University, author of children's books, and an ardent supporter of Native American rights in the United States, to produce the script. The first of the series of *Indianerfilme*, released in 1966, challenged the traditional interpretation of the myth of the American West, which both American and Karl May films propagated. Unlike the latter, *Indianerfilme* made individual Indians the central heroes of their films and portrayed white settlers as greedy and primitive, bound to eradicate the Native American nations either for pleasure or in pursuit of gold. In addition, Welskopf-Henrich's reputation as a historian and her knowledge of Native American culture were supposed to add credibility to the films as DEFA strove not only for entertainment, but also for accuracy. The uniqueness of East German Westerns lay in the emphasis upon the heroism of the Indians, rather than the cowboys and pioneers. Moreover, the *Indianerfilme* openly castigated the genocide that occurred on the American frontier.[5]

Between 1945 and 1989, films shaped people's understanding of the Cold War rivalry (one could make the argument that they still do). American cultural products dominated in both German states from the beginning of the Cold War.[6] For Germany, practically the only country that could compete with the United States in film production before World War II, the film industry had always been a significant contributor to the German national consciousness as well as to the creation of national identity. Thus, to deny the validity of films as a tool for disseminating history could condemn us to ignorance, especially because a great number of people, the younger generations in particular, learn history through the medium of cinematography. Some historians argue that cinema has been the most effective medium of history, given its diversity of approaches and the richness of imaginative experience.[7] Cinema has reached billions of viewers worldwide and most likely will continue to shape people's understanding of historical events in years to come. While historians have often focused on phenomena such as migration to demonstrate how the United States was connected transnationally, the interchange of cultures and cultural elements needs a more exhaustive examination.[8] The study of culture in a transnational context will further demonstrate that links between nations are not one-way, but reciprocal.[9] In this case, the creation of an American identity, based on the American myth of the frontier, by non-Americans for non-Americans during an ideological conflict that spanned the intersection of various cultural realms, serves as a great example of intercultural transfer. The portrayal of important national myths underwent a transformation during which national identity was negotiated and the final product, the German Western, had a tremendous influence upon Germans and provoked a response from its inventors across the Atlantic. Therefore, this book focuses mainly on the deconstruction of the major themes those powerful German Western films conveyed, supported, when available, by relevant press releases, archival documents, as well as the most recent scholarship regarding transnational, cultural, and Cold War history to demonstrate that history is a complex weaving together of coexisting histories.[10]

In 1944, 6484 movie theaters operated in Germany. Most of them were destroyed during Allied aerial attacks on German cities. By the end of 1945, 1150 movie theaters were open for business. Within a year, however, this number doubled to 2125, and grew to 3360 by the end of 1949.[11] In a world marked by destruction, the movie theaters not only entertained and informed, but they also became the center of social and cultural life, where Germans of all ages enjoyed the fantasy of the cinematic world.[12] Only two months after the war ended, newly rebuilt movie theaters were crowded again, not necessarily due to the popularity of the films, but because the theaters provided basic comforts, such as an intact roof and heat. Attendance rates of the early 1950s significantly dwarfed those of prewar Germany.[13]

The fact that the German film industry had to start almost anew, however, allowed Hollywood productions to take the lead in the German film market, which only contributed to the equating of American film characters, including Western heroes, with the American landscape and ideals, most importantly freedom, justice, and democracy.[14] Regardless of the impact of American culture upon Germany, American culture retained the status of the other, as proper German cultural values and traditions were juxtaposed against "materialist, morally risqué, or just noisy, violent, and 'uncivilized' American mass culture."[15] In essence, not only the battle was waged for the dominance of German markets, but also more importantly, the German state and religious leaders fought a battle for the cultural sovereignty of Germany, tantamount to defining the identity of the German nation.[16]

To grow up in West Germany after World War II meant a delicate equilibrium between the legacy of the high culture, the legacy of the Nazi past, and liberation, escape, and restructuring with the help of the United States. Some West Germans saw the United States as an exporter of primitive, inferior products that corrupted the youth and mongrelized German high culture and Germany's cultural integrity. West German elites condemned the United States "as the producer of Wild West and gangster films, the insidious propagator of secularized commercial culture that addressed itself directly to the viewer, bypassing the mediation of traditional cultural and religious elites."[17] West German society underwent a masculinity crisis after the end of World War II. With the high number of men killed on the battlefields, and others imprisoned in the Soviet Union in the 1950s, the crisis had a great impact on national identity. The crisis seemed severe and demanded immediate action.[18] Uta Poiger points out that men, often physically and psychologically debilitated by the war, felt they had not proven themselves as the defenders of and providers for women and children. Additionally, hardly anyone wanted to talk about the atrocities committed by the Wehrmacht.[19]

With the defeat of Nazi Germany, the quest for German identity started anew. The legacy of the Nazi past, changes to the external borders of Germany, internal administrative reforms, and enormous population movements, let alone the division into initially four occupation zones and later two distinct German states, all influenced the shaping of postwar Germanies. There are significant differences between how West Germans and East Germans understood and discussed the Nazi past. In East Germany, the "Thälmann cult" prevailed and was perpetuated through the connection drawn between Georgi Dimitrov's interpretation of fascism and the perceived aggressiveness of capitalism. According to this interpretation, fascism was considered the last and most extreme form of capitalism and so was likely to reoccur in any of the advanced capitalist societies (in West Germany in particular). In West Germany, the younger generation faced parents who had committed themselves to absolute silence regarding their involvement in the Nazi crimes.[20] How individual Germans dealt with the immediate past undoubtedly differed widely. Because both East German and West German governments actively engaged in shaping the politics of memory, including contesting and contradicting their shared history, two distant postwar German identities emerged based on memories of the Nazi past. The politics of memory has been a delicate and important point of German history, especially after the end of World War II. Not only did the West German approach to the Nazi past differ from the East German one, but there were also crucial differences in understanding the crimes of National Socialism.

In the immediate aftermath of World War II, some of the crucial political discussions revolved around the issue of German guilt. With many Germans facing potential charges of war crimes and crimes against humanity, the issue of guilt affected both Germany as a nation as well as Germans as individuals. Thus, the dilemma that required immediate attention concerned the question of who should be held responsible for what had happened, all Germans or just their leaders?[21] What constituted guilt and who was guilty? How does one distinguish those guilty from those who, though they never killed or tortured anyone with their own hands, had also become part of the Nazi killing machine? As Roderick Stackelberg pointed out, "Most Germans probably did not want to know about the death camps and the gas chambers" because "ignorance could serve as a convenient shield for the moral conscience."[22]

Few Nazis actually faced trial in West Germany. Only 6000 Nazis stood trial in West Germany between 1945 and 1992. This was an incredibly low number compared with East Germany, where about 12,000 Nazis stood trial, given that East Germany's total population was only 16 million compared with 60 million of West Germans. Thus, a great majority of Nazis escaped justice. Moreover, the 6000 Nazis convicted by West German courts seldom served their sentences. And, in the American zone of occupation alone, only 1654 party members were considered "major offenders," out of the 3.6 million party members who underwent the denazification process.[23]

The chaos in the immediate aftermath of the war also helped many Nazis, who managed to conceal their true identity, to escape punishment. Thus, perhaps as many as 80,000 Nazis found a way to transition to civilian life without ever being asked what they had done during the war.[24] Moreover, as time passed and the recent memories of the war became increasingly distant, many Germans actually began to portray themselves as victims of the Nazi regime.[25] Willy Brandt's kneeling before the memorial to the Warsaw Ghetto in 1971 dismayed some Germans, especially the conservatives, for whom "we didn't know" of the immediate aftermath of the war had its equivalent "we still don't want to know" in the 1970s and after.[26]

Despite being blood brothers, Karl May's German frontiersman Old Shatterhand could not help Winnetou, the chief of the Apache, to save his nation. This message of Karl May films may have inadvertently reflected the legacy of the Nazi past at a time when a younger generation of West Germans began asking questions about the role of their fathers and grandfathers in the Holocaust, although the latter persisted in refusing to reveal their memories. Chapters 1 and 2 examine connections between the extermination of Native Americans and the Holocaust at the time when the crimes of the Nazi past were reintroduced to the West German public through the capture and trial of Adolf Eichmann and the Auschwitz Trials of the 1960s. Also examined is East German society's attitude toward the Holocaust based on the messages *Indianerfilme* conveyed. Unlike the message of absolution that was so central in Karl May films, *Indianerfilme* condemn capitalism as the factor that led to the extermination of the indigenous peoples of North America. *Indianerfilme* indict the Western bloc and its capitalist values as a driving force for the Holocaust. The two chapters focus on the notion of genocide and elaborate on how the myth of the frontier in both Karl May films and *Indianerfilme* link the genocide of Native Americans to the Holocaust. Some historians, rather flamboyantly, go so far as to say that Karl May might have made Hitler possible. At the same time, one can also assert that *Winnetou* "functioned after the war and the Holocaust—at least phantasmatically—to undo them."[27] Whereas Chapter 1 demonstrates how Karl May Westerns conveyed implicit messages of absolution at the time when young West Germans began asking questions about their parents' lives under the Nazis, and which coincided with the trials of former Nazi officials, Chapter 2 discusses how *Indianerfilme* formed the blueprint for Socialism in East Germany and indicted the Western bloc for the crimes of genocide in both the American West and during World War II.

Chapter 3 assesses the popularity of Karl May films in West Germany and *Indianerfilme* in East Germany. Both became the most successful film series in their respective countries and elevated the actors who starred in them to celebrity status. It also explains how these actors became the German heroes of the transnational American West. Lex Barker, who played Old Shatterhand, and Pierre Brice, who played Winnetou, became the embodiment of what it meant to be German in West Germany. In East Germany there had been no actors who enjoyed the celebrity status of Gojko Mitic, the Yugoslavian actor who played lead roles in all the *Indianerfilme*. The chapter discusses the heroes they played, the values they propagated, and their significance during the ideological rivalry between the two German states. It analyzes the similarities and differences between both forms of the Western film, and compares the messages, both explicit and less conspicuous, they conveyed. Last, the chapter examines the quintessential element of the transnational Westerns: the landscape. Both genres set out to replicate the American West, but because their visions of the American West came from different sources and conveyed different messages even though both chose Yugoslavia as their filming sites, they resulted in the creation of two distinct portrayals of the American West.

Chapter 4 continues the examination of selected elements of transnationalism in German Westerns, and the relationship between Old Shatterhand and Winnetou in particular. While Karl May films and novels suggest that the demise of Native civilizations that stood in the way of the progress and the prosperity of the European colonizers was inevitable, *Indianerfilme*'s heroes manage to stand their ground and, at times, even defeat the greedy white aggressors. The chapter compares Winnetou with the Indian heroes of *Indianerfilme* and also discusses heroism on the frontier, including the treatment of African Americans, and the role of women. This chapter also discusses the concept of intercultural transfer and how studies in cultural transference not only deepen our understanding of national histories, but also inextricably point to the importance of understanding national events from a transnational perspective.

Although the German Western tradition borrowed heavily from American sources, no one contributed more to the creation of the German myth of the American frontier than Karl May. But, as Chapter 5 demonstrates, long before May began working on *Winnetou*, many Germans believed in a German–Indian affinity due to the influence of writers and linguists as well as early German–Indian interactions in Pennsylvania and Texas. The Teutonic–Indian brotherhood of German-American frontiersman Old Shatterhand, and Winnetou, chief of the Apache, became the main theme of May's Western novels. The chapter illustrates the ways in which May influenced the German perception of the American West and his contribution to the emergence of a truly national culture through the creation of an appealing and eagerly accepted image of the United States to millions of his viewers. The chapter describes the creation of the first Karl May film and how its popularity exceeded even the filmmakers' expectation, resulting in the most successful film series in West German history. Last, the chapter focuses on Welskopf-Henrich's critical examination of Karl May's works and her involvement in the cause of the American Indian Movement, as well as her contribution to the script of the first *Indianerfilm*.

The production of the first German Western intensified the cultural contest between the two German states and further deepened the cultural divide between them, thus contributing to the formation of two distinct identities. Despite the ambivalence and, in some cases, outright hostility toward Americanization, West Germany's Cold War liberal identity became intertwined with the consumption of American cultural products even before the production of the first West German Western, *The Treasure of Silver Lake*, in 1962, soon followed by the *Winnetou* trilogy. East Germany responded to the increasing popularity of Westerns in 1966 by producing its first *Indianerfilm*, *The Sons of Great Mother Bear*, followed by another 13 movies. East German Westerns, however, used the American genre and the myth of the American West to denounce the hegemony of American culture as well as to distinguish itself from both the Nazi past and its West German neighbor. By appropriating the American genre and responding to West German Westerns, DEFA Westerns contested and negotiated the meanings of German national and cultural identity.

The United States' national symbols and myths have become an international iconographic language, a visual lingua franca.[28] A case study of German Westerns demonstrates how the adversaries of the Cold War who endeavored to create two distinct and unique German identities successfully transformed the American genre of the Western. The two German states chose myths from another country located in another hemisphere to come to terms with their own dark past and articulate a vision for a better future. The subsequent creation of their own versions of the myth of the American West by non-Americans for non-Americans during an ideological conflict that spanned the intersection of various cultural realms, revolutionized the Western, as a result of which it became a transnational weapon of influence, designed to help Germans in their quest for a new identity and helping them understand what it meant to be German.[29]

1
Karl May Westerns and the Conquest of the American West

The first West German Western

Less than a century ago, the Far West was still a land which was unknown. It attracted all kinds of men; pioneers, seeking a new home; adventurers seeking excitement and gold. But the West also attracted the outcasts of society; criminals, chased by the forces of law and order; bandits; killers; tramps. And then, there were those who fought for the cause of justice. Such a man was Charles Vaillant, known as Old Shatterhand, a hunter and trapper. His friend and blood brother was Winnetou, chief of the Apaches. We shall follow them through the valleys and drags of the mountains. We shall live with them the adventure of a desperate struggle for the possession of fabulous wealth.[1]

So starts the first West German Western, *The Treasure of Silver Lake*, released in 1962. The two main characters, Old Shatterhand and Winnetou, discover the site of the ambush of a stagecoach. Following the trails, they enter a nearby town, where they promise a young man to help avenge the death of his father. It turns out that Engel, the murdered man, had half of the map that was to lead him, his son Fred, his business partner Patterson, and Patterson's daughter Ellen, to the treasure buried in the Silver Lake area. Led by Winnetou and Old Shatterhand, Engel's son Fred and two other frontiersmen know they need to leave immediately to find the bandits. They encounter an Indian village en route to the Silver Lake, a horrible site of a massacre of Indian women and children. The Colonel's band committed another atrocity while Indian men were gone hunting for buffaloes. Upon the Indian men's return, they see Old Shatterhand, Winnetou, and the others, and immediately assume they are facing the perpetrators. They continue to chase them until Old Shatterhand agrees to follow them to their camp to allow the tribal elders to decide whether Old Shatterhand told them the truth. Old Shatterhand must fight Big Wolf, a fierce warrior, to prove his innocence. He defeats his opponent, but refuses to kill him, as he wants them to believe he is a friend of the Indians. Old Shatterhand and his friends leave the Indian camp, but unbeknown to Big Wolf, some Indians decide to follow them, still unconvinced Old Shatterhand had nothing to do with the massacre of their families. At the last moment, just as a fight is about to start, Big Wolf arrives and tells the Indians that Old Shatterhand must be allowed to go, as he honorably defeated him and gained his freedom. Old Shatterhand and Winnetou tell the Indians that they are close to capturing the one responsible for the massacre. The Indians join the hunt for the Colonel. Once justice is done, they all go back to their homes, while Old Shatterhand and Winnetou ride away through the prairie in search of another adventure.

The production of the first German Western intensified the cultural contest between the two German states and further deepened the cultural divide between them, thus contributing to the formation of two distinct identities. Despite the ambivalence and, in some cases, outright hostility toward Americanization, West Germany's Cold War liberal identity became intertwined with the consumption of American cultural products even before the production of the first West German Western, *The Treasure of Silver Lake*, in 1962, soon followed by the *Winnetou* trilogy. The Karl May Westerns, next to Edgar Wallace thrillers, proved to be the most popular films of the 1960s. East Germany responded to the increasing popularity of Westerns in 1966 by producing its first *Indianerfilm*, *The Sons of the Great Bear*, followed by another 11 movies. East German Westerns, however, used the American genre and the myth of the American West to denounce the hegemony of American culture as well as to distinguish itself from both the Nazi past and its West German neighbor. By appropriating the American genre and responding to West German Westerns, DEFA Westerns contested and negotiated the meanings of German national and cultural identity. Crucially, the Holocaust and the memory of the Nazi past influenced the way the collective identity was shaped on both sides of the Iron Curtain.

West Germany and denazification

When the Allies agreed to the creation of provisional postwar zones of occupation at the Yalta Conference in 1945, no one imagined that by the end of the decade there would still be two different German states, each representing the ideological contest between capitalism and communism. Immediately after the war, Germans living in a shattered country focused on survival and could hardly remain passive as the occupying authorities decided the future of their country. By 1948, it became more and more apparent to all the parties involved that the occupying authorities' competing visions of Germany's future would result in the division of Germany into two states. Regardless of the potency of German political parties, which started developing shortly after the war ended, the former World War II allies were going to make crucial decisions regarding the postwar shape of the German state. Thus, the permanent division of Germany into two states by 1949 precipitated a quest for German identity and contributed to the emergence of competing interpretations of Germanness across the Iron Curtain.

In West Germany, the issues that had the biggest impact on the shaping of national identity proved to be the legacy of the Nazi era and the immediate results of World War II. Many West Germans doubted whether a return to "normality" was possible. Others believed that normality was not even desirable. The debates over a West German identity revolved around the question of whether West Germany was indeed an "abnormal" state due to its legal status as the successor of the Third Reich. Indeed, many Germans agreed with West German President Gustav Heinemann's assertion that Germany was a "difficult fatherland."[2]

West Germans defined their two most important diplomatic objectives as the maintenance of bilateral relationships with the Western allies and prevention of a Soviet invasion. Another goal proved to be equally important, namely, West Germans would try to rebuild their image as trustworthy members of the international community. Discussions ranged from whether the goal could be achieved through honest confrontation regarding the Nazi past to whether the West Germans should keep a low profile and avoid discussing their responsibility for the Nazi crimes. Ruth Wittlinger has shown that the West Germans found an attractive way out of this dilemma by subscribing to notions of cosmopolitanism and a post-national identity as opposed to narrow-minded and backward-looking nationalism. Focusing on the present and the future seemed more appealing than discussing the years of Nazism that many West Germans never wanted to discuss again. Thus, a commitment to universal values allowed for the creation of a new collective identity, strengthened by the economic miracle of the 1950s and based on the rule of law that guaranteed political and economic stability. In the words of the first West German Chancellor, Konrad Adenauer, West Germany would become the antithesis of the Third Reich.[3]

West Germans, however, did not neglect the fact that they were not a fully sovereign nation. Thus, regardless of the influences and popularity of American culture, West Germans did not identify the United States only with popular products such as films, Coca-Cola, or jeans and rock and roll. They also believed that they were a nation under occupation, even though they enjoyed an incomparably higher level of autonomy than did East Germany under Soviet control. The number of American troops stationed in West Germany, which tripled between 1950 and 1953 to a quarter million and was maintained at this level for almost four decades, reminded Germans on a daily basis that West Germany was not a sovereign state.[4] American GIs and the perceived "moral deterioration that followed the troops into the *Heimat*," causing a "bleeding, dangerous wound to local communities," intertwined with "an explosion of the entertainment industry."[5] Thus, not only did American troops cause distress, but they also caused open resentment, despite the economic benefits their presence brought, which accounted partially for the economic revival of the regions where they were stationed.

The ways that Germans dealt with their past changed over time, but inexorably affected the shaping of postwar German identity. Indeed, the Holocaust influenced every aspect of Germans' lives, from politics to culture. The trauma caused the people involved to question their identity, and it caused many of the perpetrators to deny and repress the memory of their crimes.[6] When the Karl May Western era began in West Germany in the 1960s, it coincided with the trial of Adolf Eichmann in Jerusalem and the Frankfurt Auschwitz trials. Thus, German Westerns and the racist stereotypes of the American West should be understood in the context of Germans' relationship with the Holocaust. For many West Germans, the frontier seemed to offer absolution and forgiveness for the genocide of World War II and a definite break with the troubling past.[7]

Following World War II, the German state underwent significant administrative changes. Not only were two German states established under the protectorate of the United States and the Soviet Union, the two newly created Germanies carried out many significant administrative reforms as well. Internal administrative changes, both prior to the creation of the two German states as well as after 1949, implemented by the German governments in their respective zones, forced some Germans to identify with newly created states without any roots in history.[8] One of the greatest powers and symbols of the might of Imperial Germany, Prussia, ceased to exist, thus postwar Germany experienced the destruction of traditional units of organization and, at the same time, it had to adjust to its new external borders. Significantly, not only did the two German states' political orientations conflict with each other, but the two states disputed which one constituted Germany territorially. Whereas West Germany did not acknowledge the Oder-Neisse border and kept the issue of national territory open, East Germany strongly criticized its western neighbor's territorial claims and used them to equate capitalist West Germany with National Socialism. The Oder-Neisse line had always been depicted as the East German-Polish border on East German maps from the inception of the GDR, though the German state was not always referred to as East Germany. Sometimes the mapmakers simply labeled it as Germany. Moreover, even a few years after the creation of the two German states, West Germany did not even appear on East German maps, since East German maps depicted the entire country as Germany. Contrary to the East German emphasis on precision, West Germany's mapmakers allowed for a great degree of ambiguity. West Germany used three different Eastern boundary lines: the border between the two German states; the Oder-Neisse border; and the border of the German Empire as of December 31, 1937, which West Germany considered to be the legal basis of a future reunited Germany. The use of the German-Polish boundary of 1937 did not become controversial until two decades after the war. West Germany eventually ceased to use the border of 1937 to represent Germany's eastern border; however, West Germany's Supreme Court ruled in 1973 that not only was West Germany the only true representative of Germany, but that the German Empire continued to exist as a legal entity. The Oder-Neisse boundary was only recognized in November 1990, shortly after the reunification of Germany.[9] Whereas on West German maps West Germany was divided into proper German Lands, East Germany was labeled as "The Soviet Zone of Occupation," and Silesia and Eastern Prussia were labeled as "German Eastern Territories under Polish and Soviet Administration."

One of the greatest postwar population movements occurred in Central Europe after World War II. More than 15 million non-Germans either occupied or resided in Germany, including millions liberated from concentration and labor camps, thousands of refugees who fled from the Red Army and territories occupied by the Soviet Union, as well as millions of soldiers of the occupying forces. Although historians still debate the numbers, over 10 million ethnic Germans either fled or were expelled from Czechoslovakia, Hungary, Yugoslavia, Romania, and Poland, including from the newly incorporated territories of the former Silesia and East Prussia, in order to do away with any new pretext for future German aggression. A great majority of the refugees fled to Western Germany, where they were often unwelcome and considered aliens, due to the political and cultural baggage they carried with them.[10] Moreover, tens of thousands of East Germans fled the newly created East German state to West Germany until construction of the Berlin Wall in 1961. Essentially, German-speaking immigrants constituted about 20 percent of the West German population.[11] In addition to the great population movement, the division of Germany, first into four occupational zones and later into two distinct states, followed by domestic administrative reforms, engendered further the quest for self-understanding of the German identity. Undoubtedly, the mass migrations of the immediate postwar era must have made people reconsider their national identity and made them ponder the meaning of their past and its consequences for their future.

East and West Germany competed with each other in another important sphere: the politics of memory. In their quest for legitimacy, nothing was as important as the legacy of the Nazi past. While West Germany saw East Germany as a continuation of the rule of totalitarianism, East Germany took pride in the alleged successful denazification within its borders. While the recent past had a great impact on ordinary citizens in both East and West Germans, they gradually ceased to become concerned with the Holocaust and Nazi crimes against humanity, but rather, as David F. Crew pointed out, with "the suffering to which ordinary Germans had been subjected during and immediately after the war: hunger, homelessness, mass rape, flight, deportation, and forced labor." In addition, the "memories of hunger and deprivation during the First World War, the postwar inflation, and the world economic depression after 1929" only exacerbated the gravity of their plight.[12] Moreover, "the combination of Hitler's 'economic miracle' (the result of the rearmament boom in the mid/late 1930s) and the first deliriously successful years of the Second World War had tantalized many Aryan Germans with the dream of a brilliant national future," which only contributed to the bitterness of the despair in the immediate aftermath of the war. Thus, the competition manifested itself in the economic dimension as well: the state whose economy would improve faster would be able to forget the hardships of the immediate postwar years and thus purge the wartime experiences, both good and bad, from its collective memory.[13] In general, then, in West Germany the population wanted simply to forget the Nazi regime and the crimes it had committed and, significantly, the government did not counteract this desire. Older generations of West Germans especially, preferred to keep silent.[14] Both German states claimed to be morally superior over the other, which, as

Thomas Lindenberger demonstrated, "helped to install a logic in Cold War Germany according to which it was impossible to address publicly the legality of the Nazi dictatorship without making reference to the vilified 'other,' " thus, "in particular during the 1950s and 1960s, the two Germanys behaved like inimical members of a family clan who each shared knowledge about skeletons in the closet of the other and were prepared to use this knowledge in public campaigns when necessary."[15]

Both West Germany and East Germany acknowledged the suffering of Germans during the war. Chancellor Konrad Adenauer and other West German politicians considered Germany a nation of victims; however, West German victimization differed significantly from East Germany's. While the issue of guilt tended to be neglected, West Germans shared stories of suffering and loss and the ethnic cleansing of German expellees from former German territories in the East, which had become part of Poland and the Soviet Union after the war. May 8, celebrated as Day of Liberation in the East, was still considered the Day of Surrender in the West. Furthermore, West Germans were incapable of accepting the Red Army as a liberating force and instead saw the advance of the Red Army into Germany and its continued presence on German soil as the precondition for replacing one totalitarian regime with another. According to this interpretation, East Germans were victims first of Nazism and then of Communism after 1945. In addition, the rape of German women by Soviet soldiers as they marched onto German soil led to the portrayal of those soldiers as inhumane and sadistic beasts, which seemed to align with Nazi stereotypes about Slav subhumans. Last, while acknowledging the genocide of Jews, Adenauer stated that "Germans had suffered too, and it was the political and moral responsibility of the West German state to address the needs of German victims who were not Jewish and whose losses had been inflicted by Allied bombs and the Red Army." Thus, those who objected to equating the suffering of the war's victims, including Jews and Communists, certainly did not receive as much attention as the German victims in postwar West Germany.[16] For East Germany, the imperialist camp led by the United States, the power that had bombed Dresden, became the enemy, whereas for West Germany, the enemy did not change; the Bolsheviks had threatened world peace long before the war and the Soviet Union threatened the free world after the war.[17]

West Germany and East Germany clearly differed in their willingness to address their troubled past. In response to Nazi crimes, distinct German identities emerged in the late 1940s and shaped the ways in which people understood what it meant to be German. The two German states came up with conflicting approaches about how the Nazi regime should be remembered. Whereas East Germany designated the Communists and Soviet soldiers as heroes, West Germans glorified those involved in the July 20 Plot, and, to a lesser degree, the Catholic students of the White Rose in Munich, and prominent churchmen such as Martin Niemöller and Dietrich Bonhoeffer.[18]

In one regard, as Konrad H. Jarausch pointed out, Germans in both East and West Germany inadvertently concurred. While images of their crimes were readily available, Germans were reluctant to discuss the roles of ordinary "decent" Germans during the war because almost everybody was implicated in one way or another. It was not until the Nuremberg Trial when Germans finally began discussing the full scope of the genocide.[19] Not only did the necessity of rebuilding a "post-fascist" society influence the decisions Germans made in the immediate aftermath of the war, Germans also had to deal with the direct consequences of the war; thus reconstruction focused on destruction, hardship, suffering, and the need to start anew. Because the individual and collective perception, recognition, assessment, and processing of wartime and postwar experiences differed, subsequently, Karen Hagemann has observed that

> considerations of the Nazi past and the Second World War in both German states were marked by a "victimization discourse" conducted on many levels, which split off individual responsibility and culpability and delegated it to "the German people" as a whole, or at least stylized individual groups of the population as surrogate victims, who explicitly or implicitly entered a "competition of suffering" with actual victims of the Nazis.[20]

The West German government insisted German society did not undergo a transformation from Nazism to democracy. Rather, it set out to disprove any connections between the two periods by "identifying the years of the National Socialist Regime as 'this un-German Germany,' as if a magical time machine had stopped German history in 1933 and resumed it in 1945."[21] At the same time, West Germans tended to blame a specific group of individuals for Nazi crimes. In fact, West German elites proclaimed ordinary Germans "innocent" while pointing to a small group of people, including Hitler and top SS officers, as responsible for all the horrors of Nazism. Indeed, the politics of memory that Adenauer pursued "combined 'extreme leniency' for the Nazi perpetrators with general 'normative distancing from National Socialism.' "[22]

Pointing to how human resources were mobilized toward reconstruction and industrial productivity, Sabine von Dirke observed that the "economic miracle" dramatically improved West Germans' living standards, further delaying serious discussions of the Nazi past. Some historians also suggest that the situation in Germany after the war, where millions of Germans faced a complete obliteration of their cities, overshadowed any possible consideration for the German atrocities committed during the war. Indeed, Roger Manvell and Heinrich Fraenkel even argue that it is impossible for anyone who never experienced the aftermath of the war to understand the impact of the devastated cities upon Germany, where the Allied bombing of its cities exceeded in scope the destruction brought about by the nuclear attack on Hiroshima and Nagasaki.[23]

In the immediate aftermath of World War II, German filmmakers produced only a few films that dealt with the legacy of National Socialism. Soon after the war, Germans began to perceive themselves as the first victims of Hitler. Increasingly, war stories began to circulate that emphasized fighting, imprisonment, evacuation, expulsion, loss, and rape. Furthermore, by excluding the Wehrmacht from a list of criminal organizations, many Germans accepted the myth that German soldiers did not commit war crimes. Rather, Germans stood behind their soldiers and, unwilling to acknowledge the atrocities they committed, they considered them defenders of their country. Thus, while stories of war and culpability emphasized German victimhood, in the 1960s a new generation began to raise questions about the involvement of their parents in the crimes committed by the Nazis.

Karl May films and the Holocaust

Karl May Westerns offered a mediated way to discuss genocide. By focusing on the conflict of English settlers with Native Americans that ended with the extermination of the latter, Germans could confront genocide, since it was not the genocide Germans had committed, but the genocide of Native Americans by Anglo-Americans, who had just recently decimated Germany's cities to rubble and dust. The Western provided absolution, or at least presented the message that genocide was not a German invention. This message of absolution, of course, seems highly suspicious since it came from a German author (Karl May) whose novels had been adopted by a German director (Harald Reinl) and resembled an American Western.[24]

The issue of the reconstruction of the German film industry after World War II became intertwined with the questions of how Nazi atrocities should be portrayed, and whether they should be portrayed at all. To denazify the film industry proved to be a difficult task. Robert R. Shandley points out that the German film industry was so "deeply implicated in the crimes of the Nazi era" that it would be "surely unrealistic to expect that the path from Nazism to a full reckoning with the past would be a short one."[25] At the same time, gradually, National Socialism ceased to be remembered as an actual experience. Rather, it became delegated to the sphere of imagination.[26] Indeed, almost 20 years after the end of the war, West German director Wolfgang Staudte noticed (paraphrasing the title of the first DEFA film discussed in the following chapter) that "the murderers are still among us, strolling out of prison cells, receiving medals for service to the Republic, being placed upon the chairs of government ministries, proves nothing but the fact that there is still something foul in our own nest, something that ought to be cleaned out."[27]

In the 1960s, first West Germany and later East Germany used the American West as the landscape where a new national identity could be formed. Karl May films also reflected the changes that German society underwent in the 1960s. The myth of the American West influenced the process of shaping identity and nation building.[28] Before the outbreak of World War I, there was a popular expression in Imperial Germany: "Karl-May-Attitude."[29] The expression encompassed a certain quantity of desired qualities of Germans. Accordingly, Germans should be patriotic as Old Shatterhand, as courageous as an Apache, as magnanimous as Winnetou, and having faith in God and Kaiser, like Winnetou's German mentor, Klekih-petra. Thus, the attitude showed a renunciation of social-democratic tendencies and it strengthened loyalty to the emperor and religiosity of the readers, as evidenced by a great number of letters from Karl May readers to the publishers and Karl May himself. There is also a significant connection between Karl May novels, their ideals, and the Imperial Germany military on the eve of World War I. Indeed, some readers compared German soldiers to May's heroes, who were hard as steel, which further points to the alleged German–Indian affinity. Members of the military subscribed to the rhetoric of German–Indian heroes as well. A German army general during World War I, Rüdiger von der Goltz, is known to have said that the skills the soldiers needed to fight effectively, such as reading enemies' traces, crawling, knowledge of terrain, and love of freedom, could best be learned from Winnetou and Old Shatterhand.[30]

During World War II the Karl-May-Attitude was very much alive. Young Germans who joined the Hitlerjugend were instilled with the same ideas derived from the reading of Karl May novels, only this time instead of the skills recommended by General von der Goltz, they handled anti-tank grenade launchers. Hitler himself wished that his generals had read Karl May novels. One of Hitler's last books read in the bunker before his suicide was apparently *Winnetou I.* At the same time, socialists such as August Bebel and Karl Liebknecht enjoyed reading Karl May's novels, which, perhaps, points to the perception of Old Shatterhand as a true German hero and to Winnetou as the symbol of the understanding of the role of nations. Indeed, one can talk about the blood-brotherhood of all readers of Karl May novels, regardless of their political affiliations and philosophies, age, and gender. For Hitler, however, May's novels articulated the superiority of the Nordic people, based on the example of Old Shatterhand.[31]

Karl May inspired Hitler throughout his life. Some historians even assert that Hitler was an ardent fan of May. Klaus Mann called May the "Cowboy Mentor of the Führer." Indeed, discussing May's role in Hitler's life, Mann wrote the following:

> one of the most ardent Karl May fans was a certain good-for-nothing from Braunau, Austria, who was to rise to impressive heights. Young Adolf was seriously smitten by Karl May whose works were his favorite, if not his only reading, even in later years. His own imagination, his whole notion of life was impregnated by these Western thrillers. The cheap and counterfeit conception of "heroism" presented by Karl May fascinated the future Führer; he loved this primitive but effective shrewdness: the use of "secret weapons" and terrible tricks, such as carrying prisoners as shields, the brutal cunning of wild animals in the jungle; he was delighted by the glorification of savages. Lazy and aimless, Adolf was perfectly at home in this dubious labyrinth created by a morbid and infantile brain. What the unsuccessful Austrian painter and potential dictator chiefly admired in Old Shatterhand, was his mixture of brutality and hypocrisy: he could quote the Bible with the greatest ease while toying with murder; he carried out the worst atrocities with a clear conscience; for he took it for granted that his enemies were of an "inferior race" and hardly human – whereas he, Old Shatterhand, was a superman, called by God to destroy evil and promote the good.[32]

One of Hitler's most famous biographers, John Toland, describes a situation when Hitler argued with his generals, overrode all their objections, and summarized the situation in the following words: "They should have read Karl May." Hitler had been impressed by the virtues of the Indian warriors and had 300,000 copies of *Winnetou* delivered to German soldiers. Toland also describes a scene in which someone who visited Hitler's summer house looked at what kind of literature Hitler chose for relaxation. Toland writes that "surprisingly, the majority of the books were the wild West novels of Karl May." Toland concludes that the books were more suitable for the visitor, who was 12, than the dictator.

Hitler's obsession with Karl May started much earlier. Some scholars believe that shortly before May's death, Adolf Hitler attended a lecture Karl May gave in Vienna. Interestingly, the lecture Hitler attended emphasized utopian pacifism and the love for humanity. Indeed, May argued that every human's task should be to become a noble human being. Other well-known Hitler biographers, including Ian Kershaw, also acknowledge Hitler's incessant fascination with May's works and that Hitler placed May's works in a special shelf in his library to honor the writer.[33]

Hitler's closest entourage also confirmed the dictator's admiration of May's works. Otto Dietrich, Hitler's confidant, stated that Hitler "had a special antipathy for novels, which he never read, and for poetry; poems were an abomination to him. In the earlier years of his reign he once more read through all the volumes of Karl May's Indian tales, which had been his favorite boyhood reading."[34] Hitler remembered different trivial information about the writer he shared with his entourage. For example, when visiting Linz, he showed Albert Speer the hotel where May had lived for almost a year. According to Albert Speer:

> Hitler would lean on Karl May as proof for everything imaginable, in particular for the idea that is was not necessary to know the desert in order to direct troops in the African theater of war; that a people could be wholly foreign to you, as foreign as the Bedouins or the American Indians were to Karl May, and yet with some imagination and empathy you could nevertheless know more about them, their soul, their customs and circumstances, than some anthropologists or geographers, who had studied them in the field. Karl May attested to Hitler that it wasn't necessary to travel in order to know the world.[35]

There are apparently three documented references which Hitler made during the war with regard to Karl May.[36] The first one comes from February 17, 1942:

> Today I read a great article about Karl May which made me very happy inside ... to May goes my first geographic knowledge ... I used to read him at candlelight and with a magnifying glass in the

moonlight. First I read (Cooper's) *Leatherstockings Tales* and *The Last Mohican,* but Fritz Seidl told me later: you have to read Karl May, there is nothing like it! The first Karl May I read was *The Ride across the Desert.* It threw me away.

The next one also comes from February 17, 1942:

There are some great books which have attracted a lot of attention. If we ignore the Bible, then of course we think of *Don Quixote* and *Robinson Crusoe.* Those two have been read all over the world. The third was *Uncle Tom's Cabin. Gulliver's Travels* also were very successful. In Germany we think of Karl May, Jules Verne, and Felix Dahn.

The last entry comes from June 13, 1943. Accordingly, Hitler said that the greatest Romanticist writer North America had was an Indian romantic, who, interestingly, happened to be German. Those remarks Hitler made about Karl May were written down by Heinrich Heim, an NSDAP (Nationalsozialistische Deutsche Arbeiterpartei) official.[37]

Interestingly, some of May's critics pointed to the similarities between the "insane game of cowboys and Indians by Germanic Karl May readers" and the social life of Nazi society. Indeed, Erich Kästner, a German writer highly critical of May, commented following his first arrest by the Gestapo in 1934 that the Germans were an "infantile Indian lust of the people" who behaved as though "they were sitting not at office desks on Prinz-Albrecht-Strasse but at campfires in the steppes... They were... cowboys and Indians, Karl May readers like their Führer..., boy scouts with bloody sheath knives, tanned redskins as blond beasts. Europe as a children's playground, wantonly trampled and full of corpses." What might come as a surprise to some, even victims of the Nazi regime, aware of Hitler's fascination with the writer, defended May. George L. Mosse argued that May did not prefigure Nazi brutality, but promoted sympathy, law, and order. Thus, although Hitler drew inspiration from May's novels, one should not go as far as to argue that there indeed existed an ideological congruency.[38]

Hitler's passion for the myth of the American West needs a little more elaboration. Karl May occupied a special place in Hitler's library. Apparently, "May opened his eyes unto the world" and Hitler, upon becoming Chancellor, might have reread his favorite authors' books and established a Karl May museum. It seems quite incredible knowing May's appeals for peace and Old Shatterhand's use of weapons and killing as a last resort.[39] Another author, Michael Burleigh, observed the following with regard to the origins of Hitler's hatred of the Jews and the "Aryan-Jew" dichotomy:

> Hitler was obsessed with an eternal struggle between two hostile forces, the "Aryan" and the "Jew," the stakes of which were the survival of mankind and the planet. The Aryan was poorly described as a wandering creative force whose destiny was to dominate lesser humans. He was a sort of "God-man."... In so far as this Aryan here could be envisaged, Hitler, an avid fan of Karl May's Westerns, did so in terms of cowboys and Indians... It was a story of racial perdition, with the fall involving "race suicide" through breeding with lesser races: the fall of man in paradise has always been followed by his expulsion.[40]

During World War II, the German army supplied German soldiers with special editions of May's novels, which, together with the works of Joseph Freiherr von Eichendorff, Johann Wolfgang von Goethe, and Friedrich Schiller, provided a suitable set of classical German writers. For example, the Bibliographisches Institut Leipzig released 80,000 copies of *The Treasure of Silver Lake* in 1943, whereas three volumes of *Winnetou* were released for the Wehrmacht soldiers in Norway, each in 10,000 copies. Furthermore, Karl-May-Verlag and Union Deutscher Verlagsanstalten regularly published Karl May's works, though any elements deemed to be pacifistic in nature were deleted from May's works, especially in the later stage of the war. Thus, on one occasion, the three-volume *Winnetou* became shortened to two volumes, and any passages that concerned religion were deleted as well. The Gestapo liquidated the Deutscher Karl-May-Bund in 1944, whose president, Gerhard Henniger, future first secretary of the Union of German Writers in East Germany, wrote the foreword for the first East German edition of *Winnetou*, later banned by East German officials.[41] However, some of May's readers might have taken to heart May's conclusion that the Indians were a dying people and thus deemed their disappearance inevitable and justified. Importantly, the characters of Winnetou and Old Shatterhand, "the archetypal 'noble savage' and the heroic, righteous, (German) arbiter of justice (endowed with nearly super-human strength, together with the anti-bourgeois, anti-capitalist rhetoric)," made his novels "fit with German imperialism in general, and fascist ideology in particular."[42]

The time of the release of the first German Western coincided with important developments in Argentina, Israel, and West Germany. On

May 11, 1960, Israeli special forces captured the SS Obersturmführer Adolf Eichmann, one of those responsible for the implementation of the "Final Solution." His trial began on April 11, 1961, and he was executed for crimes against the Jewish people, humanity, and war crimes on June 1, 1962. Moreover, as *Winnetou I* had its premiere in December 1963, the Auschwitz-trial began in Frankfurt on December 20 and lasted until August 19, 1965. Whereas the first Auschwitz Trial conducted in 1947 by the Allied-led court resulted in the execution of 21 members of the staff of the concentration camp and, following a separate trial, the execution of the first commandant of the Auschwitz concentration camp, Rudolf Höss, the second Auschwitz trial resulted in lenient sentences and even led to the acquittal of several defendants. During the Frankfurt Auschwitz Trials, 22 former guards were put on trial. Seventeen were found guilty, with five either released or acquitted.[43]

Moreover, in 1963, Rolf Hochhuth, a German author and playwright, published "the most controversial literary work of his generation," *The Deputy*. In his play, Hochhuth accused Pope Pius XII of complicity in the Holocaust.[44] Indeed, at the end of Act Four of the play, Hochhuth has the Pope state that "as the flowers in the countryside wait beneath winter's mantle of snow for the warm breezes of spring, so the *Jews* must wait, praying and trusting that the hour of heavenly comfort will come."[45] Thus, given the controversy regarding the passivity of the Catholic Church during the war, Winnetou's embracing of Christianity in the novel had to be absent from the movie version. It seems to have been impossible to West Germans to have a non-Christian victim of genocide committed by Christians to endorse their religion and race of the perpetrators on German cinema's screen at that time. The conspicuous absence of this central scene from the movie did certainly not go unnoticed by versed Karl May fans.

Although West German Westerns seemed to imitate American Westerns, they proved to be original in that they provided a stage for Native Americans. While influenced by American Westerns, "the overriding preoccupation of the May films with the 'tragedy' of the Indians' fight for survival obviously sets them significantly apart from the overt ideological concerns that have traditionally dominated the American Western."[46] Thus, assuming that Karl May films provided absolution for some West German viewers, it would be logical to assume that the images of the martyrdom and demise of the Indians, exemplified by the death of Winnetou and the Apaches, interlocked with the horrific images and the remembrance of the Nazi crimes. Furthermore, one can also conclude that May's Indian heroes were doomed to die in order to pave the way for the fulfillment of Manifest Destiny. The films might have suggested to those West German viewers that the fate of the Jews became sealed with Hitler's ascent to power and that nothing could have prevented the Holocaust. Thus, the films might have freed Germans from guilt because they made them realize the inevitability of genocide in the light of the Nazi *übermenschen* rhetoric. And, importantly, just as Winnetou and his people died at the hands of ruthless Anglo-American conquerors, the Jews were murdered at the hands of the Nazis. In both cases, no force could have altered the course of history. Last, connecting the fall of the Apaches with the Holocaust might have also suggested that no nation is flawless; even the beacon of democracy and the force that, along with the Soviet Union, destroyed Nazism, had engaged in a historically brutal conquest, dictated not only by greed but also by racism and was even founded on the annihilation of those people who had populated the nation.

Karl May Westerns did not directly concern World War II. They used the myth of the American West to convey the message of inevitable demise of Native American populations, an obstacle standing in the way of progress. While Germans did not directly connect the United States with Nazi crimes, similarities between the fate of Native Americans and Jews became a common motif. In fact, some Germans believed that American settlers anticipated Hitler and equated Manifest Destiny and its tragic consequences with the Holocaust. Moreover, in some examples, Germans pointed to the barbarity of the United States. As Dan Diner observed, "no matter how such presumptuousness equating Nazism and America was really meant, the examples certainly cannot be dismissed as quirks from the fringes," because "their deep impact, irrespective of political camp or ticket, speaks against that." Moreover, many Germans considered equating Manifest Destiny with the Holocaust a leitmotif, a recurring theme of postwar discourse on the Holocaust.[47] As an ardent Karl May fan pointed out, the German writer represented "the most brilliant example of an elemental form of literature, namely the literature of wish-fulfillment," and by "fulfilling a wish no one else had gratified so thrillingly before him, Karl May refashioned the self-image of a nation."[48]

Although Jews hardly appear in May's novels, scholars disagree about how to interpret this fact. On one hand, some argue that since May's career reached its height at the time when anti-Semitism began to escalate across Europe, the relative absence of Jewish characters might be evidence of anti-Semitism. In fact, in *Winnetou I* May compares Indians' "defective" understanding of redemption to the people of Israel. On the other hand, Karl May's second wife's first husband had been Richard Plöhn, who was Jewish. Klara May, the writer's second wife, however, joined the Nazi Party before her death in 1944.[49] Other scholars point to the fact that Isaak Hirsch, the Jewish character of Otto Ruppuis's novel *Der Pedlar*, published in 1857, influenced May's depicting of some characters in his novels. Thus, May accepted Hirsch's moral integrity, strength, and courage, and modeled his Native American heroes after the Jewish hero who was "quite a remarkable reversal for the Jew to become the loyal and selfless helper of the Teutonic hero instead of his sworn enemy."[50] Moreover, Jerry Schuchalter states that the Jewish character of the novel, Isaak Hirsch, "is elevated to a supernatural plane-like Winnetou, the stuff of myth or at least of fairy tale, his mortal qualities receding as he emerges as the avenger of moral inquiry."[51] Louis Harap, however, points out that *The Peddler* also reiterates the negative stereotype of Jews by continually focusing on their physical characteristics as well as their greed.[52] Connections between Jewish characters in Karl May's *Winnetou* novels and Jewish characters in other novels are, however, debatable, not to say far-fetched, and only those well familiar with Karl May novels could possibly notice them. Karl May films do not include any Jewish characters, although the tragic fate of the Apache Indians might have reminded West German moviegoers of the fate of the Jews.

The main question behind the making of Karl May films was: who is the right hero and where does one find him among German actors? It took an American actor, Lex Barker, to become the embodiment of the Aryan hero, Old Shatterhand, hailed by many newspapers referring to his blondness. Indeed, while West German newspapers did not allude to Nazi themes in the movies, it almost seems as if Barker's blondness became a code word for the awkwardness associated with discussing the connections between West Germans and the Nazi past, a codeword for Aryan. Newspapers labeled Lex Barker a "Hun-Christ," "a blond Hun" (the adjective Hun denoting his tallness, rather than Hun–Germanic connections, although some might have found it ambiguous), who stood for bravery, righteousness, and sincerity, and who instantaneously became every young German's hero.[53] The "apeman with a personable grin and a torso guaranteed to make any lion cringe" who succeeded Johnny Weissmuller, the Olympic swimming star, as Tarzan in 1949, became a top box-office star in Germany, playing the role of the German hero of the American West and becoming a symbol of Germanness.[54]

No German, of course, was willing to play Old Shatterhand, primarily because no actor was going to participate in an enterprise that most

likely would end in a fiasco, given the disappointing failures of the previous Karl May films released before World War II. But there was another
aspect of playing Old Shatterhand that made German actors reconsider
the role and that dealt with the legacy of the Nazi past. When it comes
to Lex Barker, those factors, including his wartime experiences and his
ideal Nazi physiognomy, do not apply. Barker was an American actor
who had fought in World War II, who had been captured by the Nazis,
and who had been held in a POW camp from which he escaped. Some
German newspapers pointed out that this American actor's blondness
"surpassed every SS-man's," thus proving the immediate reactions a
German viewer might have after watching the stories of the genocide
of a people.[55] Thus, a Princeton graduate who became a major in the
American infantry, wounded in the Africa campaign, and who spent
months in Nazi captivity as a POW, rather than a German actor, who
might have had some attachments to the Nazi system, became a German
national hero.[56]

The legacy of the Nazi past also had an impact on Karl May
Westerns' conventions. Significantly, vigorous physicality of characters was reduced to a minimum, whereas aggression and power either
belonged to the young generation or had a negative connotation
and was associated with the antagonists. Because the heroes of Karl
May films were men in their forties and older, this meant that their
West German counterparts had lived through the war and might have
belonged to the NSDAP and might even have participated in war atrocities. Thus, filmmakers avoided a direct connection between aggression
and power and the war generations of Germans that, inadvertently,
albeit implicitly, perpetuated the idea of absolution.[57] Gerd Gemünden
argues that "one can surmise that Reinl was sensitive to the fact that
May's image of a patronizing German vis-à-vis an ethnic minority would
echo unwanted memories of racial superiority. In a similar vein, much
of the missionary enthusiasm of May's German Westmänner is translated into mere action film."[58] Although the films do not emphasize
Old Shatterhand's German identity, Tim Bergfelder pointed out that his
"physiognomy (his blondness, blue eyes, and athletic body) still con-
formed to the kind of Teutonic racial stereotype that had informed the
character's description in May's novels."[59]

Although Karl May novels and films seem sympathetic to the plight
of Native Americans, not all Germans shared this sympathy. Sometimes
the West German press did not write favorably about Native Americans,
even when reporting on the activities of the American Indian Movement. For example, in a 1968 article a German writer attempted to

ridicule them, using phrases such as "Manitou's sons" or a " 'palavering chief,' who was a 'squaw,' " and concluding his article with "the German version of an Indian 'grunt': 'Uff, uff, uff.' "[60] Considering *Winnetou III*, a kitschy film for immature adults, *Frankfurter Allgemeine Zeitung* quoted a movie critic who wrote that no other films corrupted audiences and film producers as much as Karl May films, even more so, he added, than the Nazi dictatorship and the propaganda of Joseph Goebbels.[61] In other words, some film critics went so far as to declare Karl May films more damaging than the heinous film industry controlled by the Nazis. The West German press as well as ordinary Germans occasionally used sarcasm when referring to Native Americans and Karl May films. No matter how laughable the Indians were to some, however, the films conveyed important messages that registered with many viewers, both adolescents and adults.[62] That there were Germans who disliked Karl May Westerns should not come as a surprise. It would be hard to think of a film which was enthusiastically accepted by all viewers. What is important here is that regardless of how favorable Germans viewed the cinematic representation of Karl May novels, the above passage demonstrates that Karl May films inevitably made many Germans think about the still omnipresent memory of World War II and compare the genocide of Winnetou's tribe to Nazism, however timid and limited those were.

Interestingly, during his career in Europe, Lex Barker was later chosen to play the role of an ex-Nazi intelligence officer in the film *Mister Dynamit* because of his "Teutonic racial stereotype."[63] Barker admitted that the fact that he starred in German films should not come as a surprise. Referring to German World War II films, Barker pointed out (laughing as he spoke) that the Germans always acted like "boobies" (Tölpel) when it came to how cautiously they approached their Nazi past. In other words, it surprised Barker that even 20 years after the war, West Germans still tiptoed around the Wehrmacht's conduct during the war. In a sense, one can take Barker's words as another indication of the absolutory power of Karl May films. The American Aryan-looking actor, a former POW in a German camp in North Africa, and the greatest German hero starring in the most popular film series produced after the war was, indeed, surprised by the German obsession with the Nazi past. His words might have indicated that other nations that had fought Nazi Germany approved of the Germans' desire to simply move on. Given Germans' timidity and tiptoeing around the war, it should make people wonder, he added, why the war lasted more than six months instead of a quick surrender of the German forces following the American declaration of war. He also mentioned that Germany did not consist only of Nazis.[64]

While Winnetou became ennobled because he emulated his white German blood brother, the fact that Old Shatterhand became Winnetou's blood brother had tremendous significance. Thus, the blood

Figure 1.1   Pierre Brice as Winnetou (left) and Lex Barker as Old Shatterhand. Photo courtesy of United Archives GmbH/Alamy

brotherhood between the representative of the dying race and the representative of the invading race provided absolution and exoneration for the crimes committed by the conquerors on the conquered. Old Shatterhand sided with the victims, thus removing the sense of shame and guilt from contemporary Germans. Germans could then focus on the future, absolved of their past crimes. The rationale is quite simple: if one sides with the victims and is revered by them, one cannot be seen as an offender. Thus, Winnetou, the last chief of the Mescalero Apache, and Old Shatterhand, a German immigrant who becomes his blood brother, attempted to improve American–Indian relations while dealing with white profiteers, ruthless land speculators, oil and gold diggers, and railroad magnates bound on eradicating Indians from the face of the earth.[65]

Those moviegoers familiar with Karl May novels were more likely to connect the conquest of the American West with the legacy of the Holocaust. As a matter of fact, some German newspapers found the films too direct and argued that Karl May films should have been much less explicit given Germany's recent history. Some newspapers, such as *Film Beobachter*, found it inappropriate for a German film to glorify a superhuman (*die Gloriole eines üebermenschen*), since Germans knew very well that similar rhetoric brought about the rise of the Nazis and the deaths of millions of people. *Film Beobachter* even felt obliged to caution viewers as to what the intent of the filmmakers might have been and deemed it improper for children under 16 to see the film.[66]

Last, another crucial absolutory element of Karl May Westerns proved to be the participation of American soldiers in restoring peace on the frontier. Not only is absolution offered through the character of Old Shatterhand and the blood brotherhood between him and the Apache chief, Winnetou, but through the bravery of the American cavalry's actions, the viewer perceives the soldiers as heroic defenders of the Indians. The viewer also concludes that only a minority of desperados attempted to disrupt the peace on the frontier, while the government and federal troops did not cease their efforts to maintain order and justice. Because West Germans refused to acknowledge the Wehrmacht's atrocities during the war, some West German viewers might have seen their own soldiers, possibly brothers, sons, or themselves, fighting on Germany's frontiers. It is likely, then, that the actions of the American army on the frontier represented for West German viewers the actions of German soldiers. In both cases, with a few exceptions, the army restores order and uses violence only when necessary and only in the just cause.

Thus, the army does all it can to preserve the integrity of the Indian nations; however, just as the army doctor could not save Winnetou in one of the last scenes of *Winnetou III* after the Apache chief was shot in the heart, the army could not save the Indian nations against what appeared inexorable. The Native Americans were an obstacle to progress and doomed to perish in the guise of Manifest Destiny. Significantly, for the West German viewer, the *Winnetou* series revealed that it was difficult, if not impossible, to stop a well-organized and extreme minority, which, as in the case of Nazi Germany, had been responsible for tyranny and genocide. *Old Shatterhand* ends in a similar way. The major villain in this film is an army officer, Captain Bradley. Because his family had been murdered by Native Americans, he vowed to avenge their death by causing the deaths of as many Indians as possible. He also captured Old Shatterhand and seemed ready to execute him as a traitor to the white race. Despite Winnetou's desperate attempts to defeat Captain Bradley's forces, only after the arrival of the regiment's general, the de facto chief of the American army in the region, does Bradley surrender. He is taken into custody and awaits court martial. Thus, Karl May Westerns' heroes are not only Old Shatterhand and Winnetou, but also the American army, since it secured peace on the frontier and eliminated those Anglo-Americans who vowed to eradicate the Native American population. In this way, the viewer concludes that just as the army is a positive force, so is the majority of the American and, crucially, German population. There are some among them who committed atrocities, but they had been either punished, as in the case of Karl May Westerns, or tried, as in the case of the Nuremberg Trials. Significantly, the fact that West Germany became a member of NATO meant that the United States and other Western powers "were ready to see German soldiers as victims of 'Hitler's war,'" which happened at a time when more and more Germans went to the movies and every tenth movie concerned war. Apparently, "the war conquered West German film production because American imports had proven that Germans had a taste for combat films."[67] It also demonstrated the need to have a strong standing army which guaranteed restoring order on the frontier and safeguarded the uninterrupted existence of the democratic system.

Despite the popularity of the Oberhausen Manifesto that young West German directors issued in 1962, calling for a new paradigm in the movie-making industry, no other genre proved more popular at the box office in the 1960s than Karl May Westerns. Although a new generation of directors emerged, historians acknowledge that the Western proved to be extremely successful in the middle of the 1960s in Germany and the most popular genre of the decade.[68] While young directors insisted that cultural renewal meant elimination of "authoritarian" elements from postwar West German films, the popularity of the Karl May Western in West Germany proved them wrong. Karl May films simply entertained and allowed people to relive Karl May's dreams. The director of *Unter Geiern*, Alfred Vohrer, said that when he worked on the set of the film, he imagined he was 19 again.[69] Perhaps that was the most important benefit Karl May films provided. They took people back to the past where the worst memories of the 1930s and the 1940s could be explained away through the application of the German myth of the American West.

While there is a limited amount of evidence which could be found with regard to the understanding of the message Karl May films conveyed, it is safe to assume that many would conceal their feelings anyway, not to be accused of being insensitive or pro-Nazi, barely two decades after the war had ended. But that the moods and approaches to the Nazi regime were changing is perhaps best evidenced by the work of the historian Ernst Nolte, whose interpretation of the causes of the failure of democracy in Germany in the early 1930s precipitated the "Historikerstreit," a debate between academics with regard to how much revisionism is appropriate when it comes to the Nazi regime and the Holocaust. In his book *Deutschland und der kalte Krieg* (*Germany and the Cold War*) Nolte compared what happened during the Nazi regime to the ongoing war in Vietnam.[70] This book was published in 1974, just a few years after the last Karl May film was produced, while *Indianerfilme* continued to be produced until the 1980s. As a matter of fact, the same historian, having triggered the debate and being accused of revisionism, went even further in his speech at the Carl-Friedrich-Siemens-Stiftung in Munich in 1980, whose abridged version was published in Germany's biggest daily newspaper, *Frankfurter Allgemeine Zeitung* on July 24, 1980. In his speech Nolte objected to the "demonization of the Third Reich" and said that "Auschwitz is not primarily a result of traditional anti-Semitism and was not just one more case of 'genocide.' It was the fear-borne reactions to acts of annihilation that took place during the Russian Revolution." Moreover, according to him, examining the rewriting of history with regard to Napoleon, and the involvement of the United States, the beacon of democracy, in Vietnam, begged the following question: "Doesn't this situation once again force us—and this time in a less partial and isolated way—to consider revising the history of the Third Reich?"[71]

Here Nolte argued that the National Socialist atrocities against the Jews had been, in a way, but a copy of the *Gulag Archipelago*, indeed had been, a defensive reaction inasmuch as Hitler had been motivated by a subjectively justified fear of Bolshevist annihilation threats against the German people. This article immediately caused widespread indignation, as it would appear to present as much as an indirect vindication of National Socialist policies.[72]

Nolte's revisionism not only sparked the *Historikerstreit*, but also compelled Germany's most prominent politicians to express their views with regard to how the Nazi era should be remembered. While in 1985 West German Chancellor Helmut Kohl invited Ronald Reagan to the German military cemetery close to Bitburg, which contained a number of graves of members of the Waffen SS, to accentuate German–American friendship, 13 years later another German leader directly addressed Nolte's relativizing of the Nazi crimes. Addressing the 37th Congress of German Historians at Bamberg, on October 12, 1998, former president of West Germany and the first president of the unified German Republic, Richard von Weizsäcker, unequivocally pointed to those responsible for the Holocaust. Asking first "And what, after all, would it mean for us if Auschwitz could be compared with the ruthless extermination of other people?" he affirmed that "Auschwitz remains unique. It was perpetrated by Germans in the name of Germany. This truth is immutable and will not be forgotten... Historical responsibility means accepting one's own history. We must do so above all for the sake of the present."[73]

Only a year after Nolte's book sparked the historical controversy, perhaps the most anti-American *Indianerfilm* was released in East Germany. Not only was it anti-American, but it was another transnational production with an American actor, Dean Reed, writing the script and costarring next to Gojko Mitic. Thus, East Germans also found their own American star. In contrast to Lex Barker, Reed approved of burning the American flag, killing American soldiers, and showing them as cruel rapists and dispossessors. It represented the Socialist antithesis of the myth of Manifest Destiny.

2

Indianerfilme and the Conquest of the American West

The first East German Western

For a viewer familiar with the Western genre, the first East German Western, *The Sons of Great Mother Bear*, may not seem initially to differ from any traditional American Western.[1] In the opening scene, a group of Anglo-Americans are playing cards and drinking in a saloon. There are also two Native Americans present, sitting in a remote corner. The older Native American agrees to join the Anglo-Americans, while his son refuses even to acknowledge their presence. The son is also the only person in the saloon who is not drinking. His father, it appears, must have known and trusted the leading white gambler who calls him "my red brother." The friendship between Red Fox, an experienced Anglo-American frontiersman, the white frontiersman, and the older Indian proves to be fleeting once the frontiersman discovers a gold nugget in the hand of the Indian. Red Fox kills the Indian when the Indian refuses to tell him where gold can be found. Then the story follows the well-known pattern: as more and more gold-hungry whites arrive, the Indians must either leave their homeland or fight off the invaders. War appears imminent. Indeed, "if this were a Hollywood Western, John Wayne would fight off the 'redskins' single-handedly before riding off into a prairie sunset."[2] Instead, not only does Tokei-ihto manage to avenge the death of his father, but he also manages to protect his tribe from extermination by leading them to a new homeland. In the penultimate scene of the film, the young Indian, equipped only with a bow and a handful of arrows, successfully fights a few dozen whites. Tokei-ihto manages to kill many of his enemies, including the murderer of his father. Later, he returns to his tribe and leads his people across the Missouri River to their new homeland. The Indian tribes reunite, despite a short period of intra-tribal fighting, concerning the appropriate response to white encroachment upon their territories. Although Tokei-ihto manages to succeed with the help of a couple of friendly Anglo-Americans, most notably Adam Adamson, who becomes disgusted with the treatment of the Indians and helps Tokei-ihto to escape imprisonment, there is only one hero in this film: the young chief who defeats the evil white invaders.

East Germany and denazification

The process of creation of a new collective identity occurred simultaneously in West and East Germany. East Germany ratified its first constitution in 1949 and in some wording it resembled its West German counterpart. In fact, the constitution created both a socialist and a Western-style state, as it was designed "to guarantee the freedom and rights of the people... to foster social progress, to promote friendship with other nations and to safeguard peace." Aside from guaranteeing basic rights of citizens, as had its West German counterpart five months earlier, the first East German constitution emphasized that "There is only one German nationality."[3] In 1968 a new East German constitution proclaimed East Germany to be a state of workers and peasants. East German authorities thereby solidified the German division and, on paper, invoked a separate German identity. The preamble to the 1968 constitution drastically differed from its predecessor and it underscored the socialist nature of the East German state. It emphasized East Germany's responsibility to continue to follow a path of peace and socialism. It denounced the imperialism of the United States, which, combined with the capitalism of West Germany, undermined the vital interests of the German nation, namely, the establishment of socialism. It also emphasized the fact that East Germany was built upon the successes of an anti-fascist democratic and socialist revolution and it asserted consistency with the ideals of its predecessor, albeit affirming its socialist character.[4] Furthermore, Article 1 of the constitution declared that East Germany was "a socialist state of the German nation," driven in unity by "the leadership of the working class and the Marxist-Leninist Socialist Party." Last, it underscored cooperation and friendship with the Soviet Union and other socialist states, focusing especially on the economic fundamentals of Socialism, especially concepts such as "what people's hands create, they own."[5] Thus, the adoption of a revised constitution in 1968, emphasizing the achievements of socialism and the socialist identity of East Germany, affirmed the existence of the two

German states as much as, if not more than, the constitution and the creation of the two Germans states, as well as the construction of the Berlin Wall in 1961. Moreover, the constitution of 1968 made many Germans realize that the path to reunification would be difficult, if not impossible, and that the current arrangement should no longer be considered temporary. Films in both German states would reflect the prevailing values which their citizens professed as well as their attitude toward each other. Thus, while West Germans enthusiastically embraced Karl May films, in East Germany, the myth of the American West portrayed the brutal and unjust treatment of the defenseless by capitalists and fascists, thus underscoring the connection between West Germany and the Nazi past.

To detach themselves from the crimes committed by the Nazis, the two German states pointed to the number of German victims living within their borders. The East German government began equating anti-fascism with socialism by pointing to German Communists who had resisted Nazism from the beginning. The economic recovery in East Germany, however, nowhere near as rapid in East Germany as it was in West Germany, reminded many in East Germany of the deplorable conditions the last stage of the war brought about. While there was no hunger in East Germany, the government continued to ration some food items until 1958. David F. Crew demonstrated how, even in the 1960s, "shortages could assume a symbolic significance greater than their immediate material consequences" as was the case of "an East German woman who was trying to organize a wedding celebration" and who "was told that she could have one piece of butter and one bottle of condensed milk for 30–35 guests."[6]

As the possibility of reunification withered away and the two German entities became two distinct states, they competed to gain exclusive recognition of Germanness. With the implementation of East Germany's constitution in 1968 and the mutual East German–West German recognition treaty of 1972, the two states formally abandoned any intention of reunification. Shortly after the signing of the Basic Treaty between the two German states, they each joined the United Nations. Indeed, Konrad H. Jarausch has written that

> between 1951 and 1976 the proportion of the adult population who believed the Federal Republic and East Germany would never be united increased from 28 percent to 65 percent. Popular acceptance of the Oder-Neisse line (the then de facto boundary between Poland and East Germany) increased from only 8 percent in 1951 to 61 percent

by 1972. By the early 1970s about two-thirds of West Germans had come to consider European integration "more urgent" than German unification.

Significantly, the younger the respondents, the less interested they were in unification.[7] Thus, reunification no longer seemed plausible with the two German states' mutual recognition of the status quo in 1972 as well as their admittance into the United Nations the following year and the character of the relations between them in the 1970s and 1980s.[8]

Of course, the forcible removal of millions of ethnic Germans from the East had a great impact on collective identity formation. Some settled in either West or East Germany; others were left behind in what now was Czechoslovakian or Polish territories. Because it took East Germany longer to recover from the devastation and it never reached West German living standards of which many were well aware of, it must have been harder for East Germans to start all over. It must have been especially hard for those who remained in now foreign territories. There, as Andrew Demshuk has shown, they often felt "deprived of resources to rebuild a life amid a plundered, burned-out Heimat, and usually forced to leave it behind in a ruined state, expellees absorbed a profound pessimism that the beloved Heimat was physically lost, graspable only in memory." Significantly, this also had a great impact on how they perceived victims of the Nazi regime. Some of those who lived now in Poland might have sympathized with the Poles who had suffered during the war. Many, however, resented "the decline they attributed to Polish incapability and cruelty" and detesting "the lawlessness and brutality perceived in communism, seldom recognizing that a German-led war had impoverished the Polish settlers and given them cause to loathe all things German."[9] Moreover, some of them applied Nazi rhetoric to explain the loss of their territories, putting all the blame on the Slavs and comparing their takeover of the German East to the barbarity displayed by Nazi leaders. In fact, the racist attitudes toward inferior Slavs remained pervasive among those who either were expelled or found themselves living on Polish soil.[10]

In addition, the ideological foundations of both new states found their complement in mirroring policies of exclusion and inclusion. In East Germany, constructing the "anti-fascist order" implied removing a large part of the middle class from influential positions by means of criminalization and expropriation, and driving them out of the country. The integration of millions of "small" Nazis notwithstanding, a record as a National Socialist became a serious career liability. The conduct of this purge lacked the qualities of fair and just procedure; as it involved a rupture with the legal norms of the state, it was therefore highly contentious. The East German state claimed to be founded on anti-fascism as the world view par excellence that supposedly had united the resistance movements against the Nazi rule in the whole of Europe. East German governments, on the contrary, kept the issue of Nazi genocide alive by demanding that West Germany, the capitalist successor to Nazi Germany, shoulder all responsibility for the crimes of National Socialism. East Germany painted an image of a quasi-fascist regime in West Germany against which it had to protect its population through many means, including especially the construction of an "anti-fascist protective Wall" in August 1961, as officials in East Germany labeled the Berlin Wall.[11]

Regardless of the differences between them, two distinct German identities provided atonement for past crimes. East German propaganda based on anti-fascism called for East Germans to take pride in the heroic Communist resistance to Nazism and the building of a new Socialist republic. West Germans also regained pride in their country, mainly as a result of the economic miracle of the 1950s.[12]

East Germans revised the meaning of the horrors of the Nazi past along the lines of the official anti-fascist and anti-capitalist propaganda. In order to ensure that no other interpretation of the past would emerge, East Germany, from the beginning, began to depict the years under the Nazi regime in terms of a class struggle. David Kaufman points out that East Germany continued to portray the victims of the German concentration camps as almost exclusively belonging to the Communist Party, with Ernst Thälmann, imprisoned in 1933 and killed by the Nazis in August 1944, the central figure and symbol of resistance and martyrdom of Communist resistance.[13] Claiming that the noblest part of German history was its socialist traditions, East Germany also accused West Germany of merely replacing one fascist government with another. In fact, East Germans claimed to have been double victims of the war. Not only did they suffer at the hands of the Nazis, but beginning in the 1950s, they also commemorated the sufferings caused by the American and British aerial bombing of Dresden, when "Anglo-American gangsters in the skies" used "weapons of mass destructions" against German civilians. In fact, East German authorities equated the bombing of Dresden with the bombing of civilian populations of Korea during the early 1950s.[14] Others in East Germany believed that what drove the Allies carpet-bombing of Dresden was the idea to obliterate an entire city, which, in their eyes, qualified it as a Nazi-like deed. In that

they saw the British and the Americans driven by imperialistic ambi-
tions which included repudiation of the borders established at Yalta and
to conquer as much of Germany as possible. And if imperialism did not
drive the Allies to cripple Dresden and East Germany, then it must have
been advantageous to the Allies to obliterate them in order to show that
capitalism was a superior system in the postwar stage of reconstruction,
as it would allow West German cities to achieve prewar industrial output
levels higher than the crippled East.[15] Last, Germans compelled to fight
for Nazi Germany were also included among the victims, as they were
believed to have been coerced into wearing a uniform by the industri-
alists and bankers who allegedly controlled the NSDAP and who merely
used Hitler as their puppet. Accordingly, many German soldiers began
their "rehabilitation" prior to their return to Germany, transformed into
"pioneers of a new Germany," by virtue of having helped to rebuild the
Soviet Union during their captivity as POWs.[16]

The Allies ceased trials of war criminals in the late 1940s and they
even released a majority of those who had already been convicted. East
Germany increased its rhetoric of labeling West Germany as the Third
Reich's successor once officials discovered how many West German leading politicians had been active members of the NSDAP. Indeed, the
percentage of former Nazis who worked in academia, the civil service,
and the judiciary almost equaled the percentage of Nazis in those segments of society at the peak of Hitler's Germany. Mary Fulbrook asserts
that the fact that West Germans did not have to feel guilty for the atrocities committed during World War II seemed a logical consequence of
scandalously lenient verdicts in the trials of Nazis. Furthermore, former
Nazis acquitted of charges considered the verdict an act of exoneration.
Wulf Kansteiner points out that this moral equilibrium was only occasionally disrupted by political scandals that simply could not be ignored.
Thus, by ignoring questions regarding Nazi crimes, the Adenauer administration in fact planted a time bomb that exploded in the 1960s. One
can come to the conclusion that total amnesia was the foundation of
the new West German identity.[17]

Germany's first international cinematic success became the first of the
so-called "rubble" films, *The Murderers Are amongst Us*, released in 1946.
The film focused on three characters: a woman, former prisoner of a
concentration camp; a former surgeon who cannot forget the traumatic
experiences of the war on the Eastern front; and the former commander
of the surgeon's unit, who had ordered the murder of civilians, and who
is currently an owner of a big company. He expresses no compunctions
about his past crimes. Thus, even before the partition of Germany, Berlin

DEFA film studio, which the Soviet authorities licensed and sponsored, addressed the legacy of the Nazi past while connecting the past with the imperialism and corporatism of the West. In what was to become West Germany, there was no genuine attempt to address the same issue. Although two films that dealt with some Nazi crimes were released in West Germany, *Morituri* (1946) and *Long Is the Road* (1947), West German politicians and intellectuals were not interested in an attempt to give the past a thorough consideration, even though audiences, with the exception of viewers in Bavaria, found them thought-provoking and captured their attention. Although there were some exceptions among West German films in the 1950s, what seemed to have been anti-Nazi films turned out to be highly selective and historically inaccurate. For example, *The Devil's General* (1955), concerned with the Nazi invasion of Yugoslavia, completely failed to adequately present Nazi aggression. In fact, the film proved to be quite abstract and controversial, especially when an SS general crashes the bomber he pilots so that it would not be used as a weapon of mass murder. Even more significantly, the "good" SS general was inspired by the determination of a tortured pilot who, despite his physical wounds and desperate situation, was unwilling to abandon the Jewish couple whom he had been trying to help to escape.[18]

The first German films, which did bring up the topic of war crimes and destruction, quickly disappeared from German cinemas even before the creation of the two German states. Rubble films not only dared to pose the questions of guilt, both individual and collective, but they also pointed to a possibility of self-exculpation. German audiences no longer were captivated by the horrors of the war and the images of Nazism. These early films, which actually did bring up difficult questions about the Nazi past, were produced by DEFA, which after the creation of the two German states became the official film studio of East Germany. Its main tasks involved exposing and fighting fascism, engaging in a cinematic propaganda battle with the West, and promoting the humanism of Socialism. Indeed, East German films of the 1950s often offered explicit indictment of the Nazis. Films such as *Council of the Gods* (1950) focused on capitalist–fascist connections and actions that resulted in the world war.[19]

While DEFA continued to produce films that focused on social problems, often anti-fascist and ideological, West German cinema sought an escape from the images of the past. Thus, by 1949 a new genre of German film emerged that allowed West Germans to escape, as much as it was possible, from their recent past tainted by war and genocide.

In fact, the popularity of the *Heimatfilm* in the 1950s and early 1960s "extinguished the inspiration of the German cinema almost as surely as Hitler had done in 1933."[20] Thus, the popularity of the *Heimatfilm* in West Germany in the 1950s further demonstrated the unwillingness of German filmmakers and audiences to engage in meaningful discussions of their recent past. On the contrary, escapism is the one word that best characterizes the intention and the function of the most popular West German genre of the 1950s. The *Heimatfilm* "established a spatial imaginary for coming to terms with the loss of nation and for turning the Federal republic into a new homeland."[21]

Indianerfilme and the Holocaust

"Love your brother, but hate your enemies." So starts Dean Reed's song preceding the *Indianerfilm Blutsbrüder* (*Blood Brothers*), East Germany's most popular film of 1975.[22] The dreams of love and peace could not be fulfilled due to Americans' constant encroachment upon the Indian territory as well as the incessant violation of peace treaties concluded between the subsequent American governments and the Indian tribes. Thus, the film demonstrates the conflict on the frontier as Indians' just and right fight for freedom and from the very beginning the viewer sees it clearly who the good and the bad are. The film's goal was not only to explain to the viewer the true causes and ramifications of the Indian-American conflict, but also through Dean Reed, it was supposed to enhance the objectivity of the production, presenting an American "star" speaking honestly about his own country and supporting the anti-American message the film conveys. It was another DEFA production in the series of *Indianerfilme*, perhaps the most transnational of all of them. Aside from Gojko Mitic, who starred in all of the *Indianerfilme* and played the lead Native American roles, Dean Reed joined him as a disgruntled American soldier who abandoned life at a military post and rejected the army altogether, having seen the atrocities committed by American soldiers. Ultimately, Harmonika, the character played by Reed, chooses to live among the Indians and become an Indian, and fights side by side with the Indians against the American army he came to resent so much.

The opening scene, albeit somewhat chaotic, reveals what the intentions of the filmmakers were and what the viewer could expect. The viewer sees American soldiers somewhere at a camp in wintertime. Next, the viewer notices an Indian village. For some reason, the American flag can be spotted on the top of one of the Indian huts. It is not known who planted it there and for what reason. Harter Felsen, the Indian played by Gojko Mitic, is riding past the American soldiers' camp. Next he rides into the village, with kids running behind him. Soldiers seem to be following him. Once the Indians see the soldiers, they try to protect themselves and their children in particular. There is only one reason why American soldiers would enter an Indian village: to plunder and kill. An older Indian tells a group of kids to stay together as he tries to protect them by standing in front of them. Those Indians expect only one thing with the arrival of the soldiers: bloodshed. Indeed, everyone's a target; children are being shot as well. There is no reason established as to why the American soldiers enter the village and indiscriminately target everyone that moves. Harmonika is actually not taking part in the fight. He is mesmerized by the butchery conducted by his own people. He holds on to the American flag he carried as he watches people being shot, tents being set on fire, and Indians running chaotically to find some solace anywhere. He is wounded and falls off his horse, but the carnage does not cease there. Just before he loses consciousness, he sees the American flag atop of the Indian hut. He immediately breaks the flagpole he has been holding and throws his American flag to the ground.

Inevitably, the viewer might see a connection between the American raid on the Indian village and the My Lai massacre. Given Dean Read's and the Communist bloc's strong opposition to the American military's presence in Southeast Asia, this could be interpreted as connecting the past, including the conquest of the American West along with the purported unconditional support of capitalists for the Nazi regime with the most controversial contemporary issue, the Vietnam War. Indeed, there are more scenes throughout the film which suggest just that with the insistence on killing of the innocent, including children, and the immorality and avariciousness of the West. At the same time, the film presents the Indian cause as unequivocally just and, just like in other DEFA *Indianerfilme*, the Indians are the true heroes, albeit in this case, it also shows that anyone, including Americans, can undergo a metamorphosis for better if they only switch sides and throw their support behind the Indians which for all practical purposes meant the Communist bloc. Indeed, the Indians working together conduct a brave and desperate attack excellently carried out. The Indians, led by Gojko, release Indian prisoners captured during the raid. The successful operation ends with a typical element of DEFA *Indianerfilme*, placed either early or at the end of the film. The narrator begins the story about how the Cheyenne Indians were forced to abandon their homes during the Civil War due to President Lincoln's anti-Indian campaign. DEFA *Indianerfilme* often included messages read by narrators, containing actual dates, names, and events, in order to enhance the credibility of their films. While the films were supposed to entertain, they never shunned their obvious propagandistic goals of supporting the Communist system and castigating the West. A viewer better aware of history might even compare their fate to the Trail of Tears, as the Cheyenne trek through the snow-covered mountains, being defenseless and left to their own devices, having no other goal but to survive. But their survival is never certain, especially after the recent discovery of gold in Montana, which will surely trigger another wave of migration of greedy and unscrupulous Americans across the frontier.

The following scenes demonstrate the uniqueness of Harmonika, the savagery of the American army, and the brave resistance of the Natives. Harmonika is next seen riding along with two other former soldiers. When one of them falls off his horse as he tries to cross the river, he then grabs a stick and is about to beat his horse to punish it for disobedience, but Harmonika intervenes and tells him not to do it. He takes away the stick, but the other man spits at Harmonika with an expression of contempt and disbelief. Down the river, there is an Indian woman with her child. They are clearly happy and enjoying life. While Harmonika is admiring the landscape, he hears a shot has been fired. He fears it could be one of his companions. One of those soldiers kills the Indian child, while the other one is trying to drag the mother away with the probable intention of raping and killing her. The woman resists and tries to escape. If the man cannot have what he wants, the woman will no longer have a right to live. He grabs her and kills her with a knife. "Why did you do that?" Harmonika asks him. "The best Indian is a dead Indian," he hears in response, what many could immediately identify as a well-known phrase uttered by General Philip Sheridan. Harmonika watches the scene in disbelief and disgust. He watches the two bodies lying on the frozen ground as his companions depart. He then sees the woman's hand move. He does not go with his former friends. He stays behind to take care of the woman. When the woman finally regains consciousness, she sees Harmonika with a knife in his hand. Fearing he is about to finish her off, she screams; he then hits her in order to make her be quiet, for which he immediately apologizes saying that he has never hit a woman before. He wants to rescue her. He then asks his horse: "Did you know Indian women were so beautiful?"

Soon enough, Indians, led by Harter Felsen, approach Harmonika's camp. Harmonika is captured, tied up, with a rope around his neck, and he is led to the Indian village nearby and treated harshly. He has to run all the way to the Indian village and notices the body of one of his companions killed by Indians, the one who killed the woman and her child. Justice can be and has been served, even if Indians must continue to fight a more powerful enemy. They enter the village and Indians throw rocks at him. Harter Felsen announces that they captured one and killed another. He then asks the crowd whether Harmonika should die. "Yes," Indians shout. But then the Indian woman arrives and says that Harmonika had not killed anyone and that he saved her life. She turns out to be Gojko's sister. Gojko and the chief argue about what to do with Harmonika. They are afraid of white settlers and the army encroaching upon their territory contrary to the promises they had heard before. Their women and children are murdered. But the chief says that Harmonika should not be killed. "I have not killed anyone," pleads Harmonika. But the chief decides that the two are to fight. But it is a special kind of fight. Harmonika does not know yet what is going to happen to him. During the night, Gojko's sister brings Harmonika some food and a pair of shoes. Harmonika tells her he is not hungry. He does not understand the verdict the chief made. He asks Harter Felsen's sister, Rehkitz: "Why should I kill your brother and why should he kill me?" Harter Felsen notices his sister's return and finds out she went to bring food to the prisoner. She does not deny it. Harmonika begins to eat the food after the woman leaves him alone.

In the morning, Harmonika's hands are untied, but he is not set free. On the contrary, he is to fight Harter Felsen. The chief and everybody else immediately notice Harmonika's new shoes. When Harter Felsen arrives, the two are encircled by spectators. The chief brings two knives. Both Harter Felsen and Harmonika get one. The chief then addresses Harmonika: "Your life is in your hands. Run, white man, because once the sun rises, Harter Felsen will start chasing you and he will not stop until he kills you, or is killed himself." Harmonika starts running, then he stops for a while, but then resumes running. The sun rises. Harter Felsen screams and starts running after Harmonika. The sister is anxiously waiting to see how it is going to end. Whom should she support in the fight? The man she might be in love with who saved her life, or her own brother and her people? Harter Felsen is getting closer and closer. He watches Harmonika climbing the rocky hill. Harmonika loses his knife as he continues to climb but manages to reach the top. Unbeknown to him, his foot kicks a rock which falls down and hits Harter Felsen. It was an accident but Harter Felsen, who was climbing after him and seemed to be getting closer and closer, is hit by the rock and falls off the wall. Harmonika does not realize it. He finally reaches the top and grabs a stone he sees nearby, anticipating to see Harter Felsen reach the top soon too. But Harter Felsen lies down below Harmonika, unconscious. The viewer next sees Harter Felsen is being carried by Harmonika. This courageous American does not kill his Indian opponent because he does not believe it would be right, even though Harter Felsen would have killed Harmonika within a heartbeat.

Figure 2.1 Gojko Mitic: Bild 183-H0627-0018-001, Bundesarchiv. Photographer: Vera Katschorowski-Stark

When Harmonika wakes up, he is being tended to by Rehkitz. "What is with your brother," he asks? "What will be with me?" Harter Felsen, in the meantime, talks to the chief and the council. He is ashamed to be still alive, defeated and saved by Harmonika. "You will both live," says the chief. Soon enough, Harmonika finds out that he is free. During the following night, Harter Felsen enters Harmonika's tent. Harter Felsen has a knife. Deeply wounded and ashamed, he is determined to avenge his humiliation. "You could kill me, why didn't you," asks Harter Felsen.

Harmonika tells him that even though they fought each other, now they should be friends. Harter Felsen withdraws from the tent but is unsure how to behave toward Harmonika.

Harmonika seems eager to adjust to Indian ways of life. He tries to shoot an arrow, but he is quite poor at this and young Indians laugh at him. Harter Felsen picks up the arrow launched by Harmonika and he clearly does not approve of Harmonika becoming one of them. Harmonika and Rehkitz finally get to be alone. They fall in love with each other. Their relationship will be elaborated upon in the following chapters, as it is a unique rendition of relations between an American man and a Native American woman on the frontier.

Harter Felsen finally breaks the ice by telling Harmonika that he could teach him how to use his bow. Harmonika shows the Indian how good a shooter he is and pulls out his pistol, but Harter Felsen is not impressed. He does not understand how anyone could brag about being able to use the powerful weapon, which has killed many Indians. Soon enough, Harmonika marries the Indian woman and Harter Felsen approves of their marriage. Harmonika promises never to leave them and assures the tribe that he wants to be like them. But the time of harmony ends soon when Harter Felsen captures some American soldiers and brings them into the village. The Indians do not believe the soldiers when they say they are on their way to Montana and constitute no threat to the Indian tribe. The Indians think they are soon to be invaded. It is the first time that Harmonika has seen another American since the time he was captured by the Indians. Harmonika trusts the soldiers, but Harter Felsen does not. The chief lets them go as he insists that the two peoples should live in peace. But Harmonika's and the chief's naïveté will result in a catastrophe. When Indian men leave the village to go hunting, they leave women and children with no protection. The viewer probably knows what is about to happen next. When American soldiers descend on the village, it can only result in another equivalent of My Lai. The Indians return empty-handed, because buffalos have been decimated by Americans or fled and, upon their return, they see their village burned down and many people killed. Harmonika finds the body of his pregnant wife; he closes her eyes. He screams. "I never hated anyone before, but now I do. I cannot stay with you anymore after this," he tells Harter Felsen. There is only one thing that is on his mind: vengeance. He soon arrives in Montana and eventually finds the one who murdered his pregnant wife. He follows the man, sets up a trap, and is ready to shoot the man, but he does not pull the trigger. He follows the man again and watches him enter his household. "Mary, I'm home," he hears the man say. There are children too. Harmonika aims at the man, but when he sees his children, he hesitates. He then sees the woman is pregnant. So was his wife. He cries in desperation; he cannot do it. He cannot be like those who butchered his wife. He is no longer one of them, even if he is not entirely an Indian either. But one thing that clearly distinguishes him from his own kind is that he would not become a murderer.

Harmonika goes back to the town's saloon, where he earns a living by playing his harmonica. He then spends every penny on booze. A fellow soldier recognizes him and introduces him to other saloon guests and even raises money for Harmonika. A picture of him is taken by a journalist and he becomes famous. People learn about his stay with the Indians in the wilderness and want to find out more about it. That clearly enrages him, as he throws bottles off the tables, and he defends Indians by saying, "they're not barbarians." "And I will not forget," he then shouts, "you are barbarians. You killed my wife. And my child! And my friends! Leave me alone!" He sits down. Another man enters the saloon and says that they are taking the savages to a reservation. Everyone hurries to see them. Indians are being carried in a cart; the crowd approaches them, yells that they're dangerous, and mocks them. Harmonika hears it, and even though he is drunk, after a while he recognizes Harter Felsen, who sees Harmonika too. The Indian turns his head away as if in disgust upon seeing Harmonika, who, he might think, switched sides again. Harmonika tries to intervene, he grabs a woman, but her husband beats him. "Don't touch my wife!" the man yells. Harmonika falls to the ground. He once again reminisces seeing the body of his wife and the burned-down village.

Harmonika is determined to fight to let the Indians go free. At night, he overpowers one of the guards, unties Harter Felsen, who then overpowers another guard. Soldiers open fire, but they manage to escape. Following the escape, they become blood brothers. They cut their arms and hold the open wounds together as though to exchange blood.

The tribe's miserable conditions are shown again. They are desperate. "Are you ready?" Harter Felsen asks. Harmonika tells him he is now ready to kill. Harmonika and Harter Felsen fight arm in arm. But there is no end to fighting; the viewer does not see either side win. But that is perhaps the point. The viewer might assume that the fight has really never ended, rather it is still going on, in Vietnam, for example, and all over the world. The West is still trying to impose its capitalist ideology by force on other parts of the world, but after seeing the film, the viewer will have no trouble recognizing who is right in the conflict. And for the West to remedy its disastrous policies there is only one solution: follow the path of Dean Reed, the American who embraced Communism and defended the weak against capitalist aggression.

The presence of an American artist certainly attracted attention to the film. Dean Reed did not hide his personal political views and one can safely assume that the film became a manifestation thereof. The film *Blutsbrüder* was released only three years after the artist settled in East Germany. Of course, it was a great advantage for the East German government to have an American actor of some degree of recognition who could be relied upon to praise Socialist life and criticize the policies of the United States, as he did in his interview on CBS's *60 minutes* where he defended the East German government. Not only did Reed live in and praise East Germany, he also traveled to: Lebanon, spending time with Palestinian soldiers and Yasser Arafat, openly condemning Israel; Chile, to support anti-Pinochet demonstrations; and Nicaragua, where he met with President Daniel Ortega and entertained his troops during the American–Nicaraguan conflict. Perhaps most significantly, after his tour in the Soviet Union, he donated his proceeds to Aid to Vietnam, thus directly supporting the North Vietnamese Communists. When asked to justify his decision to provide financial relief to the enemy fighting American soldiers, Reed said the following:

> The people in Vietnam, and in all other countries of the world, have the right to arrange their affairs as they like, to settle their internal problems if need be by revolution. Our soldiers have no business in Vietnam, it is an aggression...I believe that every Vietnamese has the right and duty to shoot any North American soldier that sets his foot upon Vietnamese soil. He has the right and duty to shoot down any foreign plane that is flying over his country burning and maiming his women and children...Obviously, the man who is defending his land and country and home has a right to kill an intruder who is invading his home and land. That is only just.[23]

Similarly, Dean Read justified the building of the Berlin Wall as a measure to "keep Western agents and saboteurs out, not a fleeing population in." And, responding to the accusation of East German authorities' brutality, he went on to say that "the police of Dallas have shot more of its own people than the police of the G.D.R."[24] That also explains the role of Dean Reed and Harmonika in the film. Harmonika did not want to share the responsibility for the atrocities committed by his countrymen. Although he did not want to fight, he had to survive, in order to make known the truth about what happened.[25] Thus, the film is not about revenge, as Harmonika is not able to kill the murderer of his wife whom he finds. The film's conclusion is Harmonika's resolve to join the Indians in their fight for freedom, which does not happen after his wife was killed, but after he saw Harter Felsen and other Indians tied up en route to a reservation. Indeed, one East German newspaper which reviewed the film praised the ending in which viewers could see the blood brothers act together again.[26]

Figure 2.2 Dean Reed: Bild 183-J1223-0202-006, Bundesarchiv

The presence of Dean Reed served another purpose, as the film was intended not only for domestic markets and those within the

Communist bloc, but also for export to capitalist states. In fact, the Ministry of Culture approved of the film the way it was and did not ask for any additional changes to the version shown in East Germany.[27] The goal was the same as with other *Indianerfilme*: to accurately present the tragic events surrounding the history of North American Indians and to influence the historical thinking of young East Germans. In order to achieve the goal, the film was to focus in detail on the Indians' culture. While the main characters were supposed to appear likeable, nonetheless the film was to inspire young audiences to think critically about the events they watched.[28] No wonder, then, that East German papers picked up on the message the film conveyed. *Nationalzeitung Berlin* hailed *Blutsbrüder* as an "Indian film with a moral claim."[29] The "Red Sinatra," as he was called in East Germany by 1980, became the Soviet Union's and the Eastern bloc's "biggest (and first) authentic superstar."[30]

Recommending the release of the film, a reviewer for the Ministry of Culture emphasized that Dean Read, a progressive American actor and singer, set out to make a statement about the class stratification and race-related problems within the United States based on the brutal treatment of Native Americans on the part of Americans in the 1860s and the deep psychological struggle the main characters, Native Americans, have to face.[31] Here, as in Karl May Westerns, a pair of foreign actors, Dean Reed and Gojko Mitic, played the lead roles and an emphasis was put on the shaping and development of the two characters in order to accentuate the main theme, namely, the legend of the "wild" Indians and the superiority of whites in their attempt to destroy the Indians and the Indians' human and moral stance in their fight for survival.[32]

Karl May Westerns and the *Indianerfilme* became an integral part of both national cultures as well as identities. In East Germany, it meant the building of a future based on the rejection of the fascist past and taking pride in the communist resistance to the Nazi regime. In West Germany, however, it meant an emphasis on national and cultural redefinition that included the purposeful omission of Nazism from public discourse and the school curriculum.[33] In this light, it should not come as a surprise that East Germany chose Liselotte Welskopf-Henrich to write the script for the first *Indianerfilm*. She combined all the elements that DEFA desired: she had helped victims of concentration camps during the war, she had been an ardent Socialist, and she had the knowledge of the American West that added credibility to the propagandistic efforts by providing a damning response to Karl May Westerns, glorification of conquest, and portrayal of the demise of the Native American civilizations.

In these circumstances, less than two decades after the end of World War II, the first West German Western was released, soon followed by a whole series of the most successful movie series in West German history. Karl May films conveyed implicit, albeit significant, messages related to the Nazi crimes that, for many viewers, would provide absolution for their roles, voluntary or involuntary, in the Holocaust. As a response to Karl May Westerns, East German DEFA also resorted to use the Westerns in order to present its own vision of the myth of the American West, one that emphasized anti-fascism and linked National Socialism with capitalism.

Despite Karl May's popularity in Germany, East German Westerns could not have been based on Karl May's novels. Not only would they inadequately convey anti-American and anti-imperialist messages, but due to their "glorification of war and violence," as well as identification with the Nazis due to Hitler's personal fascination with Karl May, the author suffered blacklisting in East Germany.[34] *Indianerfilme* focused on the fate of the oppressed people about to be eradicated by the forces of capitalism that they equated with the destructive forces of fascism.

The *Indianerfilme* equated capitalism and fascism with greed and genocide. According to them, Anglo-Americans' avarice drove them to expand onto Native American lands, forcibly removing Native Americans from them. Those Anglo-American settlers did not hesitate to exterminate the native populations. Indeed, the *Indianerfilme* contain certain scenes in which the perpetrators' actions immediately remind the viewer of the atrocities committed and the methods applied by the Nazis. In *Apache*, Native Americans, women and children, are encouraged to come to the town market in order to collect their annual supply of flour. Only some of them, including the young chief Ulzana, find this suspicious and refuse to go. His premonition comes true when the wagon that supposedly carried tons of flour, reveals a cannon instead. Once the Native American crowds assemble at the town market, Anglo-American villains open fire on them. Native Americans cannot defend themselves because they were not allowed to bring their weapons with them. Those who survive the cannon fire are killed by Anglo-Americans, unscrupulously firing directly at them. Hundreds of Native Americans die and some of the dead lie on piles of bags of flour. This imagery might have been intended to remind audiences of similar images from Nazi concentration camps and death camps. Ulzana, who eventually decided to follow his people, managed to escape, carrying a small child. They are the two sole survivors of the massacre. In *Chingachgook, the Great Snake*, based on Cooper's *Deerslayer*, the Anglo-American frontiersman,

Deerslayer, and Chingachgook, the last Mohican chief, played by Gojko Mitic, protects the Delaware Indians against the British and French. Both European powers aim to exterminate the Native populations in order to create living space for European settlers, the concept that became known as "Lebensraum" and became the driving motive of the race-based Nazi conquest of Eastern Europe. Moreover, to effectuate this genocide of Native Americans, the European powers offer payments to frontiersmen who bring the scalps of Native Americans, including women and children. Disgusted by the horrific actions of white frontiersmen, at a certain point in the film Deerslayer turns to them and confronts them by asking: "What sort of people are you?" This question reverberates with the question posed to Germans by Allied troops who had liberated Nazi concentration camps. By emphasizing the need for collectivism, evident in *Sons of the Great Mother Bear*, the benefits of class solidarity, propagated in *Osceola*, exposing the evils of capitalism in *Chingachgook, the Great Snake*, or even by displaying the brutal methods and the slaughter of innocent Native Americans in *Apaches*, DEFA set out to discredit Anglo-Saxon capitalism and prove its complicity in genocide. Significantly, East German Indians succeed in their resistance to American and capitalist oppressors by evading annihilation. *Indianerfilme* set out to prove that not only is there an alternative to the avaricious capitalist system, but also that the alternative is based on historical accuracy and a sense of justice.

Weisse Wölfe (*White Wolves*) is an *Indianerfilm* in which the main Indian character, Weitspähender Falke, played by Gojko Mitic, does not survive. On the contrary, the final scene in which he is executed might connect the point-blank execution style with the method of mass murder perpetrated by the Einsatzgruppen on the Eastern front. At the beginning of the film the viewer, through narration, is told about the murders which the new era of industrialization in the United States engendered. The narrator even mentions some names: Rockefeller and Carnegie and how in this case industrialization meant a tragedy for the Indians of the Dakotas. In the opening scenes, an Indian village is shown. A horse collapses during a severe wintertime. The Natives will not be able to survive for too long in those circumstances. They are afraid of Americans and fear that they might be all killed but they continue going, feeding on the dead horse. In the meantime, at a fort, soldiers are discussing the Indian situation and a very well-known phrase is uttered when discussing the fate of the Natives: "order is order." The phrase was used during the Nuremberg Trials by Nazis to defend themselves against the charges of crimes against humanity and genocide. The soldiers decided that the forcible removal of Indians to reservation must continue, though another disturbing and well-known quote is uttered as well: "a dead Indian is a good Indian," to paraphrase General Sheridan. It is very obvious that the filmmakers compare the forcible relocation of the Indians and their plight to what happened during World War II. By the same token, those who both give orders and follow orders do not differ much from those who stood trial in the aftermath of the most devastating war in humanity's history. Indians argue with the soldiers about their conditions. The Indians do not want to relocate; they would rather die on their soil. The officer then tells them up front that they would get no food or water and after an argument breaks out, soldiers begin shooting at Indians, with women and children being the targets of their indiscriminate firepower. They are not the only victims of the American aggression; throughout the film there are more. Weitspähender Falke's wife is murdered as well. The American community is divided, however. There are good whites who are on the Indians' side. A young sheriff defends the Indians as well. Perhaps that could be construed as a message to the younger generations: while the corrupt sheriff fights the Indians, the young one recognizes who the real villains are and tries to protect the Natives. In the final scene, Peterson, the young sheriff, intervenes as an angry mob is about to hang an Indian they captured. He is knocked down but continues fighting, along with Weitspähender Falke, who continues to fire to allow the Indian who is about to be hanged to escape. Weitspähender Falke runs out of ammunition and tries to ride away. The bandits shoot at him and he decides to do something completely unexpected. He walks toward them face to face, even though he only has his tomahawk, surrounded by an armed mob. Weitspähender Falke kills the leader of the white bandits, but as soon as he does that, others begin firing at him, which looks like a firing squad. While Shave Head does not survive, he manages to avenge the death of his wife.

But there is another important message here as well: after the shootout, the young sheriff quits, along with his deputies. They do not want to be part of the killing machine focused on gold and profit. They do not want to work for the American government which uses Nazi methods when dealing with the indigenous. It is a strong propaganda message, even if this time Indians do not win. But the viewer knows what he or she, as an Americans or a German, should have chosen had they faced a dilemma like that. He should have chosen justice and rightness, unlike West Germans and Americans, who had instigated the Holocaust and killed off Indians, respectively. The defeat might teach more than a victory, due to the scope of its gruesomeness.

In the opening scene of *Tödlicher Irrtum* (*Fatal Error*), four Indians ride across the prairie.[35] Soon they see the sign "Welcome to Wind River City, Wyoming." The Indians freely enter the city welcomed by its residents. Apparently, the Indian riders bring some great news to the townsmen gathered at the main street, the news which the townspeople had been waiting for. Oil has just been discovered in Wyoming. It is a great time for celebration and everyone gets a drink, sings, and celebrates. Both Indians and white settlers and workers seem to equally enjoy the discovery of oil and believe that their partnership will only strengthen after it. Black gold gushes up in the air and some people even topple in it. There is a sense of cooperation. "When we all cooperate, we will all live well," says the company boss to Shave Head, the Indian played by Gojko Mitic.

As in many of the *Indianerfilme*, what follows is a scene in which a narrator situates the events in its proper context. This *Indianerfilm* made sure to remind the moviegoers that even though there was a sense of cooperation and that Indians and Americans cooperated for some time, the discovery of oil proved to be a disaster for the Natives. The next scenes show just that: An Indian cannot win. An Indian carriage is attacked. Indians cannot even win at poker. At a saloon, Indians and cowboys seem to enjoy playing poker. But the game, while providing fun for a few minutes, ends abruptly when the cowboys realize the Indian won. An Indian cannot win; he is promptly shot at point-blank in the chest and dies instantaneously. White–Indian friendship is doomed to fail too as two people, an American and an Indian, are killed in the following scene. The dead American turns out to be the town's sheriff's deputy.

Soon enough, Americans begin to exploit Indian's who begin to fight for their freedom. Shave Head then insists that Indians must cooperate with Americans if they want to survive, but that they need to cooperate with the good Americans. Can such be found, though, in Wind River City? The Indians then meet with the greedy capitalist, Mr. Allison, who owns the oil company. The chief reminds Mr. Allison of the pact. The Indians argue that the oil rig operates on their territory and due to the most recent incidents, the deal is off.

It turns out that some Indians work for the company owner and they commit atrocities against their own and the town's residents. First, they kidnap an Indian woman and tie her to a tree. Fortunately for the woman, Shave Head witnesses the kidnapping and he rescues her. The two Indians also try to set the oil fields on fire. Howard, a Sheriff's deputy, and Shave Head both fight the arsonists, even though they barely acknowledge each other's existence. The viewer might wonder what the nature of the relationship between the deputy and the Indian was. Could that deputy prove to be the good American whom Indians can trust? Could he really do that out of his conviction that Indians and Americans should bring back the spirit of cooperation? Could he become the atonement for Americans' crimes?

The two Indians who worked for the capitalist are being bashed by him. He tells them he gave them whiskey and money, but that he cannot stand their incompetence anymore. They leave embarrassed and humiliated. Shave Head witnesses them leave. Howard finds out at the saloon that the deputy had been killed. He immediately orders a drink, visibly irritated and shocked. He then leaves abruptly.

The businessmen in the meantime discuss the strategy to pursue as a response to the Indians' defiance. They have a three-day delay and the Wyoming Oil Company's bosses will not tolerate it. One of the Indians who had just been fired enters the room. He is drunk. He intends to kill the company representative, but at the last moment he is killed by one of the American's men. It is at that moment that the last of the Indians who previously supported the oil company's presence in Wyoming realizes that the company is the Indians' true enemy.

More disturbing events occur in the town. The Indian agent who was present as the capitalists discussed their response to the Indians' defiance and who witnessed the attempt to assassinate Mr. Allison is killed with an arrow to create the impression that an Indian did that. He was killed because shortly after witnessing the events, he announced to Mr. Allison that he wanted nothing to do with his dubious business. There is a fire in the city. People rush to put out the fire and they find the body of the Indian agent. People immediately want vengeance. They spot an Indian and someone immediately fires at the Native. The Indian dies, and people rejoice, kicking the dead Indian's body; a woman is seen spitting at him.

The viewer finds out Howard's true identity. He fancies a towns' resident and he asks her if she has anything against Indians. Jesseebee tells him she does not, but she does not sound convincing. She is an American living on the frontier and even though no Indian had ever done anything to her, she is supposed to be against them. Howard then reveals that he is Indian too. Shortly afterward Shave Head and Howard meet. The viewer finds out that Howard and Shave Head are brothers.

A bandit named Parker tries to kill them, but Shave Head notices him at the last moment and fires a shot which kills Parker.

The Indians debate their next move. "We cannot fight Americans," says Shave Head, "but we can show the officials how bad Americans are." During a subsequent gunfight, the oil fields are set on fire. The entire construction and oil rigs burn down. Explosions follow, and oil tanks are blown up. Finally, the oil rig collapses beaten by raging fire. The Indian party then raids a house in the prairie, in which Sheriff Jackson and one of his men are desperately looking for something. Sheriff Jackson responds to a call to come out of the house, but the other man shoots Howard. Shave Head's premonition is fulfilled. When they first met and talked, he told Howard he would be killed. Shave Head chases the killer and lassoes him. Howard dies. The sheriff, the symbol of rightness and, turns out to be a villain too. Shave Head is so angered over the killing of Howard that he moves to shoot the sheriff and the bandit who killed him, but he does not, because unlike Anglo-Americans and Nazis, Indians would not kill unarmed enemies, even after a battle. Shave Head simply rides away with Howard's body. The Indians defied the Americans and prevailed. But now they know that they can rely only on themselves. Even the sheriff and the authorities cannot be counted on in the fight for freedom and justice.

As with the discovery of gold earlier, the discovery of oil leads to the same tragic results: the Indians first try to cooperate with the Americans and sign different treaties, but stand no chance against their enemy. Thus, they really have only two choices: either to reconcile with their fate and try to adapt to the new situation, condemned to reservations, or wage a hopeless war. But the problem, according to the reviewer at *Märkische Volksstimme*, applies to the working class as well, struggling with the capitalist exploitative class. Thus, according to the scriptwriter Günter Karl, the film is not really about the conflict between Indians and whites, but the oppressed and their oppressors, the exploited and those who exploit them and through a realistic portrayal of the conflict in the late 1890s, the film is of critical importance to understand North America today.[36] The two German states shared a common past, a past that was tainted by extreme nationalism, anti-Semitism, and Nazism. Both faced the daunting challenge of denazification. In one way or another, the majority of Germans had participated in the Nazi dictatorship and felt guilt for the crimes committed in the name of Germany. From the beginning, the occupying powers understood denazification in many different ways. While the Soviets considered Nazism to be a political and structural problem, which could be solved only by structural reforms which would affect education, agriculture, and corporations, Americans considered Nazism to be an individual moral problem, which had to be dealt with through individual trials. The famous question-naire (designed to reveal one's involvement in the crimes of the Nazi regime) and subsequent trials were the American response to the prob-lem of Nazism. After the Americans turned over denazification to West German authorities in the late 1940s, hoping that they would punish those responsible for Nazi crimes, denazification came to a complete halt and evolved into rehabilitation and reintegration of Nazis into pub-lic and political life. In East Germany, denazification proved to be more far-reaching since purges in educational institutions removed Nazis from schools and universities. However, the authoritarian structures of Nazism and a drive for conformity survived past 1945 and gave Commu-nism in the East its specific shape. In general, many historians consider denazification a complete failure. The Nuremberg War Crimes Trials heard Germans blame the Nazi leadership, which had victimized an entire population. "Following orders" became the general justification for involvement with Nazi organizations. Furthermore, both Germanies were interested in integrating people with expertise such as physicians and scientists into postwar society and so overlooked their Nazi past. For most of the 1950s and 1960s, silence fell over conversations when the role of individuals in Nazism was brought up.[37] While it was impos-sible, in the face of the evidence the Allies discovered throughout the war, to deny German guilt for the crimes committed during the years of Hitler's rule, most Germans remained silent. Denazification, in general, did not have any long-term effect and most Germans were disinclined to ponder their role in these crimes.

Regardless of the ineffectiveness of their denazification policies, both West Germans and East Germans understood that the keys to legit-imization and shaping of a usable German identity were dissent and opposition to Nazism. Thus, it became a task of policymakers to equate the forebears of the present with heroes from the past and to deal with those responsible for Nazi crimes. While East Germany had its own heroes, primarily Communists, West Germans considered the men of the July 1944 Plot exclusively as heroes and forefathers of their polit-ical order. Although both East Germans and West Germans saw the main villain as Hitler, they portrayed his central role in the barbar-ity of the previous decade in different ways. Whereas West Germans perceived Hitler as "a magician leaping into German history from some-where completely different, dazzling and blinding the innocent masses and leading them off their allotted historical course," in East Germany

"Hitler was cast as but an unwitting puppet of the manipulative forces of monopoly capitalism."[38] East Germans pointed to the connection between capitalism, Nazism, and war. Accordingly, they defined Nazism as the last and final step in capitalist development. Since East Germany had moved from capitalism to socialism, Nazism could no longer occur there. West Germany, however, through its embrace of capitalism, was still in danger of becoming a Nazi state again. The fact that West Germany defined itself as the legal successor to Nazi Germany and that many former Nazis occupied leading positions in the West German civil service and in political institutions seemed to validate the opinion of the Soviet bloc that Germany could repeat the mistake of Nazism. Thus, the East German government justified the building of the Berlin Wall in order to protect East Germany and the Soviet bloc from fascism.

As the trial of Adolf Eichmann in 1961 and the Auschwitz Trial of 1963–1965 continued, Germans born after the war began to question their parents and grandparents about their actions during the Nazi period. West German Chancellor Willy Brandt's famous gesture at the Warsaw Ghetto Monument during his visit to Poland in 1970 symbolized changed attitudes and the acceptance of guilt and responsibility not only by the German people, but also by a German government. It was, however, the newly founded competition for the Prize of the Federal President funded by the wealthy industrialist Kurt A. Körber in 1973 that opened up an inter-generational discussion. Körber, together with Gustav Heinemann, initiated this competition for high-school students to research democratic traditions in German history. By 1980, however, the topics of this competition were focused on everyday life experiences of Germans during Nazism.[39]

Gradually, some Germans downplayed the German nature of Nazism while emphasizing the German suffering during the Nazi regime and World War II. To that effect, sometimes "direct parallels were drawn between German and Jewish suffering, the suggestion being that it was time the former was acknowledged and addressed just as the latter allegedly had been."[40] But while East Germany did not cease to portray itself as anti-fascist vis-à-vis West Germany, important changes did occur in West Germany in the 1960s when instead of the continuation of German-centered memory, more and more emphasis was placed on the Holocaust, especially due to the activities of the West German New Left and the generation of "sixty-eighters."[41]

3
German Westerns: Popularity, Reception, Heroines, Miscegenation, Race, and Landscape

Popularity

Not only did Karl May films prove to be the most successful film series in West German history, but they also revived the German film industry. *Kölnische Rundschau*, a West German newspaper, even headlined its review of *Old Shatterhand*, the third in the series of Karl May films, with: "Scriptwriter Karl May saves German film."[1] *Indianerfilme*, the East German response to West German Karl May films, became the most successful movie series in East Germany. Based on the popularity of the *Indianerfilme* in East Germany, as well as the fact that DEFA created *Indianerfilme* as a response to the popularity of Karl May Westerns, one might conclude that Karl May's heroes, Winnetou and Old Shatterhand, not only saved West German cinema, but also contributed to the growth of cinema in East Germany. Furthermore, Karl May films triggered a wave of interest in Westerns across the European continent on a scale previously unknown. Some of them, Italian "Spaghetti" Westerns in particular, became very successful internationally.

Were Karl May films as well as *Indianerfilme* German films, though? Perhaps they were transnational products that created transnational heroes in which both West Germans and East Germans found superheroes with whom they could identify. Those heroes embodied contemporary Germanness and became role models for many viewers. Karl May films triggered the production of successful transnational European alternatives to the American genre of the Western. Most importantly, along with the *Indianerfilme*, Karl May Westerns helped East and West Germans in their quest for a new German national identity.[2]

West German filmmakers did not engage in the futile task of separating Karl May films from Karl May novels. They knew very well that
any potential success would be due to the popularity of May's narratives of the American West. They realized that because many Germans
were familiar with the novels, the first German Westerns should avoid
discrepancies between Karl May novels and Karl May films. But one of
the challenges for filmmakers was to compress May's long novels into
two-hour films that could still portray the characters and convey the
messages Karl May intended. Given the context of the Cold War and
the relatively short time which separated the production of the first Karl
May film from the end of World War II, those messages inevitably carried into the political realm and influenced the political outlook of film
viewers.

Initially, West German filmmakers did not anticipate that Karl May
films would be so popular. As Michael Petzel points out, not only did
Winnetou save good people from evil, but he also saved moviegoers and theatergoers from a continuing decline of the West German
entertainment industry.[3] The popularity of the actors who played Old
Shatterhand and Winnetou also astonished both filmmakers and the
media. Erwin Mueller, a West German journalist, even compared the
public excitement that appearances of Pierre Brice and Lex Barker generated to the popularity of the Beatles. Young West Germans saw them
as their heroes. Recollecting how he met Brice for the first time at the age
of 15, in Elspe, North Rhine-Westphalia, Mueller wrote that it meant so
much to him that he could not refrain from crying upon seeing the actor
who played Winnetou. Many young Germans reacted in a similar way
when coming across the stars of Karl May films. Mueller wrote that it
almost felt as though Brice was the Messiah bringing Germans salvation
when he stretched his hand as if to bless the crowds.[4] Indeed, there were
two major heroes West German children identified in a survey of children between 5 and 17 years old conducted by a publisher of children's
books. Asked whom they regarded as their idol, West German children
mentioned President John F. Kennedy and Winnetou, May's chief of the
Apache Indians.[5] Thus, Karl May films realized an entire generation of
German movie enthusiasts' secret dreams by producing the cinematic
representations of their heroes' adventures.[6] Following the success of the
first Karl May film, *The Treasure of Silver Lake*, in 1962, the filmmakers
released the first of the *Winnetou* trilogy just two years later. The first
of the *Winnetou* films proved to be so successful that a year later over
9 million viewers saw its sequel, *Winnetou II*.

Karl May films became a great financial success in West Germany
and other European countries. Movie critics in the West, including the

American author Allan Eyles, praised the films in 1967 in *The Western: An Illustrated Guide*.[7] One British reviewer wrote that "the audiences had to wait for the Germans to finally produce a straightforward Western one can be enthusiastic about, with a plethora of great scenes one after another."[8] The films received many German awards, including the "Golden Screen" (*Goldene Leinwand*) in 1964, the Bambi-award in 1963 for best box-office production, as well as the award of the Federal Ministry of the Interior.[9] Some newspapers enthused about the popularity of Karl May films. *Frankfurter Allgemeine Zeitung* even wrote that it was so gratifying to see that Karl May films made the cinema cash registers all over the world ring again.[10]

Old Shatterhand, released in 1964, proved to be the most American of all Karl May films. American influences are the most visible in this film, especially the Indian–American battle scenes, due to the work of Hollywood director Hugo Fregonese as well as the casting of American actors such as Guy Madison. The film also deviates more than other films from Karl May's narrative, especially in the director's selection of events and their portrayal. Unlike Harald Reinl, the director of other Karl May films, Fregonese had not been familiar with the German writer prior to accepting the offer to direct a West German Western. Reinl, for his part, admitted that Karl May had played an important role in the life of his entire family. He also developed an interest in Indian history and had read relevant literature from the United States to broaden his knowledge. Because, he said, his family's passion was to discuss history, among other subjects, family talks often provided ideas he could use while working on the set of Karl May films.[11]

Old Shatterhand is quite exceptional in comparison to the other Karl May films. Not only was it directed by a Hollywood director, Hugo Fregonese, but it cost a record-high 6 million West German Marks and required the building of an impressive Hollywood set and an equally impressive cast. One might even question whether it was still a German Western, as it appeared more American than previous West German Westerns, primarily due to Fregonese, who brought Hollywood-style scenes such as the depiction of American cavalry in the battles. Moreover, both major Anglo-American characters were played by American actors. Lex Barker was Old Shatterhand, whereas his nemesis was acted by Guy Madison.

Reception

Thomas Jeier has concluded that the creation in 1961 of the first German Western must have appeared as sacrilege to many Americans who believed that only they could produce this most American of all film genres. The successful series of Karl May Westerns might have enraged some "bosses" in Hollywood, for whom Westerns could only be made in Monument Valley by Hollywood film studios and who did not even imagine that they would have to compete with European film studios in this genre. It should not come as a surprise, then, that in the United States the Karl May films were contemptuously called "Kraut-Westerns." An influential French film magazine, *Cashiers du Cinema*, in turn, called them "Schwarzwald-Westerns" because they did not resemble typical American Westerns. The monthly British *Film Bulletin* called them fresh, pleasurable, continental Westerns, with attractive settings, where, for a change, in the last moment the Indians come to the heroes' rescue, rather than American cavalry.[12] Moreover, these German Westerns proved popular at a time when American Westerns began to recede in popularity throughout the 1960s.[13]

Lex Barker and Pierre Brice played the two main characters, Old Shatterhand and Winnetou, in Karl May films. While introducing Brice to West German audiences, the West German press pointed out how his appearance, especially long dark hair, height, and skin tone, fit May's description of the Apache chief. While casting Lex Barker as Old Shatterhand proved to be a great decision from a commercial standpoint, it also moved filmmakers further away from a faithful representation of the hero Karl May had created. Karl May might not have even recognized Lex Barker as Old Shatterhand. Karl May described his hero (as he persistently pretended to be Old Shatterhand in real life) as having a moustache, looking ten years younger than he actually was, slim, less than 170 cm (5 feet 8 inches) tall and weighing 75 kilos (165 pounds). He also mentioned that his favorite meal was chicken with rice and that skim milk was his favorite drink. None of it sounds like anything Lex Barker would have enjoyed nor did Lex Barker, an athletic, 6 feet 4 inches man, resemble Karl May in any way.[14]

By the mid-1960s, Lex Barker and Pierre Brice became extremely popular actors in West Germany and heroes West Germans quickly came to identify with. The role of Old Shatterhand made them stars. One can only speculate whether any other role would have bestowed the same degree of popularity on them. An examination of West German press archives suggests it would have been unlikely that they would have become as popular in any other role they might have played. They fit the roles of the "Teutonic American" and the chief of the Apaches. Although they were willing to continue producing Karl May films in the 1970s, this became impossible with the death of Lex Barker in 1973.

The "Teutonic American" died at the age of 54 of a heart attack walking down Lexington Avenue in New York City. But, as a German newspaper pointed out, the death of Lex Barker, while painful and unexpected, did not mean the death of Old Shatterhand. Although the last of the series, *Winnetou and Old Shatterhand in the Valley of the Dead*, released in 1968, did not prove to be as commercially successful as its predecessors, Karl May's popularity did not end, especially since some of the actors, including Pierre Brice, continued to play Winnetou at festivals and on television, which will be discussed later in the book.[15]

When Lex Barker took on the role of Old Shatterhand, which seemed risky for a popular, albeit somewhat forgotten Hollywood actor, he did not think that he was abandoning Hollywood. Moreover, he did not believe he was going to spend the rest of his acting career in Europe, since he was still under contract to Universal Studios when he began working on the set of *The Treasure of Silver Lake* and was hoping to return to continue making films in Hollywood. One of the reasons why Barker decided to accept the role of Old Shatterhand (of whom he had never heard since he had never read a Karl May novel prior to filming) was that he did not want to be identified only and exclusively with his Hollywood role as Tarzan. For that reason he left the United States for Europe, hoping to find a new role that would have added new meaning to his career. He first traveled to Rome, believing that Italian film producers had more imagination than their Hollywood counterparts. After a conversation with the West German film producer Horst Wendlandt in Berlin, where he traveled at the invitation of an American film director temporarily staying in West Germany, he decided to accept the role of Old Shatterhand.[16] Lex Barker admitted that the first Karl May film amazed him because he concluded it truly was a great film. Although it may have seemed naïve to American audiences, he nonetheless thought it was a completely new approach to the Western and its originality certainly was one of its strengths.[17]

Similarly to Barker, Pierre Brice admitted that he was not originally enthusiastic about playing an Indian when he first read the script of *The Treasure of the Silver Lake*. Initially, he had no interest because he did not like typical American renditions of Native Americans and he believed that this film would not be any different, as he had never heard of Karl May. He even rejected a seven-year contract with Hollywood, following the success of his earlier roles in European films, because he did not want to play Indians in Hollywood Westerns. Moreover, it seemed risky to play in a German Western, having been selected by the Italian press twice in a row as the "Actor of the Year." Most film critics were quite skeptical about the potential success of a Karl May-based Western; thus he was afraid that by acting in it, he would arrest a successful career. Finally, Brice even liked the role of Old Shatterhand much better. Eventually, he decided to take part in Karl May films, which completely changed his life, and similarly to Barker's, relaunched his career. He enjoyed the fact that he was finally cast as a morally upright person as opposed to the villains he had played before.

Brice admitted that through the role of Winnetou, the French actor, less than two decades after the end of the war, learned much about Germany and Germans. In this regard, he did not differ from Barker, who also offered a new perspective on German–American relations. It would indeed be hard to find any non-German actor who wanted to play in Karl May films and who actually had heard of Karl May prior to the screening of the films, let alone read his novels. Chris Howland, a popular British actor and comedian who also played in some of the films, admitted in an interview that he had never even heard of Karl May, even though he used to read a lot. He did, however, buy *In the Desert* and placed it next to his bed while working on the set, hoping Karl May would forgive him his ignorance.[18] London-born Stewart Granger, who played the role of Old Surehand in *Among Vultures*, did not know anything about Karl May either. For him, however, the role was not just another job. He considered himself a cowboy and a rancher and enjoyed both military and Western roles. Among his better known roles was that of John Wayne's sidekick in *North to Alaska*. His role in *Among Vultures* is yet another manifestation of the transnational nature of German Western films. This British actor, living on his New Mexico ranch, came to play the German-American hero of the American West, Old Surehand, based on the story written by Germany's most popular author. The film, situated in New Mexico, the land of the Apache, was filmed in Yugoslavia, just like all other German Westerns of the era.[19]

The popularity of Karl May films manifested itself in many spheres of popular culture previously unaffected by movies. The fame of Old Shatterhand and Winnetou transcended books and movies. The German journalist Tassilo Schneider noted that it was the first time in history when fans could buy a soundtrack of a German film on record, with one of them remaining the best-selling single for 17 weeks on Germany's charts. Schneider mentions all kinds of memorabilia Karl May films enthusiasts could purchase, including "board and card games, hundreds of toys, countless comics, drawings, a coffee table, cookbooks, clothes (including socks and shoes), and a brand of cigarettes based on film motifs and characters."[20] West Germans were constantly reminded of their favorite heroes without going to the movies or even reading a book. It was enough to play a game of cards or put on a pair of socks to reminisce about the American West created by Karl May and consider the messages it conveyed.

Figure 3.1 Winnetou and Old Shatterhand inspired millions of readers and movie enthusiasts on both sides of the Iron Curtain, including the author, whose family always took the "Winnetou" tent wherever they traveled

The myth of the American West provided a context in which both West Germans and East Germans could discuss morality. Some supporters of Karl May films found it best to quote a letter from a young admirer of Winnetou to explain the moralizing effects of Karl May films. A young moviegoer wrote:

> I have learned a lot from Winnetou. Now I know that one has to appreciate friendship, that one should not immediately consider every girl a friend, that one needs to learn to know one's value, to respect others, that one needs to have some pride, and that one should not be a coward nor should one act dishonestly even towards those one does not like.[21]

A Winnetou fan wrote to Pierre Brice that she had lost faith in people, but he (Winnetou) made her believe in the goodness of people again.

People certainly came to identify with the actors and their roles. Karl May films provided a message of comfort and relief from everyday life and the troubling past, encouragement and praise to German audiences that still had not recovered from the experiences of the Holocaust and World War II. Although different generations of West Germans found different meanings in the films, they found the films optimistic and hopeful, even though they portrayed the inevitable collapse of the Native American civilizations.[22] Therefore, one could easily accept Karl Markus Kreis's observation that two contrary historical motivic themes thus influenced the German image of the United States: "the yearning for the truly existing country of America, where it was hoped the opportunities for living were better, and the sympathy for and the playfully serious identification with the ideal child of nature in the Indian."[23] In that regard, *Indianerfilme* differed tremendously from Karl May Westerns. East Germans considered *Indianerfilme* highly entertaining, even though they were more ideological than their subtler West German counterparts. Produced under the supervision of the state apparatus, *Indianerfilme* responded directly to West German messages of progress and the inevitable demise of the Natives. The *Indianerfilme* denounced the conflict between white settlers and the Native American population as proof of capitalism's destructive force and its contribution to genocide both in the American West and during World War II. *Indianerfilme* differed significantly from Karl May films in many other regards as well. The most important difference is that in East German films the good characters are predominantly the Indians, while the evil ones are Anglo-Saxons, whereas in the Karl May films, the reverse is true. Despite their differences, both series not only attracted millions of viewers, but also resulted in the creation of fan clubs, posters, and other commercial items for sale.[24]

While Karl May films became commercially successful and popular in West Germany and millions of moviegoers saw them, *Indianerfilme* proved to be equally successful proportionately to the size of East Germany, about four times smaller than its Western neighbor. People across the entire Eastern bloc could see the first *Indianerfilm*. For example, *Die Söhne der großen Bärin* was released in the Soviet Union, Bulgaria, Czechoslovakia, Poland, and Romania.[25] Because DEFA and East German officials acknowledged that most of the films would not be released in the West, they understood that their films needed to target audiences in the Communist bloc, hence the emphasis on the propagandistic nature of the genre. At the same time, DEFA set clear financial goals for the films. Filmmakers hoped that the films' entertainment value would attract enough viewers in East Germany to recover the costs of production and, possibly, make a profit. In just one week between July 30 and August 5, 1971, over 152,000 people saw *Osceola*, which brought over 275,000 Marks in profit.[26] *Weisse Wölfe* was distributed in both East Germany and other countries of the Eastern bloc. In Poland, for example, it was considered the best of the four *Indianerfilme*. Released in June 1969, it became another success for DEFA. In just one week, between July 11 and 17, over 222,000 East Germans saw the film in 72 different movie theaters during 640 screenings.[27] What is interesting is that, most likely in order to attract a greater number of moviegoers to see *Indianerfilme*, many of them were intentionally released in summer, when male youths were out of school and eagerly engaged in playing Indians and cowboys. While *Indianerfilme* became a successful response to Karl May films, unlike their West German counterparts, no *Indianerfilm* was ever released in the United States. Only within the last decade have three of them, *Son of the Great Mother Bear*, *Apaches*, and *Chingachgook, the Great Snake*, been released on DVD, thanks to the founding of the DEFA Film Library at the University of Massachusetts in Armherst. Perhaps surprisingly, no Karl May film has become available on DVD in the United States yet.

While Karl May films relaunched the career of Lex Barker and made him and Pierre Brice two of the most popular actors in West German history, *Indianerfilme* became the starting point for the tremendously successful career of the Yugoslavian-born actor, Gojko Mitic. Not only did Mitic assume the status of a celebrity, one previously unknown in East German cinema, but he also became popular in other countries of the Eastern bloc, including the Soviet Union and Yugoslavia. The former physical education student turned actor expressed his firm belief in the messages of righteousness and freedom conveyed by the *Indianerfilme*. For example, Mitic asserted in an interview that *Indianerfilme* provided role models for young male audiences. Indeed, while Mitic did not believe that the films were simplistic, he underscored the importance of a clear-cut narrative in which both adults and adolescents could easily differentiate between good and bad characters. They could thus understand what the average man should do if facing difficult circumstances in life. Interestingly, one adjective that Mitic used in the interview was purposefully emphasized by the newspaper. The newspaper found it proper to accentuate the word "common" in the phrase "common enemy" where Mitic explained Indian chief Chingachgook's determination to unite Indian tribes to fight a common enemy, as opposed to engaging in intra-tribal warfare, which could only prove detrimental to the Native Americans fighting European invaders.[28] That should not come as a surprise knowing the goal of the *Indianerfilme* was to emphasize the imperialism and racism, the two driving forces of the westward expansion.[29] Applying this rhetoric, East German authorities were only too eager to accuse the United States of having engaged in ethnic cleansing en route to the creation of a continental empire. Moreover, the United States was painted as an enemy of all Socialist states after World War II and a supporter of the fascistic West Germany, the successor to the Third Reich. DEFA also alluded to racial discrimination in the United States contrasting it with the political and cultural goals of Socialist countries and Socialist filmmakers, focused on equality and harmony.[30]

Indianerfilme sometimes focused on specific issues which DEFA filmmakers believed plagued the United States, such as corporatism. *Weisse Woelfe* illustrates the United States in the era of the rise of monopolies such as the companies founded by Carnegie, Morgan, and Rockefeller. Indeed, one newspaper called the film "a historic truth," depicting the last phase of the courageous fight for survival of the last Indian chiefs against greedy capitalists. At the same time, not only does the film illustrate the Anglo-American conquest of Native Americans, but it also shows the beginning of the class struggle between Anglo-Americans themselves on the eve of the twentieth century. In this way, the filmmakers tried to debunk what they perceived as the myth of economic progress of the late nineteenth century and draw attention to illicit actions of capitalists, destroying the lives of not only Native Americans, but also individual Americans.[31]

In order to make sure that the viewer clearly understood the anti-capitalist message, DEFA often provided a narrative at the beginning and a historical commentary at the end of films. Thus, the viewer who did not know certain events in American history could connect them with history. Moreover, DEFA directed the viewers to understand what they saw in a way compatible with the official rhetoric of the Communist state. This contrasts with Karl May films, which sometimes also narrated the beginning of films but merely to acquaint the viewer with the characters or to introduce the story. The example below demonstrates the contrasting narrations.

Winnetou	*Osceola*
"What sounds incredible today was, a century ago, a bitter, cruel reality. This was the era of the last desperate attempt of the Indian to hold his own against the white man. Pushing further and further west came the hardy pioneers, and following them were the adventurers, bandits, desperadoes. The Muscalero Apaches were friendly to other white men, but their doom was inevitable."	"This war began on December 28, 1835. It lasted seven years, cost the United States 20 million dollars, and the reputation of many generals. In this war against a small nation of 4000 Seminole Indians, 1500 American soldiers died, let alone numerous civilians. How many Indians and blacks perished, will never be known."

Karl May films point to the inevitability of the demise of Indian nations and promoted the idea of redemption by focusing on the future rather than the past. *Indianerfilme*, however, point to the agents of destruction, and how the past determines the future and how the past cannot be detached from the present. Therefore, the main difference between the two is that while *Indianerfilme* are a conspicuous indictment of capitalism and the West (the United States and West Germany in particular), Karl May films allow the viewer to understand that the genocide of the Apache was inexorable and that one needs to move on, rather than point fingers at the perpetrators, with both ideas being congruent with the positions of the authorities in the two German states.

When the first Karl May films appeared on the big screen in West Germany, it seemed as though the Winnetou-boom would never end. West Germans eagerly bought movie tickets to see Old Shatterhand and Winnetou, who, according to Karl May, were more beautiful than he could ever describe. That the movies attracted millions of West Germans and gave a boost to the declining West German movie industry demonstrates that the filmmakers managed to appeal to the imagination of the moviegoers and satisfied the fantasies of even the most devout fans of Karl May's novels.[32] The popularity of the Karl May films could serve as both a late recognition of his works and a validation of his popularity as a writer. Although Karl May had to fight critics who accused him of plagiarism and of creating false, simplistic, and stupefying images of the American West, one could argue that Germans' taste for literature did not really change for decades. Karl May's popularity had not abated since the late nineteenth century. Many West German politicians, including former President Roman Herzog and former Chancellor Helmut Kohl, admitted to being May's fans.[33] Moreover, based on the popularity of *Der Schuh des Manitou*, a recent German parody of the American West loosely based on May's works and films (somewhat similar to Mel Brooks's *Blazing Saddles*), one comes to the same conclusion regarding Karl May films, namely, that they have not been forgotten. Indeed, *Der Schuh des Manitou*, discussed in detail in the last chapter, released in Germany in 2001, and in 2002 in the United States under the title *Manitou's Shoe*, earned over 55 million dollars at the box office and has been the most successful film in German history since World War II.

Not only did Karl May Westerns trigger the production of East German *Indianerfilme*, but they also precipitated the creation of Westerns all across Europe. They boosted the making of Westerns in other countries behind the Iron Curtain. Karl May's rendition of the American West, in spite of being just one of many literary and artistic representations of the American West, certainly proved to be the most influential, not only upon Germans, but upon other Central and Southeastern Europeans as well. In 1964 in Czechoslovakia, Filmove Studio Barrandov released *Limonádový Joe aneb Konská opera*, known in the United States under the title *Lemonade Joe*. Oldrich Lipsky directed the film whose main character, Lemonade Joe, knows that he will lose his abilities as a gunslinger if he drinks alcohol and, to the enthusiasm of the persistent temperance movement, drinks only Kola-Loka lemonade.[34] In 1967 in Poland, Zespol Filmowy "Rytm" released a Polish Western, *Wilcze Echa* (*The Wolves' Echoes*), employing a typical Western convention, although the action takes place in Bieszczady Mountains in south-east Poland. It was the second Polish Western, after *Rancho Texas* (*Ranch Texas*).[35] Anyone familiar with Karl May's novels could clearly see how the German Westerns released earlier in the same decade influenced the Polish filmmakers. The narration which opens *The Wolves' Echoes* could almost serve as the opening scene of a Karl May Western:

> Bieszczady, the most remote corner of Southeastern Poland. The war lasted here three years longer than in other parts of Europe. During those three years, UPA's nationalist's bands burned towns and villages, slaughtering civilians... When shots were finally no longer heard, the land looked like a desert. It took many more years for justice and law to triumph in the area.[36]

The narration is almost identical, with the crucial differences being Poland and Bieszczady instead of the American West, and UPA's nationalists as opposed to Indians and frontiersmen. And like Old Shatterhand, the major character, Pietrek, resorts to violence only if no other solution is available, and yet, even when facing his opponents, he is capable of firing a shot which hits a bandit's weapon disarming him, instead of killing him.

Most significantly, Karl May films gave rise to the production of the "Spaghetti" Westerns in Italy. Christopher Frayling has demonstrated that Karl May films "created a commercial context which made the Italian Westerns possible." Sergio Leone, the most famous director of Italian Westerns, also admitted that "it was because of the success of the German 'Winnetou' series, directed by Harald Reinl, that the Western began to interest Italian producers." Crucially, the arrival of "Spaghetti" Westerns in the United States sparked a debate regarding the cultural roots of the American Western. Christopher Frayling pointed out that

> the fact that three of the founding fathers of the modern Western – John Ford, Fritz Lang and Fred Zinneman – were, respectively, Irish, German and Austrian by origin, was quietly forgotten (as was, presumably, the fact that an Italian "discovered" America for the Americans, and another gave his name to the continent).[37]

It should not come as a surprise that the conquest of the American West became so romanticized, since it took tough men to endure hardships and dangers along their paths. Some film historians even focus on finding connections between Old Shatterhand and Winnetou and the heroes of the American West. Describing the youngest general in American army history, George Armstrong Custer, who at the age of 24 directed the 7th Cavalry Regiment, according to one West German newspaper, should help moviegoers understand the film *Old Shatterhand*. The author argues that one can see the personification of Custer in Captain Bradley, the commander of Fort Grand. Whereas the heroism of General Custer has been greatly exaggerated and mythologized in American history, Bradley might be considered a hero by some due to his persistence to fight Apache warriors numbering in the hundreds, if not the thousands. However, his corrupt deals with the greedy and ruthless Anglo-American settlers undermine his heroic character. Moreover, Captain Bradley's opportunism exposes his joy at the death of his superior officer. With General Taylor presumably far away, Bradley assumes command of the fort and seems to undo the peacekeeping strategies of his superiors. Throughout *Old Shatterhand*, Indians killed his whole family, which is why he is driven by emotions that compel him to kill as many Indians as possible in the name of vengeance. The Winnetou-led Apaches, with the help of General Taylor, restore peace on the frontier. Bradley is discredited and arrested, and most likely faces a court martial. *Old Shatterhand* ends with a hope for peace between American soldiers and the Indians, and the crooked whites, who are the villains, are defeated.[38]

Heroism on the frontier, heroines, miscegenation, and race

There are many different approaches to defining a Western hero. What does the Western hero look like in German films? Liselotte Welskopf-Henrich's Anglo-American hero, Adam Adamson, appears experienced and inquisitive and becomes sympathetic to the plight of the Dakota Indians. He decides to help them while leaving corrupt white society in search of a better life. Thus, the film attempts to accentuate similarities between the two. While Tokei-ihto, played by the athletic Yugoslavian actor Gojko Mitic, certainly looks like a hero, Adamson is not expected to become one, albeit he also undertakes heroic acts as he frees the Dakota chief and openly rebels against the leading Anglo-American anti-Indian character, Red Fox. Welskopf-Henrich herself insisted on creating a sympathetic image of the Anglo-American hero, even though he was not as athletic as Tokei-ihto, nor as experienced a gunslinger and trapper as Red Fox. Red Fox, Welskopf-Henrich argued, should represent the prototype of the American capitalist, who embodies ruthless cynical energy, so characteristic of the manner of the American conquest of the West.[39] Thus, with the help of a good Anglo-American, the stereotypical greedy and evil Anglo-American is defeated by the Indian chief who can lead his nation to a new homeland in Canada to start the tribe's life anew. While that does not diminish the skills, bravery, and importance of Tokei-ihto in saving his own people, it is somewhat surprising that Welskopf-Henrich also insisted on the creation of a white hero, albeit much more insignificant than the Dakota chief. Perhaps it stems from Welskopf-Henrich's continuing interest in her analysis of Karl May's works, even though she detested his vision of the American West.

How does Lex Barker compare to Tokei-ihto and Adam Adamson? Lex Barker presents himself as an attractive and skillful embodiment of Old Shatterhand, as well as honest and friendly. His role as Old Shatterhand fits him perfectly, which is exactly what Karl May fans could have hoped for.[40] Lex Barker admitted that the German Westerns adhered to Hollywood standards and conventions in many regards. He also stated that, even though he was critical of certain aspects of May's rendition of the American West, he became fascinated with the character of Old Shatterhand. According to Barker, Old Shatterhand was a man who strove to do good and dared to be good, which, according to him, was what impressed people the most.[41] When asked to explain his popularity in Germany, though, Barker responded that he did not know how to explain it other than that he was probably the rare type of person that audiences found attractive. Indeed, one of the common themes that dominates letters German fans sent to Lex Barker was the notion that Lex Barker (Old Shatterhand) showed them how to be a good person in the face of adversities of everyday life.[42] Thus, the American actor Lex Barker became the embodiment of a German hero in the tumultuous decade of the 1960s. German historian Hartmut Lutz has shown that Karl May created an absolute hero, whose virtues surpassed everyone else's. Because of his qualities, he should become the hero of young Germans. Indeed, the list of his qualities is impressive: he rides the wildest Mustang, can kill a grizzly bear with only a knife, knocks people down with his fist, is the best shooter, makes quick decisions, takes charge of any difficult situation immediately, although he is neither indulgent nor self-serving.[43]

Welskopf-Henrich also pondered whether friendship between Native Americans and Anglo-Americans could be possible. She brought up many examples from history when Indians and cowboys and white settlers helped each other for no material gains. Can that be called friendship or is it a pragmatic relationship dictated by the necessity of the roughness of the frontier life? She also asked rhetorically whether the friendship between Indians and Anglo-Americans in films was true friendship or just a romantic kitsch? To prove that it indeed was possible, Welskopf-Henrich cited the example of Old Shatterhand, who, through his friendship with Winnetou, virtually became the head-chief of all Apaches.[44] The motive of blood brothers influenced some West German film producers. Harald Reinl, the director of most Karl May films and an ardent reader of Karl May's works, confessed that he and his best friend from childhood had become blood brothers as well, influenced and fascinated by the friendship between Winnetou and Old Shatterhand.[45]

Lex Barker stated that the storyline of Karl May films could be summarized in one concept: war between the Apaches, who considered signing a peace treaty with the American government, and a group of white bandits, who want to provoke the Indians and undermine the peace efforts.[46] Karl May, the author, knows that Winnetou is going to die because he stands in the way of progress. Old Shatterhand, the

German hero of the frontier, is not a naïve observer of the events of the American West and it would be hard to imagine that he was unaware of the changes occurring there. Therefore, it seems inconceivable that Old Shatterhand believed he could save the Indian nations from their ultimate demise. Does that mean he was being dishonest? Certainly not. He was willing to put his life on the line to fight for Winnetou, but it was Winnetou who died defending his friend. This was his destiny, to elevate his white blood brother's status and to make room for the coming of the superior civilization to which his white blood brother belonged.

The two heroes were certainly best friends and blood brothers, but their friendship had to be ephemeral. They were to be separated through the death of Winnetou, which is not Old Shatterhand's failure. Even the German frontiersman could not change the inevitable. Winnetou's demise is the necessary requisite for Old Shatterhand's biggest triumph. Winnetou converts to Christianity dying in Old Shatterhand's arms. Because of that, "Shatterhand is comforted to think that he had the presence of mind to administer the rites of baptism to the dying chief."[47] Winnetou does not confess to anyone else. He only confides in his German-born blood brother. It is completely inconceivable to think that May would have allowed Winnetou to die to save anyone else's life or convert influenced by an American frontiersman.

Lex Barker himself also discussed the notion of genuine Indian–Anglo-American friendship and Karl May's vision of a hero after acting in ten Karl May films. Barker stated that May had created a character he wanted to become himself and that character displayed friendship and kindness toward people. That makes Old Shatterhand not only a friend of Winnetou, but also a friend of all good people. Besides, Barker added, friendship between whites and Indians existed on the frontier for years, and thus it should not be so surprising. One can think of Jim Bowie and other trappers and fur hunters who, Barker stated, spent months among Indians and sometimes became friends for life. Barker also reminisced about his stay at the army officer school and his participation in the American campaigns in North Africa and Italy during World War II, where there was a Sioux soldier, who was the chief of his tribe, a college graduate, and had many white friends among fellow GIs. People on the frontier at the times of Karl May's stories had to rely on one another, hence friendship between Anglo-Americans and Indians was certainly possible. The French actor Pierre Brice also agreed with the idea of Anglo-American–Indian friendship. Living on a frontier can change people's views, reconcile their differences, and downplay their vices, said Brice, who had experienced interracial frontier friendship as a soldier during the war in Indochina in the early 1950s.[48] Although there are examples of friendship between Anglo-Americans and Indians in both Karl May films and *Indianerfilme*, an alliance between them could only be short-lived; Native Americans' demise was inevitable in the former, whereas violence and vengeance dominated in the latter.

Heroines, miscegenation, and race

Anglo-American women in Karl May films are neither pitch-black (evil) souls nor attractive. However, Mrs. Butler from *Treasure at the Silver Lake* reminds German women of how they suffered during World War II and its immediate aftermath. And there are more Mrs. Butlers all around the world, wherever women face times of hardships like the one on Mrs. Butler's farm, besieged by bandits.[49] American Westerns also had roles for women on the frontier. Some of them proved to be heroines, which is hardly the case in Karl May Westerns. Although American Westerns, due to their emphasis on cultural notions of masculinity, are considered the most "male" of popular film genres, they included many significant female characters who had a great impact not only on the films, but also on the leading male characters. Whereas American "female characters might appear subordinate to the western's overt narrative concerns, yet, from the blonde eastern schoolteacher to the brunette saloon girl, they have clearly have been central to the genre's ideological economy," as opposed to Karl May films where "women in general and heterosexual romance in particular are virtually absent."[50] Indeed, there is only one noteworthy woman in May's novels, Winnetou's sister, Nscho-tschi. She falls in love with Old Shatterhand and he reciprocates her feelings. There are, however, certain obstacles to their happiness. Winnetou's sister is an Indian and Old Shatterhand has strong feelings against interracial marriage. In spite of having strong objections to miscegenation, Old Shatterhand believes that once Winnetou's sister embraces Christianity and learns the white man's ways, he might be able to marry her. Winnetou's sister is ready to make that sacrifice and she prepares to leave her family and homeland to settle in New England, into what she perceives to be a strange and hostile civilization. She undertakes all this in order to please Old Shatterhand and become more of the kind of woman he could accept as a wife. The reader can only speculate how the relationship would have evolved, perhaps even May himself did not know, because they were doomed to perish. Winnetou's sister was eventually murdered by an Anglo-American bandit.[51] Thus, the marriage never occurred nor did

Winnetou's sister begin the process of acculturation to Anglo-American ways. The viewer does not know whether she would have succeeded or would have been accepted by Anglo-American women. Most important, the viewer will never know whether her efforts, even if successful, would have resulted in Old Shatterhand's approval. Her murder allowed May to cement the friendship between Winnetou and Old Shatterhand, who then combine their efforts in pursuit of the murderer of Nscho-tschi. Hartmut Lutz points out that her death solved a major problem in the novel (James Fenimore Cooper might have inspired May to choose this solution), though by no means could the reader come to the conclusion that May considered dark-skinned women equal to Europeans.[52] Moreover, in order to end the Indian–American conflict once and for all, Winnetou is willing to allow Ribanna, the woman he loves, to marry an American soldier, Lieutenant Merrill.[53]

The representation of Native American women certainly conveyed racial stereotypes. The French actress who played Old Shatterhand's fiancé-to-be and Winnetou's sister best summarized Native American women's position vis-à-vis Americans. Describing how she was to play a scene with Barker she kept telling herself: "I am very lucky. Lucky to go to school, and to learn what the whites know, so that he can love me."[54]

The whole bizarre sexual aspect of May's writings (all women get killed off, so the two blood brothers can "go it alone") is always worthy of question. The Catholic institution which employed May to write "inspirational" series of stories for young boys is surely a major parameter. But then so is May's own rather sordid sexual life of being unhappily married to Emma, who was some kind of Catholic church mouse, then being attracted to her "girl friend" Clara, a tough, very tough business woman, whom he married after her husband's death. May's relationships with women, similarly to his alleged experiences in the American West, were all a wild fantasy world with a heavy down-tow from reality. May's narcissism (Germany's second writer to attain "rock-star" fame after Goethe's success with *Die Leiden des jungen Werthers*) is perhaps a classic case of beginning to believe how readers project and inspire an author to be.[55]

The determination to avenge the death of a beloved woman is another significant similarity between Karl May films and *Indianerfilme*. A prevailing motive of the Winnetou series is Winnetou's and Old Shatterhand's retaliation following the murder of Winnetou's sister Nscho-tschi. In *Weisse Wölfe*, the Indian chief, Weitspähender Falke, played by Gojko Mitic, takes revenge against the murderer of his wife shortly before he is killed. The *Indianerfilme*, however, went much further than the motive of revenge, perhaps even further than any other Western at the time. In *Blutsbrüder*, Harmonika, a former American soldier, falls in love and marries Rehkitz, an Indian woman. It is not only the fact that he marries the Indian woman which makes it so unique. The scenes of courtship demonstrate the approval of interracial Indian–American marriages and present an Indian–American relationship as completely natural, if not superior, to a relationship between two Americans. Rehkitz's and Harmonika's relationship seems almost perfect. Their relationship progresses slowly, but the viewer can be certain that the two will fall in love with each other, even though when asked by Rehkitz if he wanted to stay with the Indians, Harmonika initially said he did not know yet. Soon enough, they begin to enjoy every moment they can spend together, even if it means riding the horse in a circle for a long time. She teaches him to whistle. He dances and screams, trying to sound like an Indian. She's infatuated by his moves. He wants to teach her to dance like Americans do. They begin to dance but what happens then is what most viewers were waiting for. They fall on the grass, he kisses her on the cheek, and then on the lips. They kiss. "I...well, forget it," he says. "What did you want to say?" she asks. "I forgot," he says. She asks him if it had anything to do with food. Or the weather? Or his family? "Or maybe," she then asks, "you want to tell me you love me?" Harmonika then finally reveals what has been on his mind: "I've never asked any woman before to marry me. But I want to marry you, live with you, and have children with you." She answers "yes" and they hug.

Before their wedding can be scheduled, Harmonika needs to discuss it with his future wife's brother. "I want to stay with you and marry your sister," he tells Harter Felsen, played by Gojko Mitic. The Indian seems to favor the idea of his sister marrying the American, but they also begin to discuss the fate of Indians given the ongoing conflict between the Indians and the Americans. "Can you kill?" the Indian asks. And he reminds Harmonika that for every white person killed, ten Indians die. "If you stay with us, it will become your fate to die with us," the Indian warns the American. "I want to stay and marry her. I will never leave you," responds Harmonika. After the wedding, which is portrayed as a comical event, where at one point Harmonika rides through a tent and part of the material stays on his head as he rides through the village, Harmonika and Rehkitz spend their first night together. Sometime later, Rehkitz tells Harmonika she is pregnant. "How do you know?" asks Harmonika. "I know it," she says. But their edenic relationship is abruptly ended by the raid of American soldiers who kill Harmonika's pregnant wife. The symbolic meaning of the murder and the raid of the village is obvious. Americans would not hesitate to kill Indians, including women and children, to exterminate them either out of greed or mere hatred of the Natives. Peace and harmony, propagated by East Germany, may be unattainable due to the avarice and wickedness of the West, which had committed similar crimes against humanity during the conquest of the Indians in the nineteenth century and, just a few years earlier, against the natives of Vietnam.

Osceola, presented in the East German press as a hit of the summer of 1971 and a realistic historic adventure story, is also not about a great Indian hero, but about presenting the true story of the Seminoles, where violence and intrigue allowed the United States to defeat the Indians after seven years of heavy fighting. In fact, newspapers suggested that each *Indianerfilm* with Gojko Mitic presented a piece of Indian history, another element of the aggressive expansionism of the Anglo-Americans. Significantly, in *Osceola*, Native Americans and African slaves fight together against white murderers, who wrought destruction and genocide.[56] Thus, *Osceola* portrays a rebellion on the part of the oppressed masses against capitalism. The Indians and African Americans combine their forces to fight their real enemy: greedy white capitalists. As with every DEFA Western, the film is not meant to merely entertain, but to have educational and propaganda value. Therefore, most DEFA Westerns make a clear division between the forces of evil (capitalist whites) and the oppressed peoples fighting for justice (Native Americans, African Americans, and occasional white characters such as Adam Adamson, who are disgusted with white ways on the frontier).

Whereas East German Westerns examine life on the frontier in a broader context, regardless of their propagandistic intentions, Karl May Westerns completely ignored ethnicities other than Indians and European Americans. The decade of the 1960s ended with important legislative victories in the United States that ultimately overturned Jim Crow segregation. Because Karl May Westerns were intended to be shown in the United States, it is logical to assume that West German filmmakers decided to avoid including African Americans, even though Karl May had not avoided the issue. On the contrary, he often expressed prejudice toward African Americans throughout his novels. While May does not discuss slavery as much as another German novelist, Friedrich Armand Strubberg, he uses similar stereotypical, derogatory discourse to describe slaves and freed African Americans. Whereas Strubberg recognized a house slave's thick lips and his ungrammatical speech, May emphasized a black servant's greed, laziness, and alcoholism. Similarly, while May does not elaborate on slavery and race as much as others, he picks up on Charles Sealsfield's idea that mixed race is as inferior as other non-white races, as it merely synthesizes negative traits of the two races. May's Indians appear more tolerant of African Americans than others, including German-American frontiersmen. Accordingly, even one of Karl May's heroes, Old Surehand, almost comparable in skills and knowledge to Old Shatterhand, although he condemns the use of the word "Nigger," is quickly told to accept it by a saloon brawler and he acquiesces, quite surprisingly for a frontiersman of his statute.[57] The inclusion of African American characters, however, might seem confusing and not necessarily sincere. While official GDR propaganda supported African Americans in their fight for racial justice and civil rights, not only were East German officials often indifferent to their fate, but they also expressed their bigotry when they thought their views would be kept secret. Furthermore, Maria Höhn and Martin Klimke have demonstrated that East Germany was "hardly a society free of racism and xenophobia" and that even those African Americans who visited East Germany were "well aware of these prejudices."[58]

Once May developed Winnetou's character, two main features became evident: first, Winnetou promoted peaceful solutions to the Anglo-American–Indian conflicts and, second, he slowly began embracing Christianity. It seems appropriate to question, as Mary Nolan did, whether "The noble savage was the best Christian – or did he become noble because he ultimately became Christian?" Yet, from the very beginning May developed the "other" United States that constituted the threat to the noble Indians and the uncivilized West: "a Yankee America of profit-hungry capitalists, markets, and materialism, technology and modernity."[59]

What makes Winnetou and Tokei-ihto heroes? It appears that there is much more to it than the notion of German–Indian affinity. It might seem initially that the same circumstances account for both Winnetou's and Tokei-ihto's heroism. In the case of Tokei-ihto, he becomes a hero because of his qualities, but most importantly because he unilaterally defends his people against the Anglo-Americans and leads them on to a new path of peace and prosperity. While Winnetou shares the qualities of Tokei-ihto, crucially, he becomes a white frontiersman's blood brother and his stature elevates the white frontiersman to the status of a frontier superhero.

Similarly, Winnetou appealed to the good in people and he was a brave, self-confident, and intelligent warrior. Nonetheless, as a West German newspaper pointed out, "What Shatterhand most admires about Winnetou's appearance are his 'European features'; the Apache chief's familiarity with the poetry of Henry Wadsworth Longfellow initially wins the white man's respect, and Winnetou's dying 'as a Christian' is clearly a source of satisfaction to Shatterhand, to May, and presumably to the historical reader."[60] Moreover, what ennobles Winnetou is "his willingness to embrace the best of European culture and blend it with the finest of his own nation."[61] Tokei-ihto, on the contrary, does not embrace Anglo-American ways. Following his battle with Red Fox and his white band from which the Indian chief emerges as victor thanks to his dexterity and bravery, in spite of being outnumbered and outgunned, the only way to rescue his people is to leave the territory where they had resided for generations and start anew in a distant land across the Missouri River. In other words, the only way to live is to move as far from Anglo-American settlements as possible. It is not possible to acculturate and assimilate. Unlike Winnetou, Tokei-ihto seems to believe that the only condition for the two races to coexist peacefully is to live in different and remote parts of the continent.

With Winnetou's ennoblement, however, comes a heavy price. While Winnetou dies fighting to assure the survival of his (and other) Indian tribes, Tokei-ihto actually achieves that goal. Not only does Winnetou die, but also while becoming a "noble" he has to give up his Mescalero identity. While wanting to become like his blood brother Old Shatterhand, he ceases to be an Apache. He is so acculturated to white ways in order to assure his tribe's survival that he no longer acts like an Apache. His actions are often influenced either by his ultimate embrace of Christianity and emphasis on peaceful negotiations rather than Apache-like propensity to fight as a matter of principle. Thus, Winnetou's renunciation of violence is yet another way in which the demise of the Indian nations proved to be inevitable.[62]

While May might make the reader think that to fight the encroaching Anglo-Americans is the right thing to do, those who actually engage in resistance to white ways do not emerge victorious. Such is not the case in DEFA Westerns. The Indians who oppose Anglo-American policies of concentration, forcible relocation, and extermination are presented as patriots, heroes. By portraying the fate of the Natives, DEFA was able to openly criticize the United States and draw connections between the American West and contemporary events, always focusing on the victims of capitalist and imperialist expansionism and its consequences, which included genocide. At the same time, the films promoted an alternative path to success, a blueprint for Socialism.[63]

Chingachgook, the Great Snake, DEFA's second *Indianerfilm*, released in 1967, loosely follows James Fenimore Cooper's *The Deerslayer*. The predominant theme of the film was the arrogance and hostility of the British and French colonists, who, using fire and sword, alcohol and low-quality products, dispossessed the Indians despite their resistance and bravery.[64] The movie focused specifically on French and British efforts to divide and conquer Native tribes. Similarly to *The Sons of Great Mother Bear*, the movie also points to the potential advantages the Natives might have had, had they united to fight the common enemy, which in both cases is exemplified by the efforts made by Tokei-ihto and Chingachgook. Indeed, Chingachgook, the last Mohican, tells the chief of the Delaware tribe that no one is invincible. He even refused to fight a Delaware Indian because he tells him that the French and the British were "fighting for their game." His arguments, however, are interpreted as proof of cowardice. Ultimately, with help from his white friend, Deerslayer, and his amazing skills and bravery, Chingachgook saves his life, his wife's life, as well as the Delaware Indians.

The film emphasizes important characteristics of the Indian-American wars: the courage and endurance of the Indians as well as the cruelty and racism of the Anglo-Americans. Indeed, the movie contains some disturbing comments made by white settlers, for example, "good Indians are dead Indians" and "Indians are not people but worthless redskins whose scalps are like wolves." The only positive white character, Deerslayer, seems completely disgusted by the racism of white soldiers and frontiersmen, and at a certain point in the movie he turns toward them and asks: "What sort of people are you?"

The film does not just focus on action and the moral imperative of the Great Snake's actions. According to Gojko Mitic, the film's role was to familiarize the audience with Indian culture. This was to add to the accuracy of the story, which, according to Mitic, may not have always been present in West German films in which "Karl May's Winnetou wears the dress of a Dakota Prairie Indian" in which "an Apache would sweat to the death."[65] Therefore, aside from trumpeting East Germany's anti-imperialist rhetoric, DEFA Westerns also set out to offer an alternative portrayal of Native Americans, contrary to the common image of the bloodthirsty savage bent on destruction, whose mere presence heralded the destruction "of all that was civilized and pure."[66]

While Karl May Westerns and *Indianerfilme* tell two completely different stories of the American West, they both use Indian characters to convey their messages: Christian redemption and absolution in the former and the (successful) struggle of the oppressed masses in the latter.[67] The appropriation of the Western ultimately served different purposes in East Germany and West Germany, even though initially the two states shared hostility toward American popular culture. The increasing popularity of the genre solidified West Germany's sense of belonging to the Western bloc. Karl May novels and films might seem anti-imperialistic but, unlike East German *Indianerfilme*, they were far from being so. Most importantly, they portrayed the inevitability of the collapse of the great Indian civilizations, even as the Indians evoke a feeling of sympathy in the readers and viewers. East Germany, in turn, used it as a propaganda tool to denounce American imperialism. While DEFA *Indianerfilme* emphasized how capitalist greed precipitated genocide, Karl May Westerns acknowledged it to be natural part of history.

Landscape

Landscape became a crucial transnational element of German Westerns. Not only did Karl May films create a multidimensional West German version of the American West, *Indianerfilme* were no less cosmopolitan than their Western counterparts. In fact, different renditions of landscape served similar purposes in both Karl May films and *Indianerfilme*. While filmmakers attempted to create authentic sites, equal in credibility and appeal to the American Southwest, which typified what a Western environment was supposed to look like, they also set out to invoke a feeling of familiarity in German viewers. That both Karl May films and *Indianerfilme* were filmed on different sites in Yugoslavia resulted in a multidimensional projection of both West German and East German Westerns. Moreover, that both Karl May Westerns and *Indianerfilme* were filmed in the former Yugoslavia showed that both West German and East German filmmakers had a similar vision of the American West. It might also demonstrate that DEFA accepted the Western conventions Karl May films created, pointing to *Indianerfilme* as a direct response and a challenge to the resulting West German projections of the American West.

The quest for authenticity seems stronger in *Indianerfilme*, whereas the effort to create a familiar and comfortable setting appears more obvious in Karl May films. This can be explained by the degree to which the films were politicized. While *Indianerfilme* clearly resonate with official anti-American and anti-capitalist propaganda of East Germany, West German films' political messages are subtle, focusing on entertainment value rather than initiating and responding to West German–East German polemics.

Karl May films not only were entertaining, but also successfully appealed to West Germans' quest for "Heimat." The film producers traveled extensively through Yugoslavia, advised by a Yugoslavian film company that they could find suitable places to film. They wanted to recreate the conditions of New Mexico and Arizona. Half a dozen architects and an army of workers tried to recreate Roswell, New Mexico, the site of *Winnetou I*, filmed in the area of Sibenik in Dalmatia. The task proved to be much harder than expected. Once they completed the building of the site, it took only one 20-minute storm and the entire site had to be rebuilt from scratch. According to the film studio release, the scriptwriter of *Winnetou I*, Harald G. Petersson, who on 50 pages elaborated on the details of the Roswell location to be recreated in Yugoslavia, believed that even Karl May would have turned green with envy if he could have seen the impressive site of the film production.[68] Indeed, many West Germans began to consider Yugoslavia "heimatlich," namely, they identified themselves with the landscape to the extent that they could see their own *Heimat* in them. Moreover, Karl May films precipitated an unprecedented wave of tourism. The popularity of Karl May films, combined with the beauty of their landscapes and how "heimatlich" they appeared, made Yugoslavia a primary tourist destination for West Germans in the 1960s. Interestingly, according to the director Harald Reinl, 90 percent of the landscape motives were found by accident.[69]

Another challenge filmmakers had to face was that, as French actress Marie Versini, who played Winnetou's sister, asserted, prior to the release of *Treasure of the Silver Lake*, only Americans made films about the Indians. To that effect, Karl May films were inevitably compared to their American counterparts and needed to prove their authenticity. But, as Versini stated, thanks to Karl May, Germany soon became an exception and precipitated a wave of interest in producing European Westerns all across the continent. Indeed, the sites in Yugoslavia were so beautiful and "original" that the crew became mesmerized by them. Lex Barker even stated that "one could think we are in California."[70] In order to authenticate the landscape, thousands of stunts, horses, and props were employed. Because of the number of horses, some movie critics even referred to the films as "neck-breaking Winnetou."[71] In the film *Old Shatterhand*, for example, the filmmakers used 600 Indian costumers, 400 American Cavalry uniforms, 14 wagons, 84 wagon horses, 300 colts produced in Milan, and many other items. Winnetou's wig was made of Indian hair and cost 2000 West German Marks.[72]

While the films include characters whose nationality is assumed to be Anglo-American, many West German viewers, familiar with Karl May, might have remembered that the main white character, Old

Shatterhand, was German-American. In fact, most of the "good" white characters were either of German or Austrian ancestry, whereas all white villains were of English descent. Moreover, actors who played in Karl May films came from many countries, including Germany, the United States, Great Britain, and France. Stuntmen who played Native Americans were usually Yugoslavians due to the fact that they had played Indians before and, most likely, due also to their complexion. Yugoslavs also became enthusiastic about Karl May films and Lex Barker reminisced that he even received a congratulatory telegram from a Yugoslav official that read: "Love and kisses, Your Tito."[73] While architects tried to recreate the American West, any viewer familiar with the American West immediately understands that it is only a replica of the original landscape. However, the blending of European and American landscapes resulted in the creation of a transnational German identity that proved so convincing that many West Germans accepted it as their imaginary "Heimat." Director Harald Reinl even stated that Karl May films were very similar to the *Heimatfilme*, the most popular West German genre of the 1950s.[74]

According to the West German media, filmmakers managed to recreate the Wild West, where "the jagged-topped mountain ranges speak and which infatuates the moviegoer."[75] While some newspapers criticized Karl May films for being too simplistic, none criticized the Yugoslavian film sites. On the contrary, they offered nothing but praise. Aside from its beauty, West German newspapers also pointed to another factor that prompted filmmakers to choose Yugoslavia. Not only did many Yugoslavs have experience playing Indians, they accepted lower wages than their Western European counterparts. The decision proved to be critical to the creation of what one newspaper hailed a "pure medium," completely worth the success at the box office.[76] This success which made the West German viewer rediscover that Heimat was indeed so beautiful.[77] Some newspapers even went further and while describing Karl May films as absolutely perfect, proclaimed that Karl May together with Lex Barker were the German superheroes.[78] Lex Barker became a German superhero thanks to his roles in transnational West German Westerns, set in a transnational setting designed to resemble the American West. Thus, films that shaped the creation of a West German identity, actually proved to be a transnational endeavor, creating a translational German hero, proclaimed as the embodiment of Germanness by West German audiences in the 1960s.

While DEFA also produced *Indianerfilme* in Yugoslavia, its objective was not the creation of an imaginary "Heimat" with which East German audiences could identify. On the contrary, East German filmmakers set out to replicate the American West and believed the credibility of their messages relied on the authenticity of the landscape. The quest for authenticity is evident in Liselotte Welskopf-Henrich's persistence in adhering to the script she wrote for the first *Indianerfilm*, *The Sons of Great Mother Bear*. In the first East German Western, the scene of crossing the Missouri River at the end of the film has great symbolic meaning. It is the beginning of the new life for the Native Americans led by Tokei-ihto as they leave the United States for Canada. Welskopf-Henrich believed that the river should have been mentioned as a formidable barrier that required great effort to overcome, serving as a symbolic obstacle en route to independence and prosperity.[79]

Other DEFA films also often focused on different elements of the film in their quest for authenticity. For example, in *Chingachgook, the Great Snake*, filmmakers put an emphasis on Indian rituals such as a lengthy tribal dance. In *Osceola*, coproduced with the Cuban film studio, ICAIC, African American actors portrayed slaves. The films also focused on American soldiers visiting white plantation owners, the images of palm trees, and even large crocodiles hungry for human flesh. All these elements combined, periodically reappearing throughout the film, constantly remind the viewer that the film depicts the tragic situation of slaves and the degeneracy of avaricious planters of the American Southeast.

Both Karl May films and *Indianerfilme* are essentially transnational productions that selected Yugoslavia as their filming sites and employed similar techniques in order to authenticate them. *Indianerfilme*, however, seem much more concerned with authenticity and replicating the American West to help them convey the message of anti-Americanism and anti-capitalism, even though they often exaggerate and distort the actuality of the American West. Karl May films, in contrast, strive to become "heimatlich" in order to appeal to the West Germans' desire to rediscover greatness and heroism. In both cases, with a varying degree of cosmopolitanism, they created two distinct transnational versions of the Wild West, which contributed to the shaping of German identity.

4
German Indian Heroes and Intercultural Transfer

Transnational heroes: Karl May films v. *Indianerfilme*

Karl May Westerns and *Indianerfilme* created national heroes with whom audiences in both West and East Germany quickly identified. In both cases, these heroes were uniquely German creations, even though the films used the American West as the setting and the myth of the American West as their narrative. Moreover, in both cases the heroes were not played by German actors nor were most of the other characters German nationals. The two most important Karl May heroes, the German frontiersman Old Shatterhand and the Indian chief Winnetou, together with DEFA Indian chiefs such as Tokei-ihto, Osceola, Chingachgook, and Ulzana, came to define what it meant to be German in the Cold War, still tainted by the omnipresent memories of the Nazi past.

Karl May's "two indefatigable adventurers," Old Shatterhand and Winnetou, "have fulfilled a need of the romantic German *Geist*," making Karl May Germany's perpetual favorite.[1] DEFA *Indianerfilme* met the expectations of East Germans who, although discouraged from reading Karl May by East German authorities, watched West German movies on West German television, still accessible despite East German authorities' efforts to block it. East Germans, too, craved their own Indian heroes to guide them through the chaos of the new postwar order. Consequently, Karl May Westerns and *Indianerfilme* created German Indians and frontiersmen, who almost overnight became the embodiment of Germanness in both German states. Whereas Germans looked at them as their national and uniquely German supermen, Old Shatterhand, Winnetou, and others were, in fact, transnational heroes operating in a transnational American West.

Not only did the movie characters become national heroes, but in both West and East Germany the actors who played them achieved the status of national heroes as well, as they became identified with the characters they played. Even in East Germany, where actors could hardly be called "stars" as understood in the West, Gojko Mitic, the actor who played the main role in all DEFA *Indianerfilme*, became a "celebrity." Of course, Pierre Brice and Lex Barker reached more audiences and certainly made more money. However, one can point to Gojko Mitic as one of the first celebrities of East German cinema, even though his salary was much less than Brice's 80,000 West German Marks per film, let alone Barker's 200,000 West German Marks per film.[2] Born in Yugoslavia to a father who had fought Hitler's army as a partisan, Mitic had moved to East Berlin in the mid-1960s after having already acted in some English and Italian productions and even in some of Harald Reinl's Karl May films, including *Among Vultures* where, along with Winnetou and Old Surehand, he led the Shoshones to capture the murderers of Martha Bauman, as described in the first chapter of this book. Mitic was thus a highly visible exception to the westward flow of East European actors and film professionals. Moreover, Mitic's off-screen qualities, including modesty and diligence, combined with his on-screen courage, personal traits such as athleticism and good looks, and character traits such as wisdom and leadership, made him "a role model for children, the dream of teenage girls, and ideal son-in-law – a particularly Teutonic form of a model Indian and model citizen." Therefore, the German historian Gerd Gemünden has argued that "the star cult that surrounded Mitic in the GDR is reminiscent of that of these famous Hollywood stars – yet another indication how a capitalist phenomenon successfully penetrated socialist culture, even if on much smaller scale."[3]

Between 1963 and 1965, following the success of *Treasure at the Silver Lake*, the Constantin studio released its cinematic adaptation of Karl May's greatest work, *Winnetou*. The *Winnetou* trilogy loosely follows Karl May's novel *Winnetou*. Although some plots and characters differ, the films include the main characters and events of the novel. The beginning of *Winnetou I* introduces the story in the same way as the book, emphasizing the inevitability of Indian demise. Both the novel and the film not only underline the heroism of Winnetou, but also foretell the inevitable collapse of his Indian nation. From the beginning of the film, the viewer can differentiate between the good Indians, such as Winnetou, who fight to protect all the Indian tribes against the white invaders, and bad Indians, who succumb to alcoholism and betray others for a stable supply of firewater and assurances of peace. There are positive white characters, but none of them equate to Old Shatterhand, Winnetou's blood brother. Furthermore, there are whites driven by greed or hatred of natives, who set out to exterminate Indians or forcibly remove them from their land, seeking gold and glory. Winnetou trusts Old Shatterhand and once they become blood brothers, he never questions Old Shatterhand's loyalty to himself or to the Apache nation. The wisdom and courage of Winnetou captivates Old Shatterhand from their first meeting. Contrary to his employer's demand, Old Shatterhand immediately agrees to the Apache's demands that they withdraw from Apache territory, where Old Shatterhand had supervised the surveying of the territory for the building of a railroad.

Despite the bravery and fighting skills of the Apache chief, Winnetou becomes the ultimate victim of white aggression. The sense of the inevitability of Indian demise is best illustrated by the feeling of doom that Winnetou confesses to Old Shatterhand shortly before the final confrontation. Unfortunately, Winnetou's premonition proves true. Throwing his body in front of Old Shatterhand to protect him, he is mortally wounded. Old Shatterhand recollects the greatest moments of their friendship and tells his Apache friend that, having defeated those who threatened them, the Apaches are now safe. Winnetou then asserts that his task of assuring his tribe's survival is done and he is ready to die.

Winnetou certainly was a great fighter, shooter, thinker, as well as a noble and just human being. But his white brother Old Shatterhand, despite his relative short presence in the American West, taught him skills that Winnetou would never have acquired had they never met, skills that allowed Old Shatterhand to outdo all frontiersmen. This had a tremendous influence on the German readers, but it also reflected Karl May's own understanding and fantasy of the American West. Karl May wanted his readers to believe that he was Old Shatterhand and that all books written about Old Shatterhand concerned his own actual adventures in the American West and Arabia. Those who may not have known him personally might have believed that his long departures did not take him to the lands he claimed to have visited. Rather, the years when hardly anyone knew where he was he actually spent in jail, but that was enough to perpetuate the myth of Karl May as an explorer and traveler.[4] Scholars have demonstrated the rehabilitative effects of his sentences, though. May used the prison time to prepare himself for a new career and worked hard behind bars to improve his writing skills.[5]

The quintessence of the friendship between the German and the Apache is the confession Winnetou makes just before he dies in the arms of Old Shatterhand. Preceded by hours of deliberate discussion,

Winnetou announces that he has become a Christian just like his white brother. This also demonstrates the inevitability of the Indian demise because, as Christopher Frayling has shown, even "the more 'cultured' Indians in the Winnetou stories (the chosen ones) are aware that the Twilight of the Gods is approaching, that they are 'The Last of the Tribe,' and that there is nothing they can do but convert to Christianity."[6] Remarkably, Winnetou's decision to convert to Christianity may in fact transcend religion. It has been suggested that the Apache's conversion stood for his ultimate embracement of Germandom, the values his blood brother Old Shatterhand professed which further points to the distinctiveness of the German–Indian affinity as well as the superiority of German frontiersmen in the American West.[7]

Although Old Shatterhand eventually became Karl May's most renowned frontiersman, he did not acquire all his skills by himself nor did he learn them all from the books. Undoubtedly, Old Shatterhand would not have become an exceptional frontiersman had he not acquired certain skills from Winnetou. In fact, Old Shatterhand acquired Winnetou's best qualities. Old Shatterhand still outshines Winnetou in any significant category, whether strength, dexterity, intelligence, or weaponry.[8] This peculiar transfer of qualities could then be summarized as follows: Old Shatterhand would not have become the most famous frontiersman had he not been taught certain skills by Winnetou. Old Shatterhand, however, perfected the skills he acquired from Winnetou and transcended Winnetou in every possible domain. This should not come as a surprise given how much effort Karl May put into perpetuating the myth that he was Old Shatterhand, in spite of creating the image of the noble, intelligent, and brave Apache chief.

Karl May Westerns do not include any white American frontiersmen other than the (supposedly) hilarious Sam Hawkens. American families, however, knew and even revered Old Shatterhand because, both in novels and in films, he protected them from Indian raids and white outlaws. He was respected by American army officers who often consulted him on military matters and sought his guidance to solve the manifold problems of the frontier, such as Indian–white relations and banditry. Indeed, although often doubting the judgment and advice of Old Shatterhand without knowing who he was, American army officers felt honored to be able to speak to and receive orders from the frontiersman once he introduced himself.

While some West German viewers might have seen Old Shatterhand as an American, for others Old Shatterhand was the embodiment of Germanness. He was a German, he possessed the best German qualities, and he exemplified the greatness of Germany. Although the Winnetou trilogy contains a great number of misconceptions about Indian customs (including the notion "*Howgh*" was "that one word" which all tribes commonly used), it does not contain some important events without which the viewer cannot fully understand the character of Old Shatterhand and his symbolic significance as far as the presence of Germans in the Wild West is concerned.[9] Significantly, the movie does not mention the fact that Old Shatterhand came from Germany; thus the viewer unfamiliar with May's novels may not consider him "The Teutonic Pioneer" he had been in May's novels.[10] Therefore, for anyone unfamiliar with May's novels watching any of the export-version of Karl May Westerns dubbed in English, it would be difficult to determine the nationality of the frontiersman. Even German critics of Karl May, including Welskopf-Henrich, pointed out that Karl May did not intend Old Shatterhand to become an American and that his German identity was unquestionable in the novels.

Old Shatterhand often visited the American West. It became his interest, his passion. He must have become deeply attached to it and the people who lived there, especially the many friends he made and the women who admired him. The American West served as a place where he could occasionally make money as a surveyor, teacher, or detective. The Wild West did not, however, become his destiny. He could come and leave and it definitely was not his homeland (*Heimat*). Moreover, once Winnetou dies, the Apache Indians, together with all other tribes, are doomed. The American West Old Shatterhand had known prior to Winnetou's death was not the same without his Apache blood brother. What used to be the land of Winnetou slowly but surely became Anglo-Saxon territory. Perhaps Old Shatterhand would have no reason to return to the new American West, where there was no more room for his blood brother Winnetou and the Indian nations they both tried to protect.

One crucial difference between Karl May films and *Indianerfilme* is the manner in which they conclude. Although both Winnetou and the Indian chiefs in *Indianerfilme* appeal to the Indians to unite in the light of the common danger, only in East German Westerns do the Indians succeed either by defeating the enemy or by finding a new homeland once they avenge the wrongs done to them. East German Westerns also attempted to emphasize historical accuracy. Not only did DEFA hire Welskopf-Henrich to write the script of *The Sons of Great Mother Bear*, but its stories were also based on historical events, even though they became distorted due to ideological imperatives. As far the authenticity of Karl

May's novels is concerned, historians have argued that "May had more success in packing his books with authentic anthropological fact, for he drew upon an exhaustive library of source materials," which, however, "does not lead to literary realism, for the factualness of his descriptions of the folkways and language of the American Indian is ultimately dissolved in the dreaming power of May's vivid imagination."[11]

Not only does the East German Westerns' storyline converge with anti-imperialist rhetoric, but the actors seem to agree with the message of the films. Gojko Mitic, the Yugoslavian actor who played the leading role in all *Indianerfilme*, pointed to the Westerns' accurate portrayal of a harsh reality. According to Mitic, "The white people invaded the land of the Indians and wanted to take away their habitat because they wanted to live there too. They wanted to build big ranches and have lots of land...basically, the whites ended taking over the country."[12] In this regard, Karl May Westerns significantly differ from their East German counterparts. While the German Indian hero, Winnetou, perishes along with his nation, Old Shatterhand continues his adventures in the American West.

Interestingly, Old Shatterhand's dominance is uncertain in *Treasure at the Silver Lake*, where no one, including Old Shatterhand, questions Winnetou's ability to lead as well as track enemies. No other Karl May Western, however, disproved Old Shatterhand's unquestionable status as the hero more than *Old Shatterhand*. As the conclusion of the film nears, Old Shatterhand finds himself tied to a pole, helplessly watching the outcome of the bloodiest battle in which Karl May heroes ever participated on the big screen. Thus, May's main hero, Old Shatterhand, who possesses not only "Atlas-like strength, amazing intellectual ability and all of the Christian virtues – but *German* blood as well" is relegated to the status of a second-tier hero during the final battle that, ultimately, saves his life.[13] Old Shatterhand does not miraculously free himself from captivity. He patiently waits until his hands are untied after the battle is over. The great frontiersman does not fire a single shot during the battle nor knock down a single enemy, while Winnetou leads his warriors to charge the heavily armed fort in a seemingly suicidal assault to free the frontiersman. Moreover, in spite of being forced to retreat twice, Winnetou does not give up and, despite heavy losses, the thought of leaving his white blood brother imprisoned and humiliated, possibly for life, does not even cross his mind.

There is another significant difference between Winnetou and the Indian heroes in *Indianerfilme*. Winnetou is not the penultimate or the last of his kind. Like Chingachgook, there are still thousands of Apache alive while he is fighting for their survival, while Chingachgook is the sole survivor of his tribe and a living proof of Anglo-Americans' genocide of Native Americans. As a matter of fact, the great leader of the Apache will die first, symbolizing the gradual defeat of the entire Indian nation. If the greatest of the Indians dies early in the American-Indian war, others, deprived of their unique chief, are destined to follow him into oblivion. Contrary to the fate of Winnetou and the Apaches in Karl May Westerns, the DEFA Indian heroes were successful, against all odds, and managed to lead their people out of danger.

Although a critic of Karl May, Welskopf-Henrich's essays help understand how Winnetou's failure and death served important functions. Winnetou, who is feared by both Indians and Anglo-Americans, develops into the chief of a powerful nation of fierce warriors. He becomes Old Shatterhand's blood brother and, because of their friendship and the skills acquired by Old Shatterhand from the Apache chief, the friendship with the most powerful Indian chief elevates Old Shatterhand's status on the frontier. In fact, Karl May books and films create situations and challenges that provide an opportunity for Old Shatterhand's elevation.[14] Thus, Old Shatterhand becomes the only blood brother of the fierce chief Winnetou, both despised and feared by Anglo-Americans, and their friendship is known across the frontier. Indeed, one is expected to see Winnetou if Old Shatterhand is in the area and vice versa. One of them, however, is doomed to perish while rescuing the other. Old Shatterhand befriended many Indian chiefs during his stay in the American West. None of them was as significant or as skilled as Winnetou. No other chief's friendship could have elevated his status to the degree that his friendship with Winnetou did. Winnetou and the Apache must die to fulfill the destiny of the Indian nations and to allow Anglo-Americans to conquer the entire continent. Moreover, in spite of being blood brothers, Winnetou must perish to ascertain the superiority of Old Shatterhand, the greatest frontiersman of the American West.

Although Karl May films and *Indianerfilme* differed from Hollywood Westerns in some regards, they resembled them in others. Most important, both Karl May films and *Indianerfilme* focused on the motive for conflict between Native Americans and white settlers. Regarding *Indianerfilme*, Gemunden has pointed out that "These films contain many of the ingredients that make for a good Hollywood western: the ambush of the stage coach, the attack on the railroad, fist fights and shoot-outs, swinging bar doors, Indians on the war path attacking an army fort, etc." Moreover, similar to Hollywood productions, DEFA *Indianerfilme* "have a clear division of good guys and bad guys – except that in the DEFA films sympathy lies exclusively with the tribe and their heroic chief (always played by Mitic) in their struggle against greedy white settlers, treaty-breaking army colonels, corrupt sheriffs, imperialist oil magnets, and plantation owners." Gemuenden's observation could also be applied to Karl May films, except that the Indian nations are doomed to perish in West German productions, whereas in East German productions, they are able to defeat their white oppressors and evade subjugation. Therefore, the motto "Indians of all lands, unite" is one of the prevailing themes in DEFA Westerns, *Chingachgook, the Great Snake* (1967), and *Osceola* (1971) in particular, leading the Indians to unite against their common white and capitalist enemy.[15]

Both West and East German Westerns, while they differ from each other and from American Westerns, rely on the American Western, which is in fact what makes them, despite their differences, quite similar. Both Karl May films and *Indianerfilme* also adopted motives prevalent in Hollywood Westerns. Both also demonstrate how entrenched the fascination with Indians was in Germany. In spite of being divided into two states belonging to different ideological spheres, both West and East Germany felt a strong connection to Indians and they chose the American West as a setting for their cultural and ideological contest, which is further discussed in the following chapter. Based on the popularity of the films and Indian novels to which so many Germans could relate, one can even describe it as existential identification which showed how much the two states actually had in common, despite the ongoing political rivalry.[16] Even the most anti-imperialist and anti-American DEFA productions, while openly castigating the Anglo-American idea of progress and the ruthlessness of the conquest of the American West, were designed to resemble American Westerns. The best example is the film *Apachen*. Aside from the culture of the Indians, their customs, the ways they hunted and lived, the film focuses on the Anglo-Americans' desire to drive Indians out of their lands by any means possible.[17] Indeed, no method seems too inhumane for Anglo-Americans. This film delivers a powerful condemnation of the Anglo-American idea of Manifest Destiny out of the five DEFA Westerns under consideration and perhaps one of the most powerful anti-American interpretations of Manifest Destiny and the American-Mexican conflict, eventually leading to the Mexican War of 1846–1848, ever displayed in cinemas around the world.

The plot revolves around the little-known massacre at Santa Rita, New Mexico. The Apaches, who arrive at the nearby village in order to obtain their annual flour allotment, are encouraged to gather at the central market in order to listen to a speech given by one of the employees of the mining company, who knows what is going to unfold. Out of the very wagon that the Indians believe has brought their flour, the white settlers roll out a canon that is soon aimed at them. The canon fires and dozens of Indians fall. The rest are gunned down by the whites. Fewer than a dozen survive, including the Indian chief Ulzana, played by Gojko Mitic. Indeed, the rounding up of the Indians in the central place of the town, eager to receive their annual supply of flour, unaware that they are to become victims of artillery fire and, finally, the killing of those who managed to survive the first wave of attack, certainly resembles methods applied by SS Einsatzgruppen following the Wehrmacht all across East Europe. Following the massacre, Ulzana sets out to avenge the death of his tribesmen.

As in previous films, the character played by Mitic ultimately succeeds. Despite being tortured by the whites (whites consider whipping him as "giving him his dessert"), the Indians unite and deal the whites a devastating blow. In the last scene, they ride their horses across the desert, just as they had at the beginning of the movie, before the first Americans arrived (significantly, as the whites are massacring the Indians, ordinary Mexican residents of the village try to help the Indians, but they become targets of the Americans as well). Despite the optimistic ending, the film includes the following poem: "Wide is the country of the Apaches... High is the sun over the desert of Chihuaha. Some ride in the morning, some ride in the evening, some ride no more. Who. Who will stop it?"

East German film producers explicitly described the objectives of their films. For example, Professor A. Wilkening, working for DEFA, wrote that *Apachen* was to present the typical imperialist expansion of the United States, during which the Native Americans were robbed of their native lands. Therefore, the film shows the history of increasing aggression, which ultimately led to a shameful business of killing Indians for money, where a scalp of a warrior brought $100, a scalp of a woman brought $50, whereas a scalp of a child brought $25. Despite the brutality and loss of life, the film shows how the Apaches resisted and, ultimately, survived.[18] Crucially, the Apaches, led by their heroic chief, managed to avenge the wrongs done to them and to save their race from the Anglo-American invasion.

The frontier conflict between Anglo-American settlers and entrepreneurs and Native American hunting and gathering populations became the dominant theme in both Karl May films and *Indianerfilme*. Moreover, there is a remarkable similarity between American Westerns, Karl May films, and *Indianerfilme*. In fact, both Karl May films and *Indianerfilme* could be considered transnational endeavors due to the involvement of actors and producers from many different countries. Karl May was a German writer; the movie producer Artur Brauner was German; the director, Hugo Fregonese, came from Argentina, albeit he had already marked his presence in Hollywood; and the main actors were American and French. Even Winnetou's sister, actress Marie Versini who appears in *Winnetou I*, was French, and while being on the production site, reported that she had to remind herself that this was a German film and that it was very important not to forget it. The important question is how German is a film where the major cast members are non-Germans, it is directed by an Argentinian, yet is based on the works of the most popular German writer with a message catering to German audiences? Lex Barker became a German superhero, but he also became an Anglo-Saxon Old Shatterhand.[19] The same applies to the *Indianerfilme*. They were often coproduced by DEFA and Czechoslovakian, Polish, or Bulgarian film studios, and included both German and non-German actors and film producers. Gojko Mitic, a Yugoslavian actor, most prominently assumed the role of the victorious Indian chiefs in the East German productions.

Based on the differences between Old Shatterhand from the novel and Old Shatterhand from the movie some German newspapers even began asking whether it was still a Karl May film. On the one hand, director Harald Reinl categorically stated that *Old Shatterhand*, directed by Argentine-born American director, Hugo Fregonese, brutalized the film to the extent that it was absolutely not a Karl May film. On the other hand, the scriptwriter of the first three Karl May films, Harald G. Petersson, asserted that they were still Karl May films. The impact of American elements had such a profound effect, however, that it provoked a debate regarding the identity of the film. Petersson also argued that the changes could be understood because the film was produced with an eye to distribution in the United States. Therefore, the filmmakers wanted to create similarities between Winnetou and Indian chiefs from both American films as well as actual characters, including Sitting Bull.[20] As a result of the mixing of different cultural elements from the two hemispheres, Old Shatterhand, while being a German superhero, simultaneously acquired more transnational features, which West German audiences may not have objected to but they may not have fully paid attention to either.

Interestingly, a similar question can be asked with regard to some American Westerns, even those considered Western icons. *High Noon,* with Gary Cooper as Marshall Cane, portrays important challenges faced by American society during the early Cold War, which just saw the beginning of the first major military conflict between the Communist and capitalist bloc in Korea. The film was directed by the Austrian director Fred Zinnemann, whose understanding of the American West prior to his arrival to the United States was greatly influenced by his fascination with Karl May's Wild West. Of course, Marshall Cane is no Old Shatterhand, nor is there any Indian hero in *High Noon*. Can the end product be really labeled as a truly American Western, even though the degree to which Karl May might have influenced it, if he did at all, can never be quantified?

Transnational history and intercultural transfer

There is no doubt that the American movie industry influenced its West and East German counterparts. American culture exerted a great impact on what was popular, produced, listened to, worn, eaten, or talked about in Europe, not only in the West, but on the other side of the Iron Curtain as well. German Westerns could serve as a great example of intercultural transfer, a concept which has been developed in Europe, and which some scholars in the United States have promoted as well. Intercultural transfer constitutes an important component of transnational history. It shows how a cultural product is simultaneously accepted by the receiving society and adjusted accordingly to meet the receiving society's needs.[21] In this case, it is the transfer of the Western, the most American of all film genres, appropriated by both West and East German filmmakers and refurbished to reflect and shape the milieu, both political and cultural, of both German states.

In his most recent book, *A Renegade History of the United States*, Thaddeus Russell has written that following World War II, "Soviet soldiers brought the virus home from the western front. It soon infected large portions of the Soviet population, then spread to other Eastern Bloc countries."[22] American culture, also labeled "American primitivism," "capitalist cultural imperialism," and "bourgeois cosmopolitanism," which the Communist authorities considered an existential threat and which ultimately helped bring down Communism, is the virus Russell discusses.[23] While culture most certainly became an effective tool of Cold War propaganda on both sides of the Iron Curtain, the cultural exchange was not marked by absolute dominance of the Western (American) products. On the contrary, the case of the American Western demonstrates the two-sided flow of intercultural transfer between camps during the Cold War. The appropriation of the American Western in both East and West Germany further suggests that this most American of all cultural products underwent significant transformations in order to fit into postwar West and East German cultures. The appropriation of the American Western also became an essential element in the construction of national identity in both Germanies.

There is no doubt that American Westerns certainly influenced German Westerns; however, intercultural transfer did not flow in only one direction. While one should not look for foreign influences in every American Western, the case of *High Noon* demonstrates that sometimes foreign influences, while often hardly conspicuous, may have had an impact upon a film through the personal experiences of the director, selection of cast, or even events that dictate that the filmmakers respond to societal pressures. Moreover, German Westerns, both in West Germany and East Germany, used the American genre of the Western and adjusted it according to their needs. Thus, while the end product was still influenced by American Westerns, in both cases they were unique interpretations of the myth of the American West and should be considered complementary to the American ones. Gemünden made the observation that

> even if DEFA was at pains to downplay the U.S. origin of the western genre, and even if the films' message was always anti-American, it was still articulated through a Hollywood genre, and one that, was quintessentially American. The emulated players were Americans too – both the historical Indian chiefs who by law had or would become U.S. citizens, and the twentieth-century actors who embodied them.[24]

A similar question could also be asked regarding the synchronization of American films. How does the fact that foreign films in German cinemas were always in the German language, with foreign actors' parts being spoken by Germans, change the identity of the film? The dialogues could often slightly differ, sometimes due to linguists' inability to translate words that do not have synonyms in another language. Sometimes, however, culture dictates which dialogues need to be altered or omitted altogether. Adjusting the dialogues might inadvertently (or purposefully) alter the meaning of the film and it may create several different interpretations of a scene or an entire film based on such modifications. All foreign actors on the site of the Karl May films were having a hard time pronouncing German sentences, yet they memorized their parts and did their best even though German viewers never heard their voices in movie theaters. Not only was it important that the characters spoke German, but also some of the actors were truly concerned about being able to communicate with the audience in German. Lex Barker, for example, wrote his speech in German following the premiere of *Winnetou I* and, pointing to his note, said with a grin: "I have to read it all."[25] While Karl May Westerns were a transnational enterprise and while they were exported to other countries, including the United States, American audiences could not have understood their implicit meaning just as they would never appreciate May's novels, so well understood by German audiences.

Despite German fascination with the American Indians as perpetuated by Karl May's novels and the movies based on his works, the acquisition of white, in this case German, identity, by the Indians is at least as important as the creation of an American identity by the German hero. Winnetou's first white friend, Klekih-Petra, is an old schoolteacher from Germany. Additionally, Winnetou becomes ennobled not necessarily because of his values, but because of "his willingness to embrace the best of European culture and blend it with the finest traits of his own nation."[26] Not only do Germans teach Winnetou literature, philosophy, as well as help him improve his fighting skills, they also represent the noble frontiersman, fighting the greedy squatters and settlers who want to take over the Indian land. Additionally, when Old Shatterhand falls in love with Winnetou's sister, Nscho-tschi, she makes the decision to go East to study and become a Christian because of Old Shatterhand's "strong feelings about miscegenation."[27]

While Karl May films include the most important characters and events from Karl May novels, some of the examples of intercultural transfer seen in his novels do not appear in movies. For example, Karl May, who most likely never even thought it would be possible to produce a cinematic version of his Wild West novels, continued to assert Old Shatterhand's German identity in novels. In Karl May films, the American actor Lex Barker plays the German frontiersman, and the viewer might consider him an American frontiersman. Paradoxically, although Karl May films shaped West Germans' understanding of what it meant to be German during the Cold War, they also avoided explicit connections to their characters' national identity as well as explicit domestic characters and settings. Tassilo Schneider correctly observed that

> although the May westerns are based on German texts, as westerns, the books and films are heavily indebted to a non-German

(American) literary tradition. In May's novels, many of the positive protagonists, including Shatterhand, are German. The films by contrast, refer only rarely to the precise origin of "the white man who came across the great water."[28]

Karl May films do not even mention Klekih-petra, the German mentor of Winnetou, whose character and sacrifice proved to be essential in bringing about the friendship between Old Shatterhand and Winnetou. There are many other examples to which one could point. Not only do the films sometimes deviate from the books on which they were based, but both novels and films projected a unique vision of the American West. While the latter were more direct, the former relied to a much greater extent on the readers' imagination, both constituted a German-American West that German readers and moviegoers accepted as their *Heimat*.

When asked why Karl May films and the character he played became so popular, Lex Barker responded that he did not know. He made, however, an important observation regarding the ways in which West German moviegoers perceived him. According to Barker, West Germans considered him a German, one of their own, which he thought was a genuine sign of appreciation, but it further demonstrates the transnational character of the West German identity he helped shape. In that sense, Barker became an agent of intercultural transfer.[29] He was an American actor, who had established himself in the United States and who became immensely popular in Europe, having bought homes in Germany, Italy, and, Spain. German audiences considered him a German superhero, who contributed to the rebirth of the Western genre in Germany and who helped Germans discover what it meant to be German during the Cold War.[30] The same could be said of Pierre Brice and Stewart Granger who also became German heroes in essentially transnational cinematic interpretations of the American West. Gojko Mitic represented the East German equivalent of a Western superhero. While the *Indianerfilme* were anti-imperialistic in nature, they were also based on the blueprint of the American Western. Describing Mitic's transnational qualities, Gemünden stated that "it could be argued that Mitic's star persona thus does not only incorporate the Yugoslav partisan, the model German, the Native American tribal hero, and the displaced Jew, but also the American."[31] *Indianerfilme* contributed to the shaping of German identity among East German moviegoers, and the process, similarly to Karl May films, but on a smaller scale, was also transnational in nature. Karl May films and *Indianerfilme* share certain crucial characteristics. Both proved to be successful in their respective countries. They both influenced generations of Germans and continue to do so even today. And most significantly, by combining and trans-ferring elements from different cultures, they both contributed to the shaping of German identity, even though they created transnational heroes operating in transnational settings, based on transnational myths of the frontier.[32]

For intercultural transfer to occur, a specific cultural product must exist. It must then be transmitted and received.[33] In this case, the spe-cific cultural product became first a Western novel, popularized in the United States by James Fenimore Cooper in the 1820s, based upon which Karl May created a German version of the myth of the American West. Next, in 1961, the first West German Western was produced, based loosely on the works of Karl May and influenced by the American Western. East Germany soon followed with the production of its own first *Indianerfilm*, based on the works of East German scholar and author, Liselotte Welskopf-Henrich, an expert on May's works and on Native American history.

Tracing its origin to 1823 when James Fenimore Cooper published *The Pioneers*, the Western is a genuinely American form of popular art. Dur-ing the upheaval of the 1890s, Americans looked for a simpler version of the United States. Their "nostalgic longing" to find a place of equality, opportunity, virtue, and idealism turned them toward the mythology of the American frontier, the "embodiment of all that was good about America."[34] After World War II, the Western played a crucial role in the cultural contest during the Cold War, both at home and overseas. Not only did it shape American identity and character, it also offered solutions to the crises that besieged American society. The Western offered something remarkable to those who never had the chance to visit the American West. It brought the myth of the frontier home to many Americans. As much as people may love it or hate it, the Western conveyed messages that moviegoers could not easily ignore.

In order to counterattack Communism and anti-Americanism, American propagandistic interpretations of the myth of the frontier became an integral element of early Cold War rhetoric. The narrative of the Western, encompassing progress, freedom, and happiness, not only safeguarded American economic, political, and military interests, but it also defined American identity.[35] The Western as well as the war film cemented national identity much more than any other cinematic form, dominating American popular culture at least until the mid-1960s. Indeed, it is the uniqueness of the Western narrative form and visual representation as well as its simplicity and clear distinction between the hero and the villain, which make it the purest and most original genre of all cinematic genres in the United States.[36] Many political commentators urged American politicians to look up to Western heroes for guidance and solutions and some American actors strongly supported the cinematic fight against Communism. John Wayne, for example, considered some of his films, and *The Alamo* in particular, a direct assault upon Communism. This seems to have been understood by the Soviets, since there were rumors among American filmmakers about attempts to assassinate Wayne, whose Westerns, though enjoyed by Joseph Stalin and other Soviet officials, dealt a blow to their propaganda efforts. Michael Munn describes a conversation between Nikita Khrushchev and John Wayne, during which

> Wayne supposedly asked the Soviet leader if it was true that the Soviets were trying to kill him. Khrushchev's response was: "That was the decision of Stalin during his last five mad years. When Stalin died, I rescinded the order." During the course of the conversation, Khrushchev also revealed why he liked watching Westerns: "I especially like the ones about the U.S. Cavalry. They remind me of how the white Americans oppressed the true natives of America."[37]

The last statement certainly points out the ambivalence and potential of these Westerns since one could identify with either the "white heroes" or the "oppressed Indians."

After World War II, the Western offered a sense of consolation and guidance for people, and Germans in particular, who were insecure about their own destiny and their values. It was more important for Germans than for the English or the French because of the complete loss of national heroes who, in one way or another, were tainted by the legacy of National Socialism as well as the unwillingness to embrace those men and women as national heroes who resisted the Nazis. In the aftermath of National Socialism, it appeared impossible to embrace even Otto von Bismarck as a national hero since he could easily have been seen as having paved the way toward the Nazi dictatorship as the concept of a German special path implied.[38] Resisters to the Nazi dictatorship were not embraced as national heroes since they could also be labeled as traitors to Germany.[39] While East Germany quickly established a cult of reverence for Communists who resisted the Nazis and turned them into national heroes by naming schools, streets, and institutions after them and made movies about them, West Germany in the 1950s was a country without credible national heroes.

The Western hero seems to have filled that void, especially for West German males.

The popularity of film, and the Western in particular, proved how intertwined cinema, politics, and economics became. The discussion of the importance of the Western during the Cold War begs the question of whether the Germans could create their identity without the influence of American culture. According to Dutch historian Rob Kroes, the quest for a common European identity benefited from the American presence, but the United States benefited from the Cold War arrangement as well, by establishing and consolidating its preponderant military, political, economic, and cultural position in Europe and its superpower status globally. The process required exposing Europeans to the American way of life and the American version of democracy through bombarding them with images of the United States, both realistic and imaginary.[40] Thus, although cinematic images of the American West influenced the formation of postwar American identity, the myth of the American frontier had a tremendous impact upon the shaping of German identities during the Cold War as well.

While examining films from a historical perspective, some scholars conclude that they constituted an important part of intercultural transfer from the very inception of cinema. Christina Haase has demonstrated that "film has been a medium with transcultural and transnational appeal" because "the history of the cinema has always been a story of complex connections and collaborations between different national and cultural traditions as well as between people of different countries, ethnicities, genders, religions, and classes."[41] Furthermore, Ian Tyrrell underscored the challenges historians face when attempting to write national histories. He has argued that no nation exists in isolation. Thus, nations (and their cultures) are created transnationally through the regional and global context of security, economic competition, and demographic change.[42] Thomas Adam has compared the task of a scholar researching intercultural transfers to archeological excavation, since most elements of modern culture are the result of contacts and exchanges. Adam suggests that "by following the path of an idea that was transferred from one culture to another, the historian recreates the transfer" and deconstructs national cultures into the elements that created them.[43]

Based on Alexander von Humboldt's extensive travels in the United States, Kirsten Belgum has concluded that "the notion of cultural transfer, like transfer in any context, presumes three things: (1) that something is being transferred, (2) that there is a point of departure for that transfer, and (3) that there is a point of arrival."[44] In addition, Belgum has emphasized the reciprocal and multilayered nature of intercultural exchanges and the fact that "the notion of a direct exchange between cultures is inadequate to comprehending the complicated relationship or mutual effects that take place between two cultures."[45]

The crucial transnational and intercultural element of the myth of the American West, incorporated and modified in German Westerns, became the Indian war, functioning as a symbolic platform concerning many social and political issues. Although the myth in the American Western differs from its German counterparts, its function remains the same. Both East and West Germany used the American myth of the frontier and appropriated it in order to define Germanness. Culture thus served a critical function for the process of the shaping of national identity, with the two competing German interpretations of the American frontier serving as an example.[46] Therefore, postwar German-American cultural history serves as a good example of intercultural transfer. Mary Nolan observed that after 1945 the German strategy for dealing with American cultural products might be summarized as becoming "Americanized while remaining oneself."[47] This proved a difficult task, especially with the concerted effort of the American government and Hollywood to control the German film market and with American cultural products assuming an essential role in everyday life.

Not only does intercultural transfer help teach about the world in which we live, it also expands our knowledge of objects, people, ideas, as well as material culture and even symbolic worlds.[48] While most scholars underscore the idea of American cultural hegemony during the Cold War, America's cultural supremacy did not prevail throughout the Cold War. The United States certainly had a great impact on European culture; European countries often blended American ideas and products with their own, creating distinctive, albeit transnational artifacts which they believed allowed them to preserve their identity even though they acknowledged their American origins. This cross-fertilization, which could also be called intercultural transfer, proves a two-sided, rather than one-sided, nature of cultural exchange between the United States and Europe.[49]

The concept of intercultural transfer offers scholars willing to transcend traditional boundaries of historical writing, an opportunity to discover the interconnectedness of cultures, regions, and polities. Furthermore, the concept of intercultural transfer helps us explain why importation of American ideas did not result in creation of a unified worldwide American culture. Since ideas and concepts that are

transferred from one society to another always undergo transformations, intercultural transfer contributes to the simultaneous convergence
and diversification of those cultures connected by transfer. As Rob Kroes
contends, the use of American icons outside the United States does
not mean that these icons carry the same meaning they did in the
American context, prior to the transfer. In fact, they often represent different ideas and meanings that were attached to them in the process of
transfer.[50] Perhaps the most important incentive to apply the concept of
intercultural transfer is the fact that said concept does not differentiate
between winners and losers. The goal of a transnational historian is not
to attempt to determine the extent to which a given culture influenced
another, which, in all actuality, is not possible anyway.[51] Studying the
transfer of cultures, or some aspects of them, deepens our understanding of the complexity of interactions between continents, regions, and
countries. This should be especially important for every historian in the
age of globalization, with the dramatic acceleration of the capability to
exchange information and products, communicate, and relocate, which
allows us to transcend boundaries both physically and mentally to the
extent it had never been possible before.

While the transnational reach of cultures in the time of Facebook,
YouTube, the creation of free-trade zones, and the disappearance of
national borders, as in the case of the European Union, seems obvious,
the transnational approach to history, while being relatively new, points
out that intercultural transfers had been occurring for centuries, first
intra-continentally, and, with the advent of the age of discovery, inter-
continentally and globally. In this case, the study of the intercultural
transfer of the Western film during the Cold War, given its immense
popularity and its appropriation and different adaptations in West and
East Germany as well as other European countries, provides context for
the study of the trans-nationalization of American popular culture during the Cold War. It emphasizes the constant refurbishment of the most
American of all cultural products, the Western film. Although we still
study and will continue to study national histories, learn the importance of national heroes, and subscribe to national myths, however
isolated, nations are nonetheless influenced by external movements
and influences and are essentially made transnational.[52] And, as Adam
demonstrated by focusing on issues such as eugenics, school reform,
and the application of the non-violent approach in the fight for independence and equality, "nation states did not emerge in a vacuum but
were the result of mutual exchanges and contacts across geographic lines
that only later, with the introduction of passports, limiting definitions

of citizenship, and the fortification of countries' geographic borders, turned into fortified political borders."[53] Examining the transfer of cultures does not intend to undermine the importance of national histories. On the contrary, applying the transnational and intercultural approaches can only lead to a better understanding of the national, how intricate the idea of nation and how intertwined national histories really are.

The production of the first West German Western intensified the cultural contest between the two German states and further deepened the cultural divide between them, thus contributing to the formation of two distinct identities. Both genres appropriated the American Western and modified it to meet their needs. Cultural influences, then, assumed a crucial component of Cold War rivalry and the transfer of the Western, a distinctly American film genre, resulted in two unique interpretations of the myth of the American frontier converging with and promoting two new postwar German identities. Historians agree that American Westerns influenced German Westerns. What is surprising, however, is how different these Westerns really were, not only from each other, but from American Westerns as well, especially because they focused on issues Germans struggled with at home, rather than being mere expressions of either Americanism or anti-Americanism.[54]

5

The Quest for National Identity

Karl May and the German–Indian affinity

"You will be my next hero," says a drunk person to an Indian who just entered the saloon, somewhere in the American West. "An Indian treasure will be the subject of my next book," the same person says a few moments later, just before he loses control of his body and his head bangs against the saloon counter. The drunkard turns out to be Karl May and the scene came from the film *Der Schuh des Manitou* (*Manitou's Shoe*), a parody of Karl May films, released in 2001. More than 8.85 million people saw the film in just two months after its release, which surpassed even *Otto-der Film* (1985), a film virtually unknown in North America, the most popular film in German history prior to 2001.[1]

Karl May films revived the German film industry in the 1960s. They precipitated the production of likewise successful *Indianerfilme* in East Germany. Four decades later, *Der Schuh des Manitou* became Germany's most popular film of all time. Even its television premiere on Pro 7 matched the earlier success of the film in movie theaters and attracted over 12 million viewers, which became the station's highest ratings in history.[2] The film did not prove successful in the United States following its release on November 11, 2002. However, Karen Durbin, a film critic for the *New York Times*, stated that *Manitou's Shoe*, along with three other recently released German films, demonstrated that "after a lone drought, Germany's once great cinema has begun to create a 'third-wave' strong enough to lap our (American) shores."[3]

The popularity of *Der Schuh des Manitou* reveals how entrenched Karl May's works have been among Germans. Although some critics might consider the film as just another spoof of *Blazing Saddles*, no other German Western, or film, for that matter, could have become nearly

106

as successful as this one. Not only did this "Western" continue the tradition of success of Karl May films in German movie theaters, but it also proved to be both a German and a transnational production, similar to its precursors over four decades earlier.

The film is a German–Spanish production, which once again proved the popularity of Karl May, the "first pop star of German literature," and the image of the American West instilled in Germans.[4] Like Karl May films, *Der Schuh des Manitou* was not filmed in Germany. Whereas the former had been filmed in Yugoslavia, the latter was filmed in Spain. It also involved a great number of foreign actors, most of whom came from Spain, but it included actors from Argentina, Turkey, and India, as well as Native Americans.

In order to understand the two competing German interpretations of the American West that helped shape German identity and the overwhelming success of German Westerns, including *Der Schuh des Manitou*, one needs to understand the importance of the German Western tradition. Germans have resorted to the American West in their search for entertainment and identity for a couple of centuries. By the time the first silent Western was made in the twentieth century, the audience had already been familiar with and eager to enjoy the genre.[5] The creation of the alleged German-Indian identity serves as another great example of how the study of intercultural transfer and transnational history helps us better understand national histories and their interdependence, both past and present.

Although Germany did not establish colonies in North America, a German diaspora developed in the Western Hemisphere by the midseventeenth century, connecting two or more societies expanding across regions and, states or between continents and encompassing various social groups, characterized by hierarchical structure and differing interests. The process occurred over a period of time and involved "clustered moves between a region of origin and a receiving region."[6] Germans had explored the North American continent along with the English and French, and often in their service during the early stages of colonization. Although most Germans who fled their homeland following devastation brought about by the Thirty Years War (1618–1648) settled in the east, in Russia and Hungary in particular, the direction of German migrations shifted westward in the course of the eighteenth century. Historians estimate that more than 100,000 Germans migrated to North America before 1800. German and Dutch settlers established the first recorded German settlement in present-day United States in Germantown, Pennsylvania, in 1683.[7] Indeed, on the eve of the American Revolution, Germans constituted a third of the entire population of Pennsylvania, and 10 percent of the population of the British North American colonies. More German migrants poured into the United States after 1815 and the number of migrants increased even more following the failed Revolutions of 1848–1849. German-speaking migrants constituted more than 16 percent of all migrants between 1830 and 1930. Consequently, German-speaking migrants and their children constituted at least 10 percent of the entire population of the United States on the eve of the twentieth century, although in some parts of the Midwest, especially Nebraska, the number was substantially higher. Aside from Nebraska, German migrants constituted more than 30 percent of the population in New York, Pennsylvania, Ohio, and Indiana. One should also mention the existence of the "German Belt" in Texas, where the Germans, whose numbers dramatically increased to 130,000 by 1887 from 11,500 in 1850, constituted more than half of all European immigrants in the state.[8] The presence of the Germans on the American frontier resulted in the creation of a great number of literary works, documenting and narrating German–Indian relations and encounters, the earliest of them being travel diaries, accompanied by an increasing number of novels throughout the nineteenth century. In fact, German-American literary works outnumbered the writings of all other ethnic groups with the exception of the English.[9]

It is difficult to generalize about the complex nature of German–Indian relations. Colin G. Calloway points out that although Germany, unlike Great Britain, France, and Spain, did not set out to colonize North America, Germans inadvertently did participate in colonizing North America even if only through their presence on the North American continent.[10] An imaginary affinity, unknown to the Indians, developed between the Germans and the Native Americans. This affinity, sometimes even characterized as a German–Indian brotherhood, contributed to the shaping of German identity through the creation of a unique German myth of the American frontier.[11] Accordingly, the German Western tradition, begun over two centuries ago with the first German accounts of the American frontier, created a unique German understanding of the American West through the literary works of German travelers and novelists, and later through the cinematic version of the myth of the American West.

Eighteenth-century German nationalist thinkers saw in the Indians of their time a reflection of the Germanic tribes and their nationalistic, constructed past. Just as the Germanic tribes had fought the Roman Empire, the Indian tribes faced the European conquerors.

The rediscovery of Tacitus's writings in the Renaissance provided the conceptual framework for German nationalism as well as character traits that could be inscribed into the story of the Indians' fight against Europeans. Accordingly, Germans and Indians shared virtues such as honesty, unflinching, even self-destructive loyalty to family, clan, tribe, and tribal leaders, utter fearlessness in battle, physical hardiness, and stoicism in the face of adversity.[12]

The rediscovery of Tacitus and other Roman and Medieval texts describing the character of ancient Germanic people were part and parcel of the Romanticists' search for the essence of a German identity. In the context of the Napoleonic Wars, scholars such as Johann Gottlieb Fichte and Jakob and Wilhelm Grimm sought to find Germanness in language, literature, and fairy tales. Linguists such as Johann Christoph Adelung and Johann Severin Vater embarked on the comparative study of languages across the globe including the languages spoken by Native Americans to determine how language developed and which languages were related. This endeavor provided the basis for creating German identity and moved Germans and Indians onto related imagined communities.[13]

The special, fanciful relationship between Germans and Indians went beyond academic discussion and the question of German identity. When German settlers sought to establish villages in Pennsylvania, they did not always follow in the footsteps of their English contemporaries. Instead, they sought to buy land through treaties and established relations with their Native American neighbors, which Germans believed were characterized by mutual recognition and trust. Conrad Weiser was the first prominent German settler who negotiated such a treaty in 1737. What is so remarkable about Weiser's treaty is that, although those German migrants were forced to rely on Great Britain's charity (for clothing, food, and passage to North America), they did not resist British policies, but rather used the British identity to their advantage. At times, German-American leadership even believed that it was more useful for offspring to learn Indian languages rather than English. Not only did the German alliance with the Mohawks threaten British control of the colony, but Germans came to behave like Native Americans and they did not consider assimilating a priority. Rather, they looked to their Indian allies to acquire the skills that would allow them to survive on the American frontier.[14] When the Adelsverein (Society for the Protection of German Immigrants in Texas, founded in 1842) moved German settlers to Texas in the course of the tumultuous 1840s, Germans again followed the example of their predecessors in New

England and concluded a treaty in 1847 with the Comanches. Proclaiming that Germans and Indians should "live together like one people of brothers," Baron Otfried Hans von Meusebach, Commissioner-General of the Adelsverein, announced to a gathering of Comanches that

> If our people will have lived together with yours for some time and we have come to know one another, it may well be that some will want to intermarry. Soon the warriors of our tribe will learn your language. If they are then so inclined and agree upon marriage, I know of no obstacle, and our peoples will become the better friends.[15]

The treaty, which German settlers proudly claimed to have never been broken, proved to be ephemeral and shortly afterwards relations between the two groups rapidly deteriorated and Comanches began raiding German settlements.

Aside from the idea of German–Indian affinity professed by German academics, the coexistence of Germans and Indians in Pennsylvania as well as the historical German-Indian treaty concluded in 1847 in Texas, the theme of affinity was also reiterated when some Germans, such as Solomon Bibo, a German from Westphalia, became Indian chiefs.[16] Moreover, Hans Rudolf Rieder expressed the following opinion in 1929 in the preface to Buffalo Child Long Lance's book:

> The Indian is closer to the German than to any other European. This may be due to our stronger leaning for that which is close to nature. Negroes, Eskimos, people of the Pacific do not possess the human qualities to arouse our friendship and inclination. The Indian, however, is model and brother for us during one of our most cherished recollections.[17]

The theme of a German–Indian affinity emphasized Teutonic–Indian brotherhood as well as the unique nature of Indian–German relations, characterized by mutual recognition and collaboration, as opposed to the racist presuppositions, violence, and exploitation that characterized the nature of the relations between the English and the Indians. The idea of German–Indian affinity proved to be "enormously attractive to May's male and female German readers, who, throughout the twentieth century, reveled in identifying alternately with kind, strong Teutonic superman and the equally kind, supple, and beautiful 'Indianer.' "[18]

Hartmut Lutz offers another explanation regarding the Germans' alleged close emotional bond to Native Americans. Because the Germans never considered Native Americans as a military threat or as economic competition, nor was Germany involved in the conquest of the American West to the same degree as England or France, there never was a need on the part of the Germans to dehumanize Indians. This, combined with the Germans' fascination with the original and primordial, contributed to the emergence of a highly romanticized image of the United States' original inhabitants.[19]

Toward the end of the nineteenth century, Europeans had an opportunity to see Native Americans, albeit in staged, unrealistic performances across Europe. Influenced by the writings of James Fenimore Cooper as well as some German writers, German audiences eagerly attended the shows, reinforcing the idea of German–Indian affinity. While they considered the Indians as noble warriors and the last representatives of a dying race, the shows only confirmed the stereotype of the Indians as savages who had to be cared for as if they were children.[20] A local Berlin paper, reporting on Buffalo Bill's Wild West tour on July 24, 1890, made the following observation:

> there's something still different, however, about the Indian races and everything that has to do with Prairie life in North America. Today, despite the fact that steamships have already put "North America" on the map of even the most casual tourists, despite the fact that things American no longer seem so "distant," so exotic, so foreign to us, Indians and everything associated with them continue to exert a powerful, indescribable force of attraction. Today, as in our childhood, we remain under the magical spell of Cooper's *Leatherstocking Tales*, and for us the names of chiefs and squaws such as "Nimble Deer," "White Dove," and the like have a sound transfigured by the actual poetry of the primeval forest.[21]

One should not neglect the importance of Buffalo Bill's visit to Germany to understand the popularization of Karl May's novels. Buffalo Bill's shows proved tremendously popular in Europe and what they brought to Europe was the dissolution of the boundaries between fiction and real life.[22] Buffalo Bill's European tours coincided with Germans' increasing appetite to meet the authentic heroes of the Wild West they had been reading about in German novels.[23] Buffalo Bill first made a tour through England, Scotland, France, and Italy, before he came to Austria and Imperial Germany in 1890–1891. He traveled east as far as the Russian border, visiting Lemberg, Krakau, and some small towns along the Russian border. In Dresden, the capital of Saxony, close to Karl May's home in Radebeul, the seating capacity stood at 17,000, yet barely half of those who wanted to see the show were admitted. Among the lucky ones admitted was Karl May. Indeed, the tour proved to be tremendously popular all across Germany.[24]

The success of the Wild West Show was made possible in part by the long tradition of Indian literature in Germany and the existing stereotypes people wanted confirmed through the shows. The shows, having met people's expectations, further made people identify with the Plains Indians and their cultures, or what they believed were their cultures. Buffalo Bill's Wild West was not the only group that toured Europe prior to the outbreak of World War I. Between 1880 and 1891, five different Wild West shows toured Germany: Labrador-Eskimos, Sioux Indians, Bella-Coola Indians, Carver's Wild America, and Buffalo Bill's Wild West. The first Indian troupe to have visited Germany, Esquimaux Indians, arrived in Germany much earlier, in 1822. No Wild West show arrived in Germany again until 1875. Wild West shows continued to tour Germany until 1914, when a Sioux Indian troupe arrived in Dresden, only a few miles away from Karl May's home. Overall, over a dozen other groups toured Europe as well between 1822 and 1914.[25]

"In the beginning was James Fenimore Cooper," wrote Ray Allen Billington. Indeed, the first of his *Leatherstocking Tales* became tremendously successful not only in the United States, but also across Europe. In Germany, two editions were published within a year after their release in 1823 in North America. To many Europeans, Cooper's portrayal of the American frontier appeared to be accurate. The popularity of his novels precipitated the popularity of European Western literature, becoming the principal image-makers for the masses of European readers. While many Americans considered Cooper's stories escapist and juvenile due to the lack of complicated narratives, for European writers he became a guru whose American Western themes guaranteed acceptance and popularity.[26] Charles Sealsfield, Friedrich Gerstäcker, and Balduin Möllhausen were probably the most popular German authors of Indian stories prior to Karl May. They used Cooper's tales as a point of reference vis-à-vis their own experience in the United States. These writers had interacted with Western tribal cultures on many occasions during their extensive travels across the American West.[27] Charles Sealsfield's novels introduced the notion of a "noble Savage" to European audiences.[28] Balduin Möllhausen, often called the German Cooper, was well known for his popular Indian novels. Influenced by Cooper, Möllhausen distinguished between good and bad Indians. While he still believed that Indians could be integrated into the civilized world, Friedrich Gerstäcker introduced the notion, later accepted by Karl May, that the Indians were doomed to perish. Both Sealsfield and Gerstäcker considered the collapse of the Indian nations inevitable, although they tended to represent the Natives as noble savages. Gerstäcker, whose representations of the Indians are rather complex, might have had more direct experience with Native American tribes than any other popular German novelist. He did not, however, share Möllhausen's enthusiasm for civilizing Indians. On the contrary, although he acknowledged that European aggression, the removal policies, and the destruction of Indian cultures precipitated Indians' degeneracy, he justified it as historically inevitable.[29]

Although often criticized for writing simplistic stories and although he never visited the American West, May possessed a personal library of over 3000 books, which contained travel literature, novels, and scientific treatises about North America and the Native Americans. In *Winnetou III*, May revealed the source of his fascination and inspiration when his alter-ego, Old Shatterhand, asked if Old Shatterhand read Cooper's novels, he responded emphatically: "Yes."[30] May's works contain many more similarities to Cooper's, pointing to the influence the American novelist had upon the shaping of May's perception of the Wild West. Cracroft points out that

> Both Cooper and May deal with the beginning of the end of the Indian nations; both follow a gradual and symbolical move westward; both have mythical heroes who symbolize a phase of history; both are fond of terribly noble and terribly evil savages; both have comic elements – Cooper's David Gamut and Obed Bat, May's Sam Hawkens; and both use sea imagery.[31]

May's works also contain a binary opposition between Indian tribes. In the case of Cooper, it was the rivalry between Mohicans and the Iroquois. In May's case, it was the antagonism between Apache and Comanche. Overall, May shares Cooper's understanding of the inevitability of the demise of Native American civilizations; thus his feeling toward them is best characterized as one of tragic sympathy. It appears, however, that while there are some good Indian tribes in May's novels, a majority of the better-known tribes such as the Comanche, Oglala-Sioux, Kiowa, and Ute are presented in a negative light.[32]

In *Winnetou I*, May seems to have responded to the idea of the Anglo-Americans' right to settle the entire North American continent by writing that "it is a cruel law, which makes the weak subjects of the strong." He reiterates, however, the notion of the inevitability of

the demise of Indian nations by adding that is how the earth was created and the natural laws had to be accepted.[33] Neither May nor any
of the Germany writers attempted to save Native American nations in
their novels. This happened only in East German movies. A similarity
also exists between how May's readers and how Möllhausen's readers
obtain information. In both cases, the writer describes what is happening through eavesdropping. Moreover, it appears that May borrowed the
narratives of initiation and rebirth from Gerstäcker's and Möllhausen's
travel accounts.[34]

Another important source for May's novels also seems to have been
a German traveler and writer, Friedrich August Strubberg, who had
spent almost a decade traveling across Missouri, Arkansas, and Texas.
Unlike other writers who came to the United States in search of adventure, Strubberg might have left Germany because of his involvement
in a duel.[35] Strubberg's hero is capable of defending himself against
three grizzly bears at one time, wresting his dog from an alligator's
jaws, and defeating dozens of Indians all by himself. May's hero, Old
Shatterhand, gained a reputation among Indians for having killed a
bear using only his knife. Last, Strubberg's hero is not only German, but
also Christian, which constitutes another important similarity between
May's and Strubberg's heroes.[36]

Coming, like May, from a poverty-stricken family, Gerstäcker also
became a significant source for some of May's literary "borrowings."
Unlike Struberg and May, who only imagined hunting a bear, Gerstäcker
actually did hunt bears. More importantly, his stories seem much more
realistic, as opposed to May's, as the former actually spent a significant
amount of time in the United States and many of his accounts reflect
his frontier experiences. May's rendition of Old Shatterhand's killing
of a bear would have either shocked Gerstäcker or made him laugh at
May's naiveté. May might have learned about the weapons for which
he became famous from Gerstäcker as well. May's inclusion of river
pirates and the similarity of the criminals' pseudonyms in *Winnetou III*
further points to his fascination with Gerstäcker's novels, in this case,
with *Mississippi River Pirates*. Another possible borrowing could be May's
idea that not only could a German frontiersman learn vital skills from
Native Americans, but, as is the case with Old Shatterhand, he could
actually become better than them. He also seems to have modeled his
descriptions of landscapes on Gerstäcker. May's emphasis on greed and
gold, in particular, derives from Gerstäcker's depiction of gold mines,
condemned as the source of evil and uprooting in American society,
subordinate to the demon gold.[37]

Unlike his predecessors, May had not visited the United States prior to the completion of his novels. He tried to cover up that fact by the incorporation of detailed geographic, botanic, and ethnographic information as well as through skillful use of existing stereotypes. His efforts to identify himself with the German-American protagonist, Old Shatterhand, probably indicate that he ceased to differentiate between reality and fiction. Against all odds, he managed to create novels that intensified German readers' curiosity for the Wild West. His Indian characters, as Cooper's, are also either good or bad, depending not only on their level of knowledge about the achievements of European civilization, but also on their approach to Christianity. There is a clear division between the good tribes of the Mescalero-Apaches and the bad tribes of the Comanche. And although Old Shatterhand needed to learn about life in the Wild West from the Apache, they were still far inferior to this German-American.

Karl May's works link the present in which Native Americans were eradicated with the past of Germanic antiquity by highlighting similarities between the brave Indian and German tribes. However, while the Germanic people proceeded into modernity, Indians remained eternally in a premodern state. Observations about Indians in Wild West shows, novels, and later movies, thus, became part of turning non-European people into objects of spectacle. For the Germans living far away from the frontier, Karl May's novels became "a natural paradise where good still triumphs over evil; where men can be men; where the ideal of the noble savage, and the apex of Western European culture mix harmoniously in May's cowboy and Indian characters, Old Shatterhand and Winnetou."[38]

May's greatest accomplishment seems to be that he introduced the concept of the American West to a German audience that had neither visited the place nor knew much about it. Essentially, May developed a distinctly German interpretation of the American West. Thus, drawing from the literary works of Cooper and German novelists, complemented by his impressive research about the culture and history of the American West, combined with the implied affinity between Germanic and Indian peoples, and enriched with the power of his imagination, Karl May created a unique German understanding of the American West. Even more significantly, May gave to the Germans, and to the young readers who grew up in a culture that valued exploration and colonial enterprise, a modern hero (Old Shatterhand) who became as important to Germans as Siegfried from the Nibelungen Song. When nineteenth-century German nationalists rediscovered Siegfried, the dragon-slayer, May, a nineteenth-century writer, created a hero who outgrew the ancient heroes in popularity. Old Shatterhand, of course, had the distinct advantage of sharing the time of its readers while Siegfried was long gone. Thus, May's writings contributed to the creation of a truly national culture that ironically focused on heroes and actions far beyond Germany's borders. His books, in the course of the nineteenth and twentieth centuries, provided an image of the United States to millions of people.

Americans are always surprised to discover the deep admiration for the Wild West among Germans of all ages. An article published in *The Economist* nicely sums up this sentiment: "When American GIs poured into Germany in 1945, they were astonished to discover that German children, after 12 years of Nazi rule, could be found decked-out in buckskins and feathers and playing 'Indians.'" *The Economist* points out that thousands of adults continue to do the same every spring in Radebeul, a quiet Dresden suburb. The weekly concludes that "the explanation for both these phenomena is Karl May (1842–1912), a Saxon weaver's son, jailbird, self-described linguist—and the man who single-handedly invented the wild west for generations of Europeans."[39]

Karl May was born on February 22, 1842, in Ernstthal, a small town in the mountainous region of Saxony, to a poor weaver family. He was the fifth child of Christiana Weise and Heinrich May. The Mays had 14 children, nine of whom did not reach adulthood. Shortly after Karl was born, he lost his sight. He regained the ability to see when he was five, thanks to successful surgery conducted in Dresden. His condition had a tremendous impact upon his development. Describing his condition, May wrote that

> I could sense people and objects, I could also smell them and hear, but it was not enough, in order to imagine what they looked like. It was an inner image. When someone talked, I heard his soul, not his body. That remained with me even after I could see. Only the one who was once blind and who possessed such a deep and powerful imaginary world, could imagine what I thought, did, and wrote.

Indeed, while some historians argue that his ability to regain sight must have been an ophthalmological miracle, others assert that regaining his sight was May's mystification concocted in a later stage of his life, designed to create an aura of secrecy.[40]

In order to escape from poverty and to deal with the death of his siblings and other family members, young Karl became an avid reader. There is an early connection between the supposed freedom the American West provided and the situation of poor German families, which, like Karl May's, might have believed that "Indians roaming the open prairie symbolized freedom at a time when feudalism practically made every individual in Europe dependent."[41] Fascinated with the distant world on the other side of the Atlantic that he read about and that often confused him, May started to learn English as he became increasingly interested in the American West. In order to pay for English lessons, he found a job at an inn. Once he became famous, he claimed to have known over 40 languages, including French, Arabic, Italian, Spanish, Greek, Latin, Hebrew, Romanian, Persian, Kurdish, Chinese, Malaysian, Hindu, Turkish, and Indian languages, including Apache, Sioux, Comanche, and Kiowa. May was a good student and while his parents hoped he might become a physician, they were too poor to send him to a medical school. Interestingly, the unrequited wish to become a doctor, or being able to heal people, frequently reappeared in May's oriental novels.[42]

At the age of 16 Karl May joined the teachers' seminary in Waldenburg, Saxony, where he committed theft for the first time in his life. He was removed from the seminary for committing more thefts a few years later and joined another one in Plauen. He assumed his first job as a teacher in Glauchau, but he was fired after just 14 days on the job for stealing a friend's watch.

After his dismissal, May committed more petty crimes, was arrested once again, and his teaching license was revoked. He was deeply saddened by that decision, but instead of correcting his behavior, he vowed revenge against the authorities for revoking his license. May wrote that since he was already labeled a criminal, he now would commit himself to living up to that expectation. It angered him so much because the revocation of his teaching license meant that his way out of poverty seemed to have been closed. He committed many more petty crimes, including theft, forgery, and fraud, for which he was sentenced to four years and one month in prison in Zwickau. At the age of 28, Karl May's life hit rock bottom. During his stay in prison, May served as a prison librarian and read adventure stories and decided that after his release he would make a living as a writer. After he was released from prison, he began to write short stories and traveled across Germany. He was arrested one more time and spent three months in jail in 1879. Once released from prison, he became one of the world's all-time best-selling fiction writers. In 1893 he completed his best-known work, the *Winnetou* trilogy, and purchased his house in Radebeul two years later at the peak of his fame.[43] While historians offered some explanations as to what pushed May to commit the petty crimes that almost ruined his life, none has come up with a credible answer. Perhaps even May himself could not explain it either.

Prior to his first and only trip to the United States, May had visited Egypt, Palestine, East Africa, as well as Ceylon and Sumatra. After he had published his famous *Winnetou* novels, on September 5, 1908, May finally embarked on a trip to the country about which he had written so much. Together with his second wife, Klara, May crossed the Atlantic aboard the passenger steamer *Grosser Kurfürst*, which arrived in New York on September 14. The Mays stayed only four days in New York. Then they took a nine-hour trip by train along the Hudson River to Albany. After three days in Albany, they traveled to Lake Erie and Buffalo. On September 24 they reached Niagara and spent ten days in the area. On October 5 they arrived in Boston. On October 18 May attended a convention organized by the German–American Union in Lawrence. On November 24 the Mays left Boston by train and arrived in New York. They left the United States later that day. They did not travel back directly to Germany, but spent an additional month in London. May, who had written so extensively about the Wild West and whose writings determined the European image of the Wild West for generations to come, did not spend a single day outside of New England. The German public did not know of May's one-month stay in London, which was covered up as an extended stay in the Wild West. Klara May explained to those who wanted to know where Karl May had spent the second part of the trip that they had decided to see the Wild West one more time. Indeed, she wrote in 1932 in her memoirs that she had done that to maintain the writer's reputation.[44] Karl May was quite disappointed with his first and only voyage to the United States, having not visited his alleged other homeland, the American West. He became quite a rich person following the success of his novels and he certainly could have afforded to visit the American West if he had wanted to. Historians can only speculate as to why he decided not to. Because May put so much effort into pretending he was Old Shatterhand, perhaps he wanted to avoid embarrassment should it become clear that he was a greenhorn rather than a frontiersman, and that the West he had created differed so much from reality.

A continuous struggle with lawsuits and scandals marked the last years of May's life. The trip to the United States was in reality an attempt to escape from these problems, rather than to visit the American West.[45] Karl May so immersed himself in his own fictional characters trying to forget his impoverished and criminal background that, by 1880, he claimed that Old Shatterhand's adventures were really the adventures he had lived through himself during his extensive travels in the United States, which, in turn, fueled even more attacks by his critics on his credibility. Indeed, Karl May tried so hard to authenticate the story of Winnetou and Old Shatterhand as the true story of his life that when asked about Winnetou's death, he even wrote a reader that "Winnetou, born in 1840, died on September 6, 1874."[*] He also wrote that he could still hear the Ave Maria, the melody during which Winnetou closed his eyes in his arms. His house and his workroom were decorated with items he called travel trophies, including many he had allegedly used as Old Shatterhand. Karl May often had himself photographed as Old Shatterhand, and carried calling cards "Dr. Karl Friedrich May, known as Old Shatterhand." The novels, always written in the first person (representing Old Shatterhand's accounts), created the impression that he was the great Old Shatterhand and had experienced all the fantastic adventures himself.[46] His critics exposed many of his lies. They made public that Karl May had not traveled to the United States before he wrote his Winnetou novels and instead had spent the time incarcerated in the Zwickau prison. Moreover, his critics also found out that May, who signed his documents Dr. Karl May, had bought his doctorate from "The German University of Chicago," run by a former barber. Bogged down by numerous libels and lawsuits, May eventually suffered a mental collapse. Even that did not stop him from perpetuating the myth of being Old Shatterhand throughout his career in his letters and public lectures, which he filled with wild stories about his adventures with Indians.[47] But, as an American book reviewer pointed out after reading May's three books, "after all, Dante had never been to Hell either, nor had Shakespeare been to Denmark or Italy." While Karl May will "never catch on in English," "such an author is clearly a phenomenon."[48]

Despite these revelations, many famous European intellectuals, politicians, and celebrities enthusiastically supported Karl May. Albert Einstein spent his entire adolescence under May's spell and was reported to have said that Karl May was "in occasional hours of doubt, of great worth to me, and I am not in the slightest ashamed of it."[49] Carl Zuckmayer became so fascinated with May's works that for a time he intended to name his daughter Winnetou.[50] A *New York Times* article from 1939 excerpts a conversation Marlene Dietrich allegedly had with James Stewart; Joe Pasternak, a Hungarian producer; and Charles Winninger, a German. While Stewart and Winninger had never heard of Karl May before, Pasternak quickly interposed to demonstrate his knowledge of Karl May and addressing Winninger, he assured him that "there really was a Karl May," and that "your father must have known about him in the old country. He was the German Nick Carter. He wrote adventure stories-five pfennig fiction. All German boys used to read his cowboy and Indian stories... He must have sold millions of those stories. They still sell, I hear." "Sure they do," interjected Marlene Dietrich, and pointed to the one she just bought in Austria for her daughter. Both Pasternak and Dietrich then agreed that May's stories made them want to come to the United States. "And here I am at last," concluded Dietrich, smiling.[51] Karl May died from a heart attack in 1912. Reportedly, his last words were: "Victory! A great victory! I see everything as rosy!"[52]

Four films based on Karl May's novels about adventures in the Middle East had already been made before World War II. The first three, *Auf den Trümmern des Paradises*, *Bei den Teufelsanbeten*, and *Die Todeskarawane*, were filmed in the 1920s. The fourth one, *Durch die Wüste*, was the first Karl May film with sound, produced in the 1930s. Neither of them, however, concerned the American West, which might explain why they failed to attract large audiences. Only in the early 1960s did West German filmmakers tackle May's successful novels of the American West. Given the amount of action and the vivid narrative of his novels, it must have been problematic for directors and film producers to write a script, let alone secure financing for creating the setup for Karl May's Wild West. Moreover, a cinematic interpretation of Karl May's novels required directors and producers to agree to delete certain parts, alter others, and yet to make sure that the film remained true to the books, which almost every German knew. Expectations of the audience were incredibly high and can easily be compared to the craze for the Harry Potter novels and movies in the first decade of the twenty-first century. It was not an easy task, especially given Karl May's stature as a writer and the number of plots and characters he had developed in his novels. At the time when the number of moviegoers continued to decrease, the Constantin film studio turned to Karl May novels in hopes of reviving the film industry and, unbeknown to them, released the most popular film series in the history of postwar West German cinema.[53]

The person credited with the idea of filming a Karl May Western is the Constantine film producer, Horst Wendlandt. He admitted that he considered the idea for a few weeks and a seemingly insignificant conversation made him realize that the idea might be worthwhile. While on a business trip, he asked a hotel maid whether she knew Karl May. She immediately said yes and mentioned two titles of May's books, *The Treasure of Silver Lake* and *Winnetou*. He realized then that everybody in

Germany knew Karl May and that May's heroes were omnipresent in German culture. Thus, the Constantin studio and Wendlandt set out to do something that was believed to be possible only in Hollywood: the production of a successful Western.[54] Even Wendlandt admitted later in an interview that he was afraid that the Western might not have turned out as popular as he was hoping for, or, even worse, it might have been an utter failure. His view was shared by some of the people involved in the project. Considering the risk associated with the filming of the first Karl May Western, Wendlandt alluded to Winnetou and Old Shatterhand, Karl May's heroes, besieged and under assault in a seemingly hopeless situation, who did not worry about their situation; rather, they were concerned with the fate of their attackers once they counterattacked. Wendlandt realized that the film industry had to fight to overcome the crisis, just as Karl May's heroes had fought for their survival. He also believed that he had selected the right actors to play the leading roles. Just before the film was released, the producers were asking each other whether there would be 5 million Germans willing to see the movie to cover the expenses associated with the making of the most expensive film of the year. Some even considered Wendlandt a dead man, meaning that no film studio would ever again entrust him with producing a motion picture. As it turned out, following the premiere of the film in Stuttgart on December 12, 1961, the film became a huge success. The entire country was excited about the first postwar Karl May film. Some film critics asserted that the country had never experienced the kind of excitement the release of the first Karl May Western generated. Already after three months of screening, the film turned in profits. The film also brought almost a quarter of a million Marks within just eight weeks of screening in Antwerp, whereas four weeks of screening in Italy brought almost a quarter of a million Marks. Sixty-eight thousand people saw the film in Paris within just two weeks. It proved to be a tremendous success both in and outside West Germany.[55] Tassilo Schneider, a German journalist, pointed out that two of the Karl May Westerns were among the top-five most successful films in West Germany at the end of 1963, the other three being the popular crime films based upon the English author Edgar Wallace's detective stories films.[56]

Horst Wendlandt knew that the potential success of the first West German Western depended on the selection of the lead actors. It appeared impossible to have a German actor play either Winnetou or Old Shatterhand. Old Shatterhand, who appeared in May's novels as a superhuman right out of Friedrich Nietzsche's writings, was tall, blue-eyed, and with blond hair, could not be played by any German actor given the recent Nazi past and its racial stereotypes. The idea that such a person would face the dying race of Indians, less than two decades after the Holocaust, which was still not a topic of recognition or discussion among many West Germans, seemed impossible. The American actor Lex Barker, who had become famous for playing Tarzan, seemed to be the perfect solution to this dilemma. He had already starred in an American Western and was a fairly well-established actor in Europe. Although he seemed to be a perfect candidate for the role of Old Shatterhand, Barker initially was not enthusiastic about playing in a German "Wild West adventure film." He did not see how he could develop as an actor in a German version of the genre that Hollywood had been filming for six decades. Barker simply did not believe a German Western could possibly become a success, nor did he think the German studios had the potential to film it.[57] His wife, Irene Labhart, who was aware of May's iconic status in Germany, encouraged him to accept the role. Barker, however, still hesitated. Having read the script, he especially did not like the amount of dialogue, which he believed would feminize his role by making his character engage in numerous conversations. He eventually agreed and accepted the DM 120,000 contract. The relatively unknown French actor Pierre Brice agreed to play Winnetou. Thus, the producers found two perfect actors for these two roles, a blond, blue-eyed and Hun-looking German hero Lex Barker, and a gray–green-eyed, Pierre Brice, with facial features resembling those of the Apache chief, Winnetou.[58]

Movie fans immediately became enthusiastic about the tall, blond, and athletic Barker, who became the most popular American actor in Germany in the 1960s.[59] Similarly, Brice became so popular as Winnetou that he never found another meaningful role in his career. *The Treasure of Silver Lake* began the series of successful West German, and later, European Westerns, as well as provided West Germans with a couple of German and non-German great heroes with whom moviegoers found it easy to identify.[60] The movies accomplished the impossible: they turned a deeply nationalistic topic into a transnational enterprise through the selection of non-German actors. Moreover, the movies were produced in Yugoslavia, meaning they crossed the East–West divide. Lex Barker even stated, while working on the set of *The Treasure of Silver Lake*, that once American filmmakers saw the landscape of the German Westerns, it would not be too long until the first American Western would be made in Yugoslavia, which would cost them much less to produce. A Yugoslavian film company, Jadran-Film, immediately offered its assistance, since Karl May's novels were immensely popular not only in the German-speaking countries, but also in the entire Eastern bloc. The suitability of Yugoslav landscapes encouraged filmmakers to follow through, thinking that they had found the perfect scenery between the Karavanke Mountains in Slovenia and the mountainous area of Macedonia to rival that of the American West. This region proved to be so beautiful that it fed into the hunger of West Germans for distant landscapes and encouraged people to imagine a world beyond their own.[61]

The Treasure of Silver Lake was a test case to see whether Karl May novels were worth filming at all. Film producers believed that the appealing title combined with the popularity of Karl May novels would contribute to the success of the film, which, in turn, would lead to the creation of a whole series of Karl May films. *The Treasure of Silver Lake* proved to be tremendously successful not only in West Germany, but also throughout Europe. Seventeen more cinematic adaptations of the novel were made in just six years following the film's release in 1961. It was "the first continental postwar film that did not imitate the American Western but instead adapted it to specific national heritage, here Karl May's romantic version of the West." Thus, the film became "a singular achievement for a national cinema that, by the early 1960s, was facing economic catastrophe."[62] Former Hollywood star Lex Barker did not believe that American film companies would purchase the film and distribute it in the United States. He even stated that it would be more likely for an Eskimo family to buy a refrigerator than for a Hollywood company to distribute a German Western in the United States. He was wrong. Three years after the premiere the film was released in the United States, albeit it did not become a success. The Rialto-film promptly signed a new contract with Barker assigning him the role of Old Shatterhand for future Karl May films. Horst Wendlandt reminisced that the viewers immediately idolized the two main actors, Barker and Brice. Thus, a dream pair of actors was born. The risk paid off as more than 17 million West Germans saw the film at the movie theater.[63] A reviewer for the *Düsseldorfer Nachrichten* was certainly correct when he commented on February 27, 1963, that "once the villains were dead, Old Shatterhand and Winnetou rode away to find a new adventure. This film will certainly not be the last one and more will soon follow."[64] The 1960s proved to be a tremendously successful decade for the Karl May Westerns, providing West Germans entertainment and two great heroes they came to identify with amid an identity crisis caused by World War II and the Cold War.

How successful the Karl May Westerns became was further demonstrated by the reaction of the East German officials. Less than three years after the release of *The Treasure of Silver Lake*, East Germany released its first *Indianerfilm*, *The Sons of Great Mother Bear*, providing an alternative interpretation of the myth of the American West, which was part and parcel of the construction of an East German identity. Thus, the cinematic representation of the myth of the American West precipitated a cultural rivalry, which produced two distinct interpretations of what it meant to be German.

Liselotte Weslkopf-Henrich and East Germany's response to Karl May films

East Germany produced its first *Indianerfilm* as a response to the tremendously popular series of Karl May Westerns in West Germany, which became the most successful film series in postwar German history. Like their West German counterparts, East German filmmakers selected Yugoslavia as the filming site. The decision to film in Yugoslavia proved to be crucial to the success of the endeavor, not only because the scenery met the producers' expectations, but also because there were many Yugoslav actors who already had experience playing Indians. East German authorities intended to portray *Indianerfilme* as an international enterprise; therefore the DEFA chose Josef Mach, a Czech director. The films also became the starting point of the great career for the Yugoslavian actor Gojko Mitic, who played the lead role in all *Indianerfilme* produced in East Germany between 1966 and 1983.[65] The DEFA also hired actors and staff from other countries of the Eastern bloc, including Poland and the Soviet Union. At the time DEFA released *The Sons of Great Mother Bear* in 1966, it had not decided whether it would be a one-time endeavor or whether a series of films would follow. East German filmmakers did not foresee that their film would become such an astonishing success and result in the creation of a tremendously popular series of *Indianerfilme*, spanning two decades. *The Sons of Great Mother Bear* provided East German enthusiasts of Native American history a significant source of reference and encouraged them to continue their interests in the subject. It also captivated those who previously did not share a passion for Native American history. More than 10 million people saw the film in movie theaters, which is a spectacular number, given the fact that only about 16 million people lived in East Germany at that time. The film challenged the conventional interpretation of the myth of the American West, where white settlers were portrayed as righteous and lawful, and Native Americans as aggressive, unreasonable, cruel, and primitive. East German filmmakers did not intend to make yet another Western film in which Indians would simply get slaughtered. They set out to focus on individual Native American heroes and made them the central point of the story convergent with the dictum of the Socialist state's anti-imperialist (and anti-American) rhetoric. They also wanted the film to portray the conquest of the American West realistically; thus they realized they had to cooperate with experts on the ethnology, history, and culture of Native Americans. Furthermore, they believed that in order to differentiate *Indianerfilme* from the plethora of Western films and to raise their credibility, the films would be based on real historical events. By meeting the demands for adventure films and satisfying the interests of young Germans in the history of the American West, the DEFA managed to create a series of *Indianerfilme*, which proved to be a commercial success while propagating the "correct" vision of the history of the American Indians, compatible with the official rhetoric of GDR foreign policy. This vision placed the Indians as the central figures who were finally given a voice to offer an alternative version of the European conquest of the United States. In actuality, the main theme of the DEFA's Westerns became a history of class conflict in the American West, where, according to Günter Karl, a leading writer of the DEFA's studio Roter Kreis that produced the *Indianerfilme*, the historical truth converged with the theoretical principles of the socialist system.[66] To call it an *Indianerfilm*, as opposed to a Western, served an important function of clearly separating the film from any other traditional Western, and Karl May Westerns in particular.

In order to authenticate the film, the DEFA decided to ask Liselotte Welskopf-Henrich, a Professor of Classics and Ancient History at Humboldt University in Berlin, as well as an outspoken defender of the American Indian Movement, to write the script. The filmmakers also approached Lothar Dräger of the Leipzig Museum of Ethnology to supervise the work on Indian customs and outfits.[67] While Welskopf-Henrich's intention was to present an original, realistic portrayal of a frontier event, the film turned out to be a subjective interpretation of the events under consideration. Its simplifications, one-sidedness, and obvious anti-imperialism led to many distortions. Nevertheless, viewers considered it entertaining, exciting, and educational, and tended to overlook its obvious drawbacks.[68] Most importantly, *Indianerfilme* articulated the "deeper-seated processes of identification that resonated with postwar constructions of national and cultural identity." They "attested to what it means to be East German in the 1960s and 1970s" through their emergence as a "discursive site where meanings of national and cultural identity were negotiated and contested...a battleground not only between whites and reds, but also between state ideology, studio fantasy production, and spectatorial identification."[69]

Several literary forms shaped East Germans' understanding of history as well as their perception of the socialist state. Many East Germans expressed their pride in the rebuilding of the state following the destruction of the fascist regime and the war had brought about. Postwar East German literature often shared these points of view, including literature for children and young adults. One of the writers who debuted during the postwar period was Liselotte Welskopf-Henrich. Although her early novels, published in the mid-1950s, dealt with the fight against fascism, her later novels focused on the fate of the North American Indians in the nineteenth and twentieth centuries. Her trilogy, *The Sons of the Great Mother Bear*, published in 1963, followed by four other novels based on socio-ethnographic studies as well as personal experiences, proved to be successful portrayals of the Native Americans' fight for freedom and equality.[70] Due to the popularity of her novels as well as her connections with the members of the American Indian Movement and expertise on the matters of Native Americans in the United States, East German authorities chose Welskopf-Henrich to write the script for the first East German Western released in 1966.[71]

Liselotte Welskopf-Henrich was born on September 9, 1901, in Munich. From the age of four, she demonstrated enthusiasm for stories, especially those in which suffering, oppressed peoples found help from brave rescuers. As a student, she often told stories to her friends. Her passion for stories later developed into storytelling. Her family moved to Berlin in 1913, a city she considered "horrible." She studied economics, history, and philosophy at Humboldt University in Berlin and received her doctoral degree in economics in 1925. The hyperinflation of 1923 and the death of her father prevented her from continuing her academic career in the second half of the1920s. Welskopf-Henrich had to work for some time at a store to support her mother and herself because the family had lost all of its savings due to rampaging inflation. Paradoxically, she chose to major in economics rather than history or philosophy because she believed this academic field would prove more useful as the economic situation continued to deteriorate. With the Nazis' ascent to power in 1933, her prospects for an academic career seemed more distant than ever, especially since she refused to join the NSDAP. When an academic position became available, she was blocked from applying for it. During the war, she managed to maintain contact with and help some inmates at two camps: the concentration camp at Sachsenhausen and the labor camp at Lichterfeld. A year after the end of the war, she married August Rudolf Welskopf, who had been an inmate at Sachsenhausen, where he had become a Communist, and actively engaged in resistance toward the Nazis. She gave birth to Rudolf Welskopf, their first and only child, two years later. Immediately after the war ended, she received a significant position in the Berlin District Administration and joined the Communist Party of Germany. In 1949, she was finally given the opportunity to begin her academic career at Humboldt University. In 1959, she defended a second dissertation in ancient history (the *Habilitation*), which is a prerequisite for becoming a full professor. Welskopf-Henrich was selected as the first female member of the German Academy of Sciences in Berlin. She died on June 16, 1979, six months after the death of her husband. Welskopf-Henrich subscribed to a Marxist interpretation of history, but distanced herself from a rigid application of Marxist principles to history, which explains why her publications received little attention within the East German academic community.[72]

As an author of Indian novels, she set out to create a new form of Indian literature. Her goal was to examine white–Indian relations from the perspective of Native Americans. She wanted to replace the Karl May narrative where a good Indian had to be a friend of whites and a bad Indian had to be the enemy of whites, progress, and civilization. In her novels, she portrayed Native Americans the way she believed they deserved it, so that readers could learn about them not only through ethnographic studies, but also through historical novels grounded in scientific research.

Welskopf-Henrich also became involved in politics. After World War II, she contributed to the efforts of rebuilding East Germany, though she did not unconditionally support the new political system. The relationship between state officials and the professor proved to be quite complex. In contrast to the black and white image of good Communist resisters versus former Nazis, which dominated East Germany's understanding of the Nazi period, Welskopf-Henrich wanted a reasonable, honest, and open discussion about the German past and the involvement of Germans in the Nazi system and in Nazi crimes. She also criticized the ineffectiveness of the economic system of the GDR and set out to fight against nepotism and bureaucracy. Ultimately, Welskopf-Henrich ceased to cooperate with the DEFA because she became dismayed by the "stupid factual mistakes" that "upset and shocked her." She even "threatened the film company with a lawsuit if they should

ever try to break the copyright act and make any other movie" following
The Sons of Great Mother Bear.[73]

With Welskopf-Henrich's cooperation, DEFA Westerns became a significant propaganda tool for the Communist regime, even though East
Germans did not question established genre conventions and in many
regards modeled their film on American Westerns.[74] One should not,
however, consider Welskopf-Henrich a tool of those who created Communist propaganda. Although committed to Socialism and the GDR,
there is no evidence to link her activities with those of East German
foreign policymakers.[75] As a committed Socialist, she gradually became
increasingly disappointed with how East Germany implemented Socialist ideals, especially following the Hungarian Uprising in 1956. The
Prague Spring of 1968 exasperated her even more. On both occasions,
Welskopf-Henrich illegally donated money and supplies, which had to
be smuggled out of the GDR to her Hungarian and Czechoslovakian
colleagues. Still, the GDR offered her a chance to achieve her goals, and
only after the demise of fascism and the creation of a Socialist state was
she finally able to realize her dream of becoming a university professor.
This does not mean she was a passive member of the Communist Party,
nor does it mean that she became so disappointed with the system that
she left the party. She was able to use the freedom she had to help those
whom she chose to aid. In fact, she became a difficult person for the
GDR leadership to deal with since she sometimes criticized the Socialist system. At the same time, however, the East German authorities did
not consider her a potentially dangerous figure. Her Stasi files are rather
insignificant. The East German Ministry for State Security followed her
activities for only two years beginning in 1972 after her fourth trip to
North America. The files were closed the following year.[76]

Liselotte Welskopf-Henrich visited North America five times, in 1963,
1965, 1968, 1970, and 1974. Altogether, she spent around two-and-a-
half years traveling across the North American continent. Prior to her
visits, often supervised by an official from the Bureau of Indian Affairs,
she had met Native Americans stationed in Berlin. Welskopf-Henrich
even planned to hire residents of Wood Mountain in Canada to play
the Indian parts of the first East German Western. She visited the members of the American Indians Movement at Alcatraz in 1970. Eventually,
the FBI even interrogated her about her Native American connections
for a few hours following the events at Pine Ridge, South Dakota. While
Welskopf-Henrich was not denied a visa to enter the United States,
for political reasons, some of her colleagues were. On one occasion,
in order to display her solidarity with those whose applications were

denied, Welskopf-Henrich chose not to travel to Indiana for the Fourth Congress of the International Economic History Association in 1968.[77] She described herself as an ethnologist as well as an ancient historian, who understood Native American history as well as the current situation of Native Americans from both a historical and a personal perspective.[78] According to Elsa Christina Mueller, in her novels Welskopf "reached a rather remarkable level of approximation to a true depiction." However, Mueller also points out that "Welskopf's critical representation of the United States (which might still carry some anti-Americanism) easily serves the ideological East-West controversy which is supposed to make socialist Europe look like the better future option."[79]

It took Welskopf-Henrich 17 years to complete her first Indian story. She often incorporated new material into them, especially as she gained access to more and more biographies of Native Americans. She also admitted in her letters that she needed more experience, knowledge, and time. Her main objective for writing the novels was to give voice to the oppressed. *The Sons of Great Mother Bear* was initially an anti-fascist novel, which Welskopf-Henrich had already begun working on during World War II. After two major revisions, the third and final version articulated her vision of the future of Socialism in East Germany. Thus, although the two main characters, Adamson, a white farmer, and Tokei-ihto, the Dakota chief, were not initially fond of each other as long as Adamson's goal was to find gold. Having observed the treatment of the Dakota tribe, Adamson understood that, as a proletarian, he was closer to the oppressed Indians than to the white capitalists. Adamson's efforts to free Tokei-ihto mark the beginning of their alliance as well as their friendship, which ultimately leads to their victory. They also highlight the main difference between her writing and Karl May's. Welskopf-Henrich believed that her imagination, thanks to the experiences of the struggle of the working class, allowed her to find the right path to Socialism, whereas May's imagination and his great talent to tell stories became corrupted by capitalist influences to the point where they became useless.[80]

Welskopf-Henrich corresponded with and befriended some of the most influential members of the American Indian Movement (AIM). She believed that the trials of the AIM represented a quest for the human rights of Native Americans and other minorities. The Wounded Knee Legal Defense understood the importance of bringing foreigners into the trials of Native Americans accused of breaking federal laws in 1973 on the Pine Ridge Reservation in South Dakota. Native Americans, including Russell Means and Dennis Banks, leaders of the movement, protested against the treatment of Native Americans. Their protest resulted in an armed stand-off with local and federal law enforcement units that lasted 71 days. Members of the AIM also occupied the symbolic site of Wounded Knee where in 1890 the American army had killed more than 150 Sioux, including women and children. The Wounded Knee Legal Defense contacted Welskopf-Henrich because they believed that the support of influential people could help the cause of imprisoned Native Americans. They also explained to Welskopf-Henrich that "for the non-Indians on the Committee our Commitment has been an educational experience in learning about the values of Native Americans in comparison to our own upbringing and what we were taught to believe."[81] It appears that, apart from her strong support for the cause of the Native Americans, Welskopf-Henrich never ceased to be curious about their culture and history.

One of the leaders of the AIM, Russell Means, together with his wife and eldest daughter, visited her at her house in Berlin-Treptow.[82] Shortly before his trial, Welskopf-Henrich assured him of her support, however helpful an East German at the time of the Cold War could be. Interestingly, when writing to Russell Means and many other Native Americans, Welskopf-Henrich often referred to herself as the "grandmother" who knew the Indians and their problems very well and who would continue to talk to young people all over the world in order to inform them of the conditions of Native Americans in the United States. Her efforts were not limited to mere comforting. In the case of Means, she promised to distribute the letter he had written to her earlier, which she believed would help the defense at the trial of the members of the AIM. Welskopf-Henrich admitted to Means that "the letter you gave me is already in more than a thousand copies spread over several countries and we continue to make it even better-known."[83]

Welskopf-Henrich wrote in her letter to Means that although she was aware of the fact that he had many Indian names, the name she would give him would be Toke-ihto-man, one who "goes first, straight through." Toke-ihto became the name of the young Indian chief in *The Sons of Great Mother Bear*, the role played by the Yugoslavian actor Gojko Mitic. Welskopf-Henrich assured Means that "we all, friends of Indian people, will never forget Wounded Knee (1890–1973) even if some goons forbid and hinder the celebration of the graves." This clearly demonstrates a major important motive for her scriptwriting: to commemorate and expose the brutal treatment of the native population by white settlers and American troops. Indeed, some Native Americans even expressed their willingness to come to Germany to see the motion picture. W.I.C. Wuttunee, a Native American attorney, expressed his confidence that "I am sure you have given a proper portrayal" of the Native American cause.[84] One can assume that the visits of the prominent members of the AIM must have been closely monitored by the American government, which also only reluctantly granted foreigners visas to visit Native American reservations.[85]

Not only did Welskopf-Henrich offer her assistance and support to the AIM, but she also tried to help imprisoned Native Americans. Because many members of the movement knew her, some Native Americans contacted her from prison by sending letters to her in Berlin. In one such letter, an inmate discussed the harsh conditions he had to endure while being imprisoned. He also replied to Welskopf-Henrich's question about a comparison he had made in a previous letter between slavery and the status of Native Americans. The inmate explained that the Indians were in economic slavery, and that due to hunger, Native Americans welcomed death as a savior. Moreover, he pointed out that he was aware of the fact that it was hard for people from other countries to believe that the United States, the richest country in the world, which spent billions of dollars to go to the moon, would allow people to starve to death.[86]

What did those inmates expect from Welskopf-Henrich? She managed to help them in various ways. First of all, she sent them money by postal orders. Having traveled to the United States and Western Europe, she was able to acquire American currency, which she could send to Native Americans from West Germany. East Germans were not allowed to freely dispose of Western currencies, whether American dollars or West German Marks. They had to deposit them in the state-controlled central bank (Staatsbank der DDR). Thus, sending Western currency was not only impossible, but also illegal. Western visitors to East Germany were obligated to exchange certain amounts of currency upon arrival depending on the number of days they were going to stay.[87] Welskopf-Henrich freely mentioned in her letters the sums of money she sent to Native Americans in the United States. The recipients also acknowledged and thanked her for the donations in their letters to her. It would be hard to argue that she was not aware of existing currency laws. Moreover, although she saw an economic advantage stemming from living in a Socialist country, where "inflation cannot infiltrate our country," she admitted that "we are a socialist country" and "our money is not privately exchangeable."[88] Her activities, then, point to her devotion to the Native American cause and her willingness to bypass the East German laws in order to help her Native American friends. Doing this, she risked her career and personal freedom, especially since it is highly likely that the Stasi was aware of the money transfers she made. Her correspondence with Native Americans was understandably monitored. It is possible that because state officials did not consider her dangerous, they allowed her to continue her activities, especially since they targeted the American government through her support of the AIM at the time when the Native American movement was engaged in direct, sometimes violent, confrontations with the federal government.

Second, Welskopf-Henrich sent packages to Native American communities, primarily clothes. For example, one package sent to South Dakota included coats, jackets, and trousers. As H. Glenn Penny pointed out, when examining the direction of the flow of goods during the Cold War, one is sure to recognize the velocity of "care packages moving across the geographic and political divide from west to east," and thus consider the packages sent to the Indian reservations in the United States as "unlikely, even absurd proposition, one that many Cold Warriors might try to explain away as the work of naïve idealists, some sort of clever political ploy, or simply an extension of similar efforts to support so-called 'third-world peoples' in places such as Vietnam or Angola." It does not mean, however, that her humanitarian efforts should be equated to her support of official policies of East German governments.[89] Interestingly, it was a time when the East German government officially supported American Communist and civil rights activist Angela Davis, imprisoned in 1970 for the shooting in a courtroom in California. East German schoolchildren were asked to paint postcards and send them as a sign of protest to the American government, asking for the release of the "heroine of 'the other America.'"[90] East Germany started no such campaign on behalf of the Native American population. Welskopf-Henrich acted independently and defied official laws of the Socialist state to send money to the United States. Unlike other East German intellectuals, imprisoned for *Devisenvergehen* (crimes related to convertible currency), she was never questioned about her illegal money transfers. The reason why she was never questioned or stood trial for making illegal money transfers at a time when other intellectuals did is not clear. One can only speculate that the East German government's foreign policy goals converged with her involvement in the Native American cause, which might have overshadowed her occasional, albeit explicit, illegal activities.

Welskopf-Henrich met with several Indian prisoners during her visits to the United States. Perhaps most importantly, she tried to help the inmates understand their legal status and its implications. By asking many direct questions regarding their sentences, witnesses, charges, she attempted to direct the inmates to take the necessary steps toward freedom, though she informed them that given the circumstances, the fight for freedom would be a long and difficult one. While admitting that it was easy to talk and much more difficult to follow up with actions she compared the Native Americans' status to her life in Nazi Germany, remembered as "one big jail." She expressed hope that the inmates would not have to wait 12 years, as she had waited in Germany for Allied liberation.[91] Welskopf-Henrich also expressed her disillusionment with the American government, which did so little for the Native Americans.[92]

Welskopf-Henrich's involvement in the AIM certainly demonstrates her commitment to the cause of the Native American organization. She genuinely believed she was an important part of the movement and that her support, whether monetary or in the form of letters, packages, or just advice, could bring positive changes to the Native Americans' struggle for civil rights. She corresponded and met with some prominent members of the movement both in the United States and in East Germany. It is possible, however, that she may not have played as important a role as she thought she did. It is difficult to validate her actual significance due to the scarcity of Native American sources even mentioning her. Regardless of how insignificant the leaders of the AIM perceived her to have been, one can conclude that she thought she was an integral part of the Native American struggle for civil rights. Moreover, although her advice, letters, or monetary donations did not prove to be crucial factors leading to the success of the movement, they certainly meant a lot to her as well as the individual recipients, such as an imprisoned Native American who found the support he needed in her letters, or an impoverished Dakotan who finally had adequate clothing to survive harsh winters. Most importantly, one should consider her work for the DEFA in the making of *The Sons of Great Mother Bear* as an important stage in her fight for Native Americans' civil rights. Regardless of how much recognition her efforts actually received, it is fair to say that had she not been so involved in the Native American cause, the DEFA may not have chosen her to write the script for the first *Indianerfilm*, nor would she have fought the DEFA so vigorously to present Native Americans' history and struggle accurately.

Welskopf-Henrich also tried to reach many important American politicians who, according to her, might have been able to improve the conditions of the Native Americans. She sent one of the many letters she wrote to President Jimmy Carter. In her letter, she introduced herself as a scientist and a writer whose novels reached millions of young people on both sides of the Iron Curtain. She pointed out that while he committed the sacrilegious act of arrogance by stealing the land from a defenseless Indian tribe, he was also the only man who could prevent this from happening again. While asking the president to right the wrongs done to the Indians in the United States, Welskopf-Henrich asked him whether he knew that the Indians were forced to live in the slums of the cities. She contended that what had been done to the Indians could not be God's work, but it was truly the work of the Devil.[93] To make the message more personal and straightforward, Welskopf-Henrich reminisced about the hardships Germans had endured during the years of the Nazi regime. Yet, she wrote, being almost powerless, she risked her life to save other people's lives. In a letter to an American attorney, Sanford Ray Rosen, Welskopf-Henrich argued that since President Carter talked so much about people's rights, he should understand the rights of the Indian nations fell under the same category as well. Despite the harshness of the letters, Welskopf-Henrich expressed her conviction that the president would not allow the worst to happen. Perhaps she truly believed that President Carter could be the one to undo the injustices done to Native Americans.[94] At the same time, growing more and more disillusioned with Socialism in her home country, she distanced herself from Marxism-Leninism and concluded that Marxism and Indigenism, the rights of native peoples to their land, were not compatible. Moreover, she even alleged the GDR, as much as the rest of the world, including the United States, shared the blame for the plight of Native Americans. She implicated the GDR as much as Western powers since she believed the whole world did not seem to care about the AIM. Her limited efforts to make people aware of the situation as well as efforts helping to fight injustice proved to be ineffective.[95]

Welskopf-Henrich believed that what distinguished her from Karl May was the fact that her works approximated the reality of life on the Great Plains and that she was not afraid to discuss the immorality of the conquest of the American West. While Karl May's works might seem sympathetic toward the plight of the Indians, he nonetheless pointed to the inevitability of the collapse of the Indians nations, which were mere obstacles to the progress of white Western society. Welskopf-Henrich, by contrast, set out to approach the conflict from a Native American perspective, as she believed the German perception of Native American society and culture needed a better review. Thus, not only did she strive to present the fight between the Sioux and the whites realistically and accurately, but she also wanted to demonstrate to the world that the Indians were not just part of a long past history, but that their struggle for the improvement of their peoples continued and would continue for years to come.[96]

In a letter to Chris Spotted Eagle, an important member of the AIM, Welskopf-Henrich offered her critique of the works of Karl May. She exposed May's ignorance of the historical context in which he had placed his characters. Indeed, Welskopf-Henrich asserted that when May wrote *Winnetou* and his subsequent novels, he refused to acknowledge the fact that the wars waged by Red Cloud, Crazy Horse, Sitting Bull, and Geronimo had been fought "for their tribe, their country, their freedom and their children." Moreover, she accused May of creating "a fantastic 'Head-chief' of all Apache, who gave up resistance and switched his allegiance to a white man," thus becoming a passive character, devoid of a cause and legacy. Therefore, the Apaches, convinced by Winnetou, agreed to something they would never have agreed to otherwise. They allowed Old Shatterhand to survey the land, which paved the way for Anglo-Americans to claim it as their own. Thus, despite the initial hatred of all white settlers, who, among others, killed Winnetou's father and sister (as well as his German-born teacher), Old Shatterhand became Winnetou's blood brother and "Winnetou ordered even his Apache-warriors to complete the railroad construction so that Karl May (Old Shatterhand) could receive his salary." According to Welskopf-Henrich, May's fantasies began affecting his writing once he began studying the nature and history of foreign countries. While labeling May's works as "travel tales," she reiterated the notion that although May had always referred to his characters in the first person, none of the adventures he described in his books was realistic. She also expressed her disappointment with the enormous popularity of Karl May's works, in spite of the proven cases of plagiarism and the tendency to make up facts.[97]

The correspondence between Welskopf-Henrich and Chris Spotted Eagle is important for another reason. The Native American had his own film production company and was curious about Karl May and his interpretation of the myth of the American West while he was working on the AIM/NIEA Treaty Film Project. The major obstacle to the realization of his project was lack of funding. He expected the project to cost over 80,000 dollars. Welskopf-Henrich sent him 100 dollars in 1975 to help support his film production company, but advised Spotted Eagle to use the money for whatever purpose he deemed necessary, including support for the imprisoned Russell Means. Interestingly, the two had met at Welskopf-Henrich's house in Berlin-Treptow, where the Native American appreciated "the quiet informal atmosphere" as opposed to New York, which was "such a busy, busy place." The relationship between Welskopf-Henrich and Spotted Eagle further demonstrates her closeness to the most influential members of the AIM as well as the significance of her support. Moreover, the fact that Spotted Eagle had visited her is truly remarkable and also points to her importance as a transatlantic patron and supporter of the Native American cause.[98]

In an essay entitled "About the Karl May Problem" ("*Zum Karl May Problem*"), Welskopf-Henrich explained her disapproval of Karl May's interpretation of the myth of the American frontier.[99] She admitted that she had learned about Karl May from a friend when she was ten years old. Because May had spent some time in prison, she first asked her mother whether she would be allowed to read his books. Her mother told her that she should not read books written by an ex-convict. At the age of 11, Welskopf-Henrich, together with her friends, like many other German children, would "play Indians." The "chief" of their Indian "band," however, told her at some point that she could no longer play with them, because she had not read any of Karl May's books. The following day, she began reading *Winnetou I*, hidden among junk in the attic. She was then allowed to rejoin the band and even became the undisputed wife of the chief. At first, she was overwhelmed by May's talent to tell stories. She read the Indian stories, as well as May's stories of the Middle East, and she did not deny that even at the moment when she wrote the essay on the problems of Karl May, she could still pronounce some of the hardest and most exotic names such as "Hadschi Hale Omar Ben Hadschi Abdul Abbas Ibn Ben Hadschi Dawuhd al Gossarah." What made her become so critical of May, then? Not only did she detest the male-oriented stories of Old Shatterhand, but also she could not believe how vain, conceited, and simply unbearable the stories were. Significantly, how could Karl May, she wrote, put himself in a position where he knew everything best, much better than any other human being? The initial resentment of Karl May's works came from what she perceived as his arrogance and egotism. She stated that "she simply could not stand him." Another reason for her resentment of May was his superficial representation of Native Americans, including the Apache chief, and his dog-like devotion to the white frontiersman. She also stated that the many contradictions May's books contained filled her with a strange feeling of confusion. Ultimately, having finished reading May's works, she decided she had to present a more desirable history. According to her, when she started studying Indians, discerning the truth about Indians became the sacred oath of her childhood.[100] Welskopf-Henrich argued that in May's novels, the only Indian who evoked sympathy was the one who befriended a white person. Conversely, the Indian who defended his land became an object of hate. Already as a child, she had come to the conclusion that the friendship between Old Shatterhand and Winnetou was hypocritical, and she could not understand the Indian's unconditional and unquestioning friendship toward the white intruder.[101]

Welskopf-Henrich's Indian hero, Tokei-ihto, became a role model for many young Germans, thus partly replacing the shoddy heroes such as Winnetou and Old Shatterhand. East German officials certainly appreciated the popularity of the novels and the films, which denounced American and West German imperialism. As the German film historian Gerd Gemünden pointed out, the shifting of the narrative from the Anglo-Americans to the Native Americans proved compatible with the GDR's denunciation of imperialism; thus "the fate of the Native Americans provided a showcase of what it means to be a victim of capitalist expansionism, the consequences of which can range from unequal trade, theft, and deceit to willful starvation, random murder and organized genocide." In this regard, the film also proved to be a blueprint for a better Socialist German state, where clashes were not won on the battle fields, but at the bargaining tables. This view was so typical for all East German *Indianerfilme*.[102]

Conclusion

One can often see cowboys, walking past the sheriff's office in Pullman City, visited by more than a million people every year. But this Pullman City is located northeast of Munich, close to the Bavarian town of Eging am See. Those cowboys will, too, eagerly enter the Black Bison Saloon, but instead of saying "I'll have a beer," they will say "Ein bier, bitte." According to *The New York Times*, Pullman City "is a compendium of mythic iconography engrained in the global psyche by well over a century of hugely popular adventure stories, movies, television shows and travelling Wild West extravaganzas."[1] Moreover, it typifies the mythical German–Indian affinity, still ever so popular among Germans, perpetuated by Karl May novels and their cinematic interpretations.

Shortly after the first Karl May film was produced in West Germany, East Germany responded with the production of its own *Indianerfilme*. Western products during the Cold War era often served as a "powerful referent" for the Communist governments. As Michael David-Fox observed, "The West was not only an attractive rival, but in other ways, an inextricable part of the fabric of those societies," whose constant goal was to catch up and overtake implicitly adopted "Western yardsticks to measure industry, technology, or consumer goods." Therefore, David-Fox adds,

> East-West interactions under communism deserve to be recognized as transnational history of a distinctive kind: layered onto long-standing preoccupations preceding the communist era, buffeted by exceptionally intense political and ideological ambitions and constraints, and centrally caught up with the geopolitical and systemic confrontations triggered by the Bolshevik Revolution and the Cold War.[2]

The Cold War rivalry between West Germany and East Germany began instantaneously following the creation of the two states after World War II. Both German states attempted to construct a new German identity which precipitated a new state- and nation-building phase. Not only did their respective governments attempt to convince their citizens that their own state was the legitimate one, but they also competed with each other for worldwide recognition.[3] Undoubtedly, one of the many fields of contestation was how to remember Nazism. In this regard, most Germans on both sides of the Iron Curtain were focused on the suffering to which they were subjected, rather than the crimes they had committed.[4] The competition for legitimacy between the two German states can be evidenced through the highly popular Western films produced during the Cold War, which conveyed messages regarding the recent past and articulated visions for the future.

There is no doubt, as Rob Kroes pointed out, that in the early twentieth century, American mass culture "was already pollinating shores on the other side of the Atlantic Ocean, creating some interesting cultural hybrids in the process."[5] One of the most popular hybrids of the Cold War era became the German Western, performing similar functions in both West and East Germany, albeit conveying different, often conflicting messages. Although West Germans considered the heroes of Karl May films as the embodiment of Germanness, the films created transnational heroes who transcended national borders. By the same token, while East Germans considered the *Indianerfilme* as a uniquely German response to the allegedly mongrelized West German films, they, too, created transnational heroes perceived as the quintessence of Cold War Germanness. The case of German Western films serves as an example of how American culture was "re-contextualized and re-semanticized to make it function within expressive settings of their own making" by agents of intercultural transfer, audiences, and producers.[6]

The popularity and significance of German Westerns clearly demonstrate why historians should become aware of the possibilities transnational forces create. Historians should also understand that they have to "redefine models for understanding the nature of cultural and social identities and the interplay between them in various global settings" as they increasingly deal with new forms of blended identity and transnationalism in the era of global capitalist expansion and new communication technologies, resulting in fluid patterns of cultural migration, assimilation, and group consciousness.[7] Gerd-Rainer

Horn and Padraic Kenney best substantiated the reasons for studying transnational phenomena. According to them:

Transnational history is no miracle cure. History is always concrete, and for obvious reasons any satisfactory answer to virtually any significant question will need to address and untangle the web and intermixture of transnational, national, and local influences. But what we are also saying is that, given a transnational historical phenomenon, it would be wholly surprising if transnational causes would be merely incidental in more than a few exceptional cases.[8]

What is so unique about the German Westerns is that the German case cannot be compared to any other Cold War instance. As Thomas Lindenberger has shown,

it is evident that these differing experiences remained much more intimately linked to each other than were the experiences of other European states separated from the other half of the continent by the Iron Curtain. Some historians suggest that in no other country did the Cold War predicament maintain such as presence in everyday life as in Germany and that in no other country was concrete knowledge about the conditions of life under the "other" system so widespread, both among elites and specialists and among those segments of the population that happened to have relatives on the other side.[9]

Moreover, following the unification of Germany, the *Indianerfilme* and Karl May films, despite their differences, helped bring the two German states together and the German–Indian affinity remained as strong as ever, as evidenced by the popularity of *Der Schuh des Manitou*. The film bridged the distinctions between the former antagonistic film genres: Karl May films and *Indianerfilme*. This symbolic meaning can be best seen in the role the former East German star Gojko Mitic played after the unification of the two German states. At the time of the release of *Der Schuh des Manitou*, Mitic performed the role of Winnetou in the immensely popular, traditional annual celebration of Karl May's works at the Karl May Festival at Bad Segeberg, in former West Germany. Thus, as Martin Wolf wrote in *Der Spiegel*, Gojko Mitic "was promoted from the chief of East German Indians to Winnetou of all Germans. Now he rides in the happy hunting grounds."[10]

It does not really matter that the film never became a success overseas, in the United States in particular, and that it, along with May, has been ridiculed by Western audiences. Karl May films and the writer himself have had a tremendous impact on millions of Germans, as well as Eastern and Southern Europeans, for over a century. Readers and moviegoers eagerly embraced the image of the United States May created, even though a great majority of them had never traveled to the United States. What explains the success of May's stories is that through his stories of the American West May created an image of the United States which registered with many people's dreams, provided an escape from daily life problems, and entertained them, all the while helping them navigate through life and discover who they are, such as a few hundred *Indianisten*, who have been meeting annually in Cottbus since 1973. For them, and many other Germans and Karl May enthusiasts, their annual celebrations are more than a hobby. When they "play Indians," they celebrate what the American Wild West still stands for as it had for over a century since Karl May published his *Winnetou* novels: freedom, limitless space, and adventure; a dream for a better life.[11]

Notes

Introduction

1. Richard Cracroft. "World Westerns: The European Writer and the American West." In *A Literary History of the American West*. Fort Worth: Texas Christian University Press, 1987, 159.
2. Chuck Laszewski. *Rock 'n' Roll Radical: The Life and Mysterious Death of Dean Reed*. Edina: Beaver's Pond Press, Inc., 2005, 106. *Jadran in Profile*. Zagreb: Publicity Dept. Jadran Film, 1986, 2.
3. May's first works published in the United States were translated by Marion Ames Taggart and published by Benzinger Brothers. Retrieved from http://onlinebooks.library.upenn.edu/webbin/book/lookupname?key=Taggart%2C%20Marion%20Ames%2C%201866-1945.Cook, 70. Meredith McClain, as quoted in Danica Tutush, "The Strange Life and Legacy of Karl May." In *Cowboys & Indians*, September 1999, 155.
4. Michael Petzel. "Deutsche Helden: Karl May im Film." In *Karl May im Film: Eine Bilde Dokumentation*. Christine Unucka, ed. Dachau: Vereinigte Verlagsgesellschaften, 1980, 11–12. "Grün-goldene Erfolgsgeschichte – 90 Jahre Karl-May-Verlag." Rolf Derrnen. *Karl May & Co.* Nr. 92 (Juni 2003), 7.
5. Leonie Naughton. *That Was the Wild East: Film, Culture, Unification, and the "New" Germany*. Ann Arbor: The University of Michigan Press, 2002, 28. Christopher Frayling. *Spaghetti Westerns: Cowboys and Europeans from Karl May to Sergio Leone*. New York: I.B. Tauris, 2006, 114.
6. Tony Shaw. *Hollywood's Cold War*. Amherst: University of Massachusetts Press, 2007, 1.
7. Robert A. Rosenstone. *History on Film/Film on History*. Harlow: Pearson Longman, 2006, 3–4.
8. Ian Tyrrell. *Transnational Nation: United States History in Global Perspective since 1789*. New York: Palgrave Macmillan, 2007, 8.
9. Ibid., 8.
10. Thomas Bender. "Introduction: Historians, the Nation, and the Plenitude of Narratives." In *Rethinking American History in a Global Age*. Thomas Bender, ed. Raleigh: University of North Carolina Press, 2002, 9.
11. Hermann Glaser. *Deutsche Kultur 1945–2000*. München: Carl Hansen Verlag, 1997, 159.
12. Ibid.
13. Heide Fehrenbach. *Cinema in Democratizing Germany: Reconstructing National Identity after Hitler*. Chapel Hill: The University of North Carolina Press, 1995, 2.
14. Richard Maltby and Ruth Vasey. " 'Temporary American Citizens': Cultural Anxieties and Industrial Strategies in the Americanization of European Cinema." In *"Film Europe" and "Film America": Cinema, Commerce and Cultural*

Exchange 1920–1939. Andrew Higson and Richard Maltby, eds. Exeter: University of Exeter Press, 1999, 39. Thomas H. Guback. *The International Film Industry, Western Europe and America since 1945*. Bloomington: Indiana University Press, 1969, 106.

15. Diethelm Prowe. "German Democratization as Conservative Restabilization: The Impact of American Policy." In *American Policy and the Reconstruction of West Germany, 1945–1955*. Jeffry M. Diefendorf, Axel Frohn, Hermann-Josef Rupieper, eds. New York: Cambridge University Press, 1993, 457.

16. Uta Poiger. "Fear and Fascination: American Popular Culture in a Divided Germany, 1945–1968." In *Kazaaam! Splat! Ploof! The American Impact on European Popular Culture since 1945*. Sabrina P. Ramet and Gordana O. Crnkovic, eds. Boston: Rowman & Littlefield Publishers, Inc., 2003, 58. Fehrenbach. *Cinema in Democratizing Germany*, 6–7.

17. Poiger. "Fear and Fascination," 64. Christina Haase. *When Heimat Meets Hollywood: German Filmmakers and America, 1985–2005*. Rochester: Camden House, 2007, 399.

18. Fehrenbach. *Cinema in Democratizing Germany*, 95–117.

19. Uta Poiger. "A New, 'Western' Hero? Reconstructing German Masculinity in the 1950s." In *The Miracle Years: A Cultural History of West Germany, 1949–1968*. Hanna Schissler, ed. Princeton: Princeton University Press, 2001, 413.

20. Dorothee Wierling. "Mission to Happiness: The Cohort of 1949 and the Making of East and West Germans." In *The Miracle Years: A Cultural History of West Germany, 1949–1968*. Hanna Schissler, ed. Princeton: Princeton University Press, 2001, 116–117.

21. Jost Hermand. *Kultur im Wiederaufbau: Die Bundesrepublik Deutschland 1945–1965*. München: Nymphenburger, 1986, 42. Frank Stern. "Film in the 1950s: Passing Images of Guilt and Responsibility." In *The Miracle Years: A Cultural History of West Germany, 1949–1968*. Hanna Schissler, ed. Princeton: Princeton University Press, 2001, 267.

22. Roderick Stackelberg. *Hitler's Germany*. New York: Routledge, 1999, 271.

23. Ibid., 279–280.

24. Ibid., 275.

25. Moishe Postone. "After the Holocaust: History and Identity in West Germany." In *German History after 1945*. In *Coping with the Past: Germany and Austria after 1945*. Kathy Harms, Lutz R. Reuter, and Volker Duerr, eds. Madison: The University of Wisconsin Press, 2005, 233–234.

26. Ibid., 236–237.

27. Katrin Sieg. "Ethnic Drag and National Identity: Multicultural Crises, Crossings, and Interventions." In *The Imperialist Imagination: German Colonialism and Its Legacy*. Sara Friedrichsmeyer, Sara Lennox, and Susanne Zantop, eds. Ann Arbor: The University of Michigan Press, 1998, 303.

28. Rob Kroes. "American Empire and Cultural Imperialism: A View from the Receiving End." In *Rethinking American History in a Global Age*. Thomas Bender, ed. Raleigh: University of North Carolina Press, 2002, 304.

29. Barton Byg. "DEFA Traditions of International Cinema." In *DEFA: East German Cinema, 1946–1992*. Sean Allan and John Sandford, eds. New York: Berghahn Books, 1999, 22–26.

1 Karl May Westerns and the Conquest of the American West

1. *Der Schatz im Silbersee* (*The Treasure of Silverlake*). Rialtofilm Preben Philipsen/Jadran-Film, 1962. Dr. Harald Reinl, director.
2. Ruth Wittlinger. *German National Identity in the Twenty-First Century: A Different Republic after All?* New York: Palgrave Macmillan, 2010, 2–7.
3. Ibid., 4–5.
4. "Global U.S. Troop Deployment 1950–2003." Retrieved from http://www.heritage.org/research/.
5. Maria Höhn. "*Heimat* in Turmoil: African-American GIs in 1950s West Germany." In *The Miracle Years: A Cultural History of West Germany, 1949–1968*. Hanna Schissler, ed. Princeton: Princeton University Press, 2001, 146.
6. Dominick LaCapra. *History and Memory after Auschwitz*. Ithaca: Cornell University Press, 1998, 8–9.
7. Konrad H. Jarausch. *After Hitler: Recivilizing Germans, 1945–1995*. New York: Oxford University Press, 2006, 6. Gerd Gemünden. "Between Karl May and Karl Marx: The DEFA Indianerfilme." In *Germans & Indians: Fantasies, Encounters, and Projections*. Colin G. Calloway, Gerd Gemünden, and Suzanne Zantop, eds. Lincoln: University of Nebraska Press, 2002, 249.
8. Nigel Thomas. "Germany and Europe." In *Modern Germany: Politics, Society and Culture*. Peter James, ed. New York: Routledge, 1998, 196–199. Joachim Whaley. "The German Lands before 1815." In *German History since 1800*. Mary Fulbrook, ed. New York: Arnold, 1997, 15–37. Mark Roseman. "Division and Stability: The Federal Republic of Germany, 1949–1989." In *German History since 1800*. Mary Fulbrook, ed. New York: Arnold, 1997, 365–390. Michael Balfour. *West Germany: A Contemporary History*. New York: St. Martin's Press, 1982, 11–15.
9. Guntram H. Herb. "Double Vision: Territorial Strategies in the Construction of National Identities in Germany, 1949–1979." In *Annals of the Association of American Geographers*. Vol. 94, No. 1, March, 2004, 140–149.
10. Koppel S. Pinson. *Modern Germany: Its History and Civilization*. New York: The Macmillan Company, 1964, 534–535.
11. Ibid., 534–535. Mary Fulbrook. "Ossis and Wessis: The Creation of Two German Societies." In *German History since 1800*. Mary Fulbrook, ed. New York: Arnold, 1997, 411.
12. David F. Crew. "Consuming Germany in the Cold War: Consumption and National Identity in East and West Germany, 1949–1989." In *Consuming Germany in the Cold War*. David F. Crew, ed. New York: Berge, 2003, 1–2.
13. Ibid.
14. Leonie Naughton. *That Was the Wild East: Film, Culture, Unification, and the "New" Germany*. Ann Arbor: The University of Michigan Press, 2002, 12–13. Sabine von Dirke. *"All Power to the Imagination." The West German Counterculture from the Student Movement to the Greens*. Lincoln: University of Nebraska Press, 1997, 12–14. David Kaufman. "The Nazi Legacy: Coming to Terms with the Past." In *Modern Germany: Politics, Society and Culture*. Peter James, ed. New York: Routledge, 1998, 126. Roger Manvell and Heinrich Fraenkel. *The German Cinema*. New York: Praeger Publishers, 1971, 125–126.

15. Thomas Lindenberger. "Divided but Not Disconnected: Germany as a Border Region of the Cold War." In *Divided but Not Disconnected: German Experiences of the Cold War.* Tobias Hochscherf, Christoph Laucht, and Andrew Plowman, eds. New York: Berghahn Books, 2010, 19–21.

16. Ibid., 30–35.

17. Hermann Glaser. *Deutsche Kultur 1945–2000.* Muenchen: Carl Hanser Verlag, 1997, 19. Alon Confino. *Germany as a Culture of Remembrance: Promises and Limits of Writing History.* Chapel Hill: The University of North Carolina Press, 2006, 82–91. Robert G. Moeller. "The Politics of the Past in the 1950s: Rhetorics of Victimization in East and West Germany." In *Germans as Victims: Remembering the Past in Contemporary Germany.* Bill Niven, ed. New York: Palgrave Macmillan, 2006, 35–37.

18. Mary Fulbrook. "Re-presenting the Nation: History and Identity in East and West Germany." In *Representing the German Nation: History and Identity in Twentieth-Century Germany.* Mary Fulbrook and Martin Swales, eds. New York: Manchester University Press, 2000, 177–178.

19. Konrad H. Jarausch, Hinrich C. Seeba, and David P. Conradt. "The Presence of the Past: Culture, Opinion, and Identity in Germany." In *After Unity: Reconfiguring German Identities.* Konrad H. Jarausch, ed. Providence: Berghahn Books, 1997, 50–51. Glaser. *Deutsche Kultur 1945–2000,* 47.

20. Karen Hagemann. "Home/Front: The Military, Violence and Gender Relations in the Age of the World Wars." In *Home/Front: The Military, War and Gender in Twentieth-Century Germany.* Karen Hagemann and Stefanie Schuler-Springorum, eds. New York: Berg, 2002, 27.

21. Confino. *Germany as a Culture of Remembrance,* 82–91.

22. Wulf Kansteiner. *In Pursuit of German Memory: History, Television, and Politics after Auschwitz.* Athens: Ohio University Press, 2006, 6–7.

23. von Dirke. *"All Power to the Imagination,"* 12–14. Manvell and Fraenkel. *The German Cinema,* 99.

24. Ruth Wittlinger. "Taboo or Tradition? The 'German as Victims' Theme in the Federal Republic until the mid-1990s." In *Germans as Victims: Remembering the Past in Contemporary Germany.* Bill Niven, ed. New York: Palgrave Macmillan, 2006, 63–65. Moeller, "The Politics of the Past in the 1950s," 43–60.

25. Robert R. Shandley. *Rubble Film: German Cinema in the Shadow of the Third Reich.* Philadelphia: Temple University Press, 2001, 8. Michael Geyer and Miriam Hansen. "German-Jewish Memory and National Consciousness." In *Holocaust Remembrance: The Shapes of Memory.* Geoffrey H. Hartman, ed. Cambridge: Blackwell, 1994, 177.

26. Shandley. *Rubble Film,* 177.

27. Frank Stern. "Film in the 1950s: Passing Images of Guilt and Responsibility." In *The Miracle Years: A Cultural History of West Germany, 1949–1968,* 276. Richard McCormick. "Memory and Commerce, Gender and Restoration: Woflgang Staudte's Roses for the State Prosecutor (1959) and West German Film in the 1950s." In *The Miracle Years: A Cultural History of West Germany, 1949–1968.* Hanna Schissler, ed. Princeton: Princeton University Press, 2001, 266–267.

28. John Belton. *American Cinema/American Culture.* New York: McGrawHill, 2005, 259. Michael Petzel. "Deutsche Helden: Karl May im Film." In *Karl May*

im Film: eine Bilddokumentation. Christian Unucka, ed. Dachau: Vereinigte Verlagsgesellschaften, 1980, 1–2.

29. Helmut Fritz. *Roter Bruder Winnetou: Karl May als Erzieher. Eine Sendung zum 150. Geburtstag des Dichters.* Siegen: Die Universität-Gesamthochschule-Siegen, 1992, 16–19.

30. Ibid.

31. Ibid.

32. Klaus Mann. "Cowboy Mentor of the Führer." In *The Living Age,* November 1940, 217.

33. Colleen Cook. "Germany's Wild West Author: A Researcher's Guide to Karl May." In *German Studies Review,* 67. John Toland. *Adolf Hitler.* Garden City: Doubleday & Company, Inc., 1976, 13, 317, and 604. Rolf Bernhard Essig and Gudrun Schury. *Alles ueber Karl May: Ein Sammelsurium von A bis Z.* Berlin: Aufbau Verlagsgruppe, 2007, 68–69. Frederik Hetmann. *Old Shatterhand, das bin ich: Die Lebensgeschichte des Karl May.* Weinheim: Beltz Verlag, 2001, 277–278. Ian Kershaw. *Hitler: A Biography.* New York: W.W. Norton & Company, 2008, 7–9. Robert G.L. Waite. *The Psychopathic God: Adolf Hitler.* New York: Basic Books, Inc., Publishers, 1977, 11.

34. Otto Dietrich. *The Hitler I Knew: The Memoirs of the Third Reich's Press Chief.* New York: Skyhorse Publishing, 2010, 123.

35. Albert Speer. *Spandau: The Secret Diaries.* New York: Macmillan Publishing Co., Inc., 1976, 168 and 348.

36. Gerhard Linkemeyer. *Was hat Hitler mit Karl May zu tun?* Ubstadt: KMG-Presse, 1987, 5.

37. Werner Jochmann, ed. *Adolf Hitler Monologe im Führer Hauptquartier 1941–1944: Die Aufzeichnungen Heinrich Heims.* Hamburg: Albrecht Knaus Verlag, 1980, 281–282 and 398.

38. As quoted in Karl Markus Kreis. "German Wild West: Karl May's Invention of the Definitive Indian." In *I Like America: Fictions of the Wild West.* Pamela Kort and Max Hollein, eds. New York: Prestel, 2007, 265–269.

39. Ambrus Miskolczy. *Hitler's Library.* New York: Central European University Press Budapest, 2003, 67–68.

40. Michael Burleigh. *The Third Reich: A New History.* New York: Hill and Wang, 2000, 93.

41. Norbert Honsza and Wojciech Kunicki. *Karl May-Anatomia Sukcesu: Zycie-Tworczosc-Recepcja.* Katowice: Wydawnictwo Slask, 1986, 218–219.

42. Tassilo Schneider. "Finding a New Heimat in the Wild West: Karl May and the German Western of the 1960s." In *Journal of Film and Video,* Vol. 47, No. 1–3, (Spring–Fall 1995), 53.

43. "Auschwitz Trials." Retrieved from Jewish Virtual Library. http://www.jewishvirtuallibrary.org/jsource/judaica/ejud_0002_0002_0_01612.html.

44. Hannah Arendt. *Responsibility and Judgment.* New York: Schocken Books, 2003, 214–217.

45. Rolf Hochhuth. *The Deputy.* New York: Grove Press, Inc., 1964, 220–221.

46. Schneider. "Finding a New Heimat in the Wild West," 57.

47. Dan Diner. *America in the Eyes of the Germans: An Essay on Anti-Americanism.* Princeton: Markus Wiener Publishers, 1996, 133–136.

48. Frederic Morton. "Tales of the Grand Teutons: Karl May among the Indians: Grand Teutons." In *New York Times,* January 4, 1987.

49. Jeffrey L. Sammons. *Ideology, Mimesis, Fantasy: Charles Sealsfield, Friedrich Gerstäcker, Karl May, and Other German Novelists of America.* Chapel Hill: The University Press of North Carolina Press, 1998, 239–240.
50. Jerry Schuchalter. *Narratives of American and the Frontier in Nineteenth-Century German Literature.* New York: Peter Lang, 237–238.
51. Ibid., 238.
52. Louis Harap. *The Image of the Jew in American Literature: From Early Republic to Mass Immigration.* Philadelphia: The Jewish Publication Society of America, 1974, 78.
53. H. Lutz. "Die Populärste Romanfigur der letzten 50 Jahre: Frauenidol als Old Shatterhand/Hollywood star Lex Barker in der ersten deutschen Wild-West-Verfilmung." Microfilm. Textarchiv des Deutschen Filminstituts, Frankfurt. D-ck. "Old Shatterhand und Winnetou als Filmstars: Von Millionen mit Spannung erwartet: Die Karl-May-Verfilmung 'Der Schatz im Silbersee.'" Microfilm. Textarchiv des Deutschen Filminstituts, Frankfurt. Guenter Seuren. "Karl-May-Renaissance im Kino." *Deutsche Zeitung,* Stuttgart/Koeln, December 17, 1963. Textarchiv des Deutschen Filminstituts, Frankfurt. "Europa: 'Winnetou.' Ein Farbiger CinemaScope-Film." *Darmstaedter Echo,* December 21, 1963. Textarchiv des Deutschen Filminstituts, Frankfurt.
54. "Lex Barker Dies, Tarzan of Movies: Was 10th to Play the Role, Succeeding Weismuller." *New York Times,* May 12, 1973.
55. Brigitte Jeremias. "Winnetou I: Die Karl-May-Erfolgsfilm-Serie läuft." *Frankfurter Allgemeine Zeitung,* December 17, 1963. Textarchiv des Deutschen Filminstituts, Frankfurt.
56. Karl-Heinz Kukowski. "Lex Barker aus der New Yorker High Society: Hollywoods Tarzan, unser Old Shatterhand." *Welt,* May 25, 1987. Textarchiv des Deutschen Filminstituts, Frankfurt.
57. Oliver Baumgarten. "Euro-Gunfighter: Karl May und die deutsche Eurowestern-Erfolgswelle (1962–1968)." In *Um Sie weht der Hauch des Todes. Der Italo-Western – die Geschichte eines Genres.* Georg Seesslen, Hans, Schifferle, and Hans-Christoph Blumenberg, eds. Koeln: Schnitt Verlag, 1998, 16.
58. Gemünden, "Between Karl May and Karl Marx," 32–34.
59. Tim Bergfelder. *International Adventures: German Popular Cinema and European Co-Productions in the 1960s.* New York: Berghahn Books, 2005, 183.
60. Aribert Schröder. "They Lived Together with Their Dogs and Horses: 'Indian Copy' in West German Newspapers 1968–1982." In *Indians and Europe: An Interdisciplinary Collection of Essays.* Christian F. Feest, ed. Lincoln: University of Nebraska Press, 1999, 532.
61. "Reiten für Deutschland: Winnetou III – frei nach Karl May." In *Frankfurter Allgemeine Zeitung,* November 11, 1965. Archiv des Deutschen Filminstituts/ Deutschen Filmmuseums. Frankfurt.
62. Roland Märchen. "Das Große Karl-May-Lexikon." In *Film dienst,* 13/2000. Archiv des Deutschen Filminstituts/Deutschen Filmmuseums. Frankfurt.
63. Jan Distelmeyer. "Mister Dynamit – Morgen küsst euch der Tod (1967)." In *Fredy Bockbein trifft Mister Dynamit: Filme auf den zweiten Blick.* Christoph Fuchs und Michael Toeteberg, eds. München: Edition text und kritik, 2007, 184–185.

64. Christoph Dompke. "A-uuah-uuah! Für Fans: Die Lex-Barker-Biographie." *Film*, 8/2003, 54. Archiv des Deutschen Filminstituts/Deutschen Film-museums. Frankfurt.
65. Schneider. "Finding a New Heimat in the Wild West," 52–53.
66. "Old Shatterhand." *Film Beobachter*, Nr. 19/64. Archiv des Deutschen Filminstituts/Deutschen Filmmuseums. Frankfurt.
67. Robert G. Moeller. "Victims in Uniform: West German Combat Movies from the 1950s." In *Germans as Victims: Remembering the Past in Contemporary Germany*. Bill Niven, ed. Houndmills, Basingstoke: Palgrave Macmillan, 2006, 45.
68. Reiner Pommerin. "Some Remarks on the Cultural History of the Federal Republic of Germany." In *Culture in the Federal Republic of Germany, 1945–1995*. Reiner Pommerin, ed. Herndon: Berg, 1996, 11.
69. Alfred Vohrer. "Ich bin jetzt wieder 19." Microfilm. Textarchiv des Deutschen Filminstituts, Frankfurt.
70. Ernst Nolte. *Deutschland und der kalte Krieg*. Muenchen: R. Piper & Co. Vorlag, 1974, 463–471 and 522–529.
71. Ernst Nolte. "Between Historical Legend and Revisionism? The Third Reich in Perspective of 1980." In *Forever in the Shadow of Hitler? Original Documents of the Historikerstreit. The Controversy Concerning the Singularity of the Holocaust*. James Knowlton, ed. Atlantic Highlands: Humanities Press, 1993, 1–15.
72. Wolfgang J. Mommsen. "The Germans and Their Past: History and Political Consciousness in the Federal Republic of Germany." In *German History after 1945*. In *Coping with the Past: Germany and Austria after 1945*. Kathy Harms, Lutz R. Reuter, and Volker Duerr, eds. Madison: The University of Wisconsin Press, 2005, 233–234.
73. Volker Duerr. "Introduction." In *Coping with the Past: Germany and Austria after 1945*. Kathy Harms, Lutz R. Reuter, and Volker Duerr, eds. Madison: The University of Wisconsin Press, 2005, 19–20.

2   *Indianerfilme* and the Conquest of the American West

1. *Die Söhne der großen Bärin* (*The Sons of Great Bear*). DEFA Film Studios, 1965. Josef Mach, director.
2. Gerd Gemünden. "Between Karl May and Karl Marx: The DEFA *Indianerfilme*." In *Germans & Indians: Fantasies, Encounters, Projections*. Colin G. Calloway, Gerd Gemuenden and Susanne Zantop, eds. Lincoln: University of Nebraska Press, 2002, 243.
3. Retrieved from http://www.documentarchiv.de/ddr/verfddr1949.html.
4. Ibid. Mary Fulbrook. "Ossis and Wessis: The Creation of Two German Societies." In *German History since 1800*. Mary Fulbrook, ed. New York: Arnold, 1997, 421.
5. Retrieved from http://www.documentarchiv.de/ddr/verfddr1968.html#0.
6. David F. Crew. "Consuming Germany in the Cold War: Consumption and National Identity in East and West Germany, 1949–1989." In *Consuming Germany in the Cold War*. David F. Crew, ed. New York: Berge, 2003, 1–2.
7. Konrad H. Jarausch, Hinrich C. Seeba, and David P. Conradt. "The Presence of the Past: Culture, Opinion, and Identity in Germany." In *After Unity:*

Reconfiguring German Identities. Konrad H. Jarausch, ed. Providence: Berghahn Books, 1997, 40–41.

8. Michael Balfour. *West Germany: A Contemporary History*. New York: St. Martin's Press, 1982, 161–162, 177–178. Inge Chistopher. "The Written Constitution: The Basic Law of a Socialist State?" In *Honecker's Germany*. David Childs, ed. Boston: Allen & Unwin, 1985, 15–19, 29–30. Mary Fulbrook. *A Concise History of Germany*. New York: Cambridge University Press, 1991, 212–213. Mike Dennis. *The Rise and Fall of the German Democratic Republic 1945–1990*. Harlow: Longman, 2000, xi.

9. Andrew Demshuk. *The Lost German East: Forced Migration and the Politics of Memory, 1945–1970*. New York: Cambridge University Press, 2012, 98–99.

10. Ibid., 105–109.

11. Leonie Naughton. *That Was the Wild East: Film, Culture, Unification, and the "New" Germany*. Ann Arbor: The University of Michigan Press, 2002, 12–13. Sabine von Dirke. *"All Power to the Imagination." The West German Counterculture from the Student Movement to the Greens*. Lincoln: University of Nebraska Press, 1997, 12–14. David Kaufman. "The Nazi Legacy: Coming to Terms with the Past," 126. Roger Manvell and Heinrich Fraenkel. *The German Cinema*. New York: Praeger Publishers, 1971, 125–126.

12. Jarausch, Seeba, and Conradt. "The Presence of the Past." 47.

13. Kaufman. "The Nazi Legacy." 129. Sabine Behrenbeck. "The Transformation of Sacrifice: German Identity between Heroic Narrative and Economic Success." In *Pain and Prosperity: Reconsidering Twentieth-Century German History*. Paul Betts and Greg Eghigian, eds. Stanford: Stanford University Press, 2003, 134–135. Dorothee Wierling. "Mission to Happiness: The Cohort of 1949 and the Making of East and West Germans." In *The Miracle Years: A Cultural History of West Germany, 1949–1968*. Hanna Schissler, ed. Princeton: Princeton University Press, 2001, 112.

14. Robert G. Moeller. "The Politics of the Past in the 1950s: Rhetorics of Victimization in East and West Germany." In *Germans as Victims: Remembering the Past in Contemporary Germany*. Bill Niven, ed. New York: Palgrave Macmillan, 2006, 29–30.

15. Bill Nevin. "The GDR and Memory of the Bombing of Dresden." In *Germans as Victims: Remembering the Past in Contemporary Germany*. Bill Niven, ed. Houndmills, Basingstoke: Palgrave Macmillan, 2006, 113.

16. Moeller. "The Politics of the Past in the 1950s," 29–30.

17. Hans Kundnani. *Utopia or Auschwitz: Germany's 1968 Generation and the Holocaust*. New York: Columbia University Press, 2009, 12–15. Mary Fulbrook. *Representing the German Nation. History and Identity in Twentieth-century Germany*. Manchester: Manchester University Press, 2000, 186. Michael Geyer and Miriam Hansen. "German-Jewish Memory and National Consciousness." In *Holocaust Remembrance: The Shapes of Memory*. Geoffrey H. Hartman, ed. Cambridge: Blackwell, 1994, 176–177. Wulf Kansteiner. *In Pursuit of German Memory: History, Television, and Politics after Auschwitz*. Athens: Ohio University Press, 2006, 7–8.

18. Manvell and Fraenkel. *The German Cinema*, 104–117.

19. Sabine Hake. *German National Cinema*. New York: Routledge, 2002, 99–106. Manvell and Fraenkel. *The German Cinema*, 121–123.

20. Ibid., 112–113.

21. Hake. *German National Cinema*, 118.
22. Ariana Harner. "Values in Conflict: The Singing Marxist." In *Colorado Heritage*, Winter 1999. *Blutsbrueder (Blood Brothers)*. DEFA, 1975. Werner W. Wallroth, director.
23. Chuck Laszewski. *Rock 'n' Roll Radical: The Life and Mysterious Death of Dean Reed*. Edina: Beaver's Pond Press, Inc., 2005, 1–5 and 101–105.
24. James M. Markham. "U.S. Folk Hero for Soviet Bloc." In *New York Times*, January 10, 1984.
25. BArch, DR1-Z/20713. VEB DEFA Studio für Spielfilme, Babelsberg, den 8.4.75. Hauptdirektor-Stellungnahme zum Film "Blutsbrüder."
26. Ibid. Günter Sobe. "Ein Taugenichts im wilden Westen: Indianerfilmjubiläum bei der DEFA." *Berliner Zeitung*.
27. BArch, DR1-Z/20713. Ministerium fuer Kultur Hauptverwaltung Film. "Blutsbrüder."
28. Ibid. Kulturpolitische Arbeit mit dem Film. Berlin, den 9.4.1975. Stellungnahme zum Spielfilm "Blutsbrüder" den VEB DEFA Studio für Spielfilme.
29. BArch, FilmSG1/20713 Blutsbrüder. Heinz Hofmann. "Indianerfilm mit moralischem Anspruch: 'Blutsbrüder' mit Dean Reed and Gojko Mitic." *Nationalzeitung Berlin*.
30. Harner. "Values in Conflict: The Singing Marxist."
31. BArch, DR1-Z/ 20713. Künstlerische Produktion, Berlin, den 8.4.1975. Stellungnahme zum staatlichen Zulanssungsvorfahren zu "Blutsbrüder" am 10. April 1975.
32. Ibid. Stellungnahme für die Staatliche Abnahme "Blutsbrüder" and Inhalt (von Studio Uebernommen).
33. Heide Fehrenbach. *Cinema in Democratizing Germany: Reconstructing National Identity after Hitler*. Chapel Hill: The University of North Carolina Press, 1995, 4–5.
34. Colleen Cook. "Germany's Wild West Author: A Researcher's Guide to Karl May," In *German Studies Review*, Vol. 5, No. 1, February 1982, 76.
35. *Toedlicher Irrtum (Fatal Error)*. DEFA, 1969. Konrad Petzold, director.
36. BArch, FilmSG1/17156 *Tödlicher Irrtum*. Heinz Hofmann. "Tödlicher Irrtum"-Höhepunkt der Trilogie historisch-konreter Indianerfilme." *Märkische Volksstimme*, Potsdam.
37. Koppel S. Pinson. *Modern Germany: Its History and Civilization*. New York: The Macmillan Company, 1964, 540–545.
38. Ibid., 546–554. Fulbrook, "Ossis and Wessis." 413, Mark Roseman. In "Division and Stability: The Federal Republic of Germany, 1949–1989." In *German History since 1800*. Mary Fulbrook, ed. New York: Arnold, 1997, 375, Mary Fulbrook, *A Concise History of Germany*, 177–178, Patrick Major. "Introduction." In *The Workers' and Peasants' State: Communism and Society in East Germany under Ulbricht, 1945–1971*. Patrick Major and Jonathan Osmond, eds. New York: Manchester University Press, 2002, 3–4.
39. Willy Brandt. *My Life in Politics*. New York: Viking, 1992.
40. Andrew H. Beattie. "The Victims of Totalitarianism and Centrality of Nazi Genocide: Continuity and Change in German Commemorative Politics." In *Germans as Victims: Remembering the Past in Contemporary Germany*. Bill Niven, ed. Houndmills, Basingstoke: Palgrave Macmillan, 2006, 151–153.
41. Ibid.

3 German Westerns: Popularity, Reception, Heroines, Miscegenation, Race, and Landscape

1. "Old Shatterhand in Zahlen: Drehbuchautor Karl May rettet den deutschen Film." *Kölnische Rundschau*, April 4, 1964. Archiv des Deutschen Filminstituts/Deutschen Filmmuseums. Frankfurt.
2. "Zu unserem Titelbild: 'von der Barker-Familie autorisiert.'" *Karl May & Co.*, Nr. 92 (Juni 2003), 4. Archiv des Deutschen Filminstituts/Deutschen Filmmuseums. Frankfurt.
3. Michael Petzel. "Deutsche Helden: Karl May im Film." In *Karl May im Film: eine Bilddokumentation*. Christian Unucka, ed. Dachau: Vereinigte Verlagsgesellschaften, 1980, 11.
4. Erwin Mueller, as reported in Helmut Fritz. *Roter Bruder Winnetou: Karl May als Erzieher. Eine Sendung zum 150. Geburtstag des Dichters*. Siegen, 1992, 20–21. Archiv des Deutschen Filminstituts/Deutschen Filmmuseums. Frankfurt.
5. "Kennedy Is Hero No. 1 for German Children." In *New York Times*, October 31, 1965.
6. "90 Jahre Winnetou: Im Jubilaeumsjahr reitet e rim Oelprinz und in Winnetou III." Ringpress. Dokumentation. Microfilm. Archiv des Deutschen Filminstituts/Deutschen Filmmuseums. Frankfurt.
7. Oliver Baumgarten. "Euro-Gunfighter: Karl May und die Deutsche Eurowestern-Erfolgswelle (1962–1968)." In *Um Sie Weht Der Hauch Des Todes: Der Italowestern – die Geschichte eines Genres*. Görg Seesslen, Hans Schifferle, and Hans-Christoph Blumenberg, eds. Koeln: Schnitt Verlag, 1999, 15.
8. "Kernige Männerfreundschaft: 'Winnetou' – zum drittenmal Reinls Karl-May-Verfilmung." In *Frankfurter Rundschau*, December 7, 2000. Archiv des Deutschen Filminstituts/Deutschen Filmmuseums. Frankfurt.
9. Retrieved from http://www.imdb.com/title/tt0056452/maindetails.
10. "Reiten für Deutschland: Winnetou III – frei nach Karl May." In *Frankfurter Allgemeine Zeitung*, November 11, 1965. Archiv des Deutschen Filminstituts/ Deutschen Filmmuseums. Frankfurt.
11. "Winnetou – 3. Teil: 'Ich liebe das Abenteuer.'" Constantin Film Studio Archives. Microfilm. Archiv des Deutschen Filminstituts/Deutschen Filmmuseums. Frankfurt.
12. Thomas Jeier. *Der Western-Film*. Muenchen: Wilhelm Verlag, 1995, 189–191.
13. Tassilo Schneider. "Finding a New Heimat in the Wild West: Karl May and the German Western of the 1960s." In *Journal of Film and Video*, Vol. 47, No. 1–3, (Spring–Fall 1995), 54–55.
14. Erika Kempe-Wiegand. "Die große Mayerei." In *Westdeutsche Allgemeine*, Essen, June 1, 1963. Archiv des Deutschen Filminstituts/Deutschen Filmmuseums. Frankfurt.
15. Jobst Fechter. "Winnetous Geheimnisse – ausgeplaudert." Ringpress. Dokumentation. Microfilm. Archiv des Deutschen Filminstituts/Deutschen Filmmuseums. Frankfurt. Jörg Kastner. *Das große Karl May Buch: Sein Leben-Seine Bücher - Die Filme*. Bergisch Gladbach: Bastei-Verlag, 1992, 265. Petzel. "Deutsche Helden: Karl May im Film." 17–18.
16. "Lex Barker: Lollo konnte seine Karierre nicht aufhalten." Ringpress. Dokumentation. Microfilm. Archiv des Deutschen Filminstituts/Deutschen Filmmuseums. Frankfurt.

17. Ibid.
18. Joe Hembus. "Wie gut sind die Karl-May-Western? Ein paar nette Wörte für Shatterhand und Winnetou." Constantin Film Studio. Dokumentation. Microfilm. Archiv des Deutschen Filminstituts/Deutschen Filmmuseums. Frankfurt. Pierre Brice. *Mein wahres Leben*. Bergisch Gladbach: Gustav Luebbe Verlag, 2004, 10–11 and 240. "Vom Filme über die Bühne zum Hörspiel: Interview mit Chris Howland." *Karl May & Co.*, Nr. 92, 34. Archiv des Deutschen Filminstituts/Deutschen Filmmuseums. Frankfurt.
19. Don Shiach. *Stewart Granger: The Last of the Swashbucklers*. London: Aurum, 2005, 218–219.
20. Schneider. "Finding a New Heimat in the Wild West," 50–51.
21. "Winnetou – 3. Teil: Mehr Wert als Moralpauken." Constantin Film Studio. Dokumentation. Microfilm. Archiv des Deutschen Filminstituts/Deutschen Filmmuseums. Frankfurt.
22. "Winnetou – 3. Teil: Brief an Winnetou: 'Sie haben mire den Glauben an das Gute wiedergegeben...'" Constantin Film Studio. Dokumentation. Microfilm. Archiv des Deutschen Filminstituts/Deutschen Filmmuseums. Frankfurt.
23. Karl Markus Kreis. "German Wild West: Karl May's Invention of the Definitive Indian." In *I Like America: Fictions of the Wild West*. Pamela Kort and Max Hollein, eds. New York: Prestel, 2007, 249–252.
24. "Ein Stück deutsch-deutsche Geschichte: eine Sonderausstellung widmet sich den Indianerfilmen in Ost und West." *Karl May & Co.*, Nr. 92, 26–27. Archiv des Deutschen Filminstituts/Deutschen Filmmuseums. Frankfurt.
25. BArch, DR1-Z/15609. Ministerium fuer Kultur. Hauptverwaltung Film. Antrag auf Filmzulassung – Teil II – "Die Söhne der großen Bärin."
26. BArch, DR1-Z/ 2315. Besucher-Ergebnisse der DEFA Filme *Osceola*. Berlin, den 5.10.1971.
27. BArch, DR1-Z/19036. Besucher-Ergebnisse der DEFA Filme *Weisse Wölfe*. Berlin, den 30.7.1969.
28. BArch, FilmSG1/2315 *Chingachgook – Die große Schlange*. "Tokei-ihto und Chingachgook: Pressegespräch mit dem jugoslawischen Schauspieler Gojko Mitic," July 4, 1967.
29. Gerd Gemünden. "Between Karl May and Karl Marx: The DEFA Indianerfilme." In *Germans & Indians: Fantasies, Encounters, and Projections*. Colin G. Calloway, Gerd Gemuenden and Suzanne Zantop, eds. Lincoln: University of Nebraska Press, 2002, 244.
30. BArch, DR1-Z/19036. Stellungnahme zur staatlichen Zulassung des DEFA-Spielfilmes "Weisse Wölfe," January 20, 1969.
31. BArch, FilmSG1/19036 *Weisse Wölfe*. "Historisch Wahr: Das letzte Abenteuer des Falken im 4. DEFA-Indianerfilm." *Märkische Volksstimme, Potsdam*, July 24, 1969.
32. "90 Jahre Winnetou: Im Jubiläumsjahr reitete rim Oelprinz und in Winnetou III." Ringpress. Dokumentation. Microfilm. Archiv des Deutschen Filminstituts/Deutschen Filmmuseums. Frankfurt.
33. N. Richter. "Karl May:...sogar Literatur. Späte Anerkennung für den phantasievollen Sachsen/Der Schatz im Silbersee," ein deutscher Großfilm. Constantin-Verleih, Microfilm. Textarchiv des Deutschen Filminstituts,

Frankfurt. Roland Märchen. "Das Große Karl-May-Lexikon." In *Film dienst*, 13/2000. Textarchiv des Deutschen Filminstituts, Frankfurt.

34. *Limonádový Joe aneb Konská opera (Lemonade Joe)*. Filmove Studio Barrandov. Oldrich Lipsky, director, 1964.
35. *Wilcze Echa (The Wolves' Echoes)*. Zespol Filmowy "Rytm." Aleksander Scibor-Rylski, director, 1967.
36. Ibid.
37. Sergio Leone as quoted in Christopher Frayling. *Spaghetti Westerns: Cowboys and Europeans from Karl May to Sergio Leone*. New York: I.B. Tauris, 2006, 39 and 115.
38. "Indianerfresser Custer." In *Ringpress*. Archiv des Deutschen Filminstituts/ Deutschen Filmmuseums, Frankfurt, Microfilm.
39. Archiv der Berlin-Brandenburgischen Akademie der Wissenschaften, Nachlass Liselotte Welskopf-Henrich (ABBAW), Folder 121.
40. Peter Martin. "Unser Porträt: Lex Barker." In *West. Allgem.*, June 30, 1963. Archiv des Deutschen Filminstituts/Deutschen Filmmuseums, Frankfurt.
41. "Kannste was, biste was! Ein Gespräch mit Lex Barker." In *Hamburger Echo*, December 22, 1963. Archiv des Deutschen Filminstituts/Deutschen Filmmuseums, Frankfurt.
42. "Lex Barker: Lollo konnte seine Karriere nicht aufhalten." In *Ringpress*. Archiv des Deutschen Filminstituts/Deutschen Filmmuseums, Frankfurt.
43. Hartmut Lutz. *"Indianer" und "Native Americans." Zur social- und literarhistorischen Vermittlung eines Stereotyps*. New York: Georg Olms Verlag, 1985, 330–331.
44. ABBAW, Folder 147.
45. "Winnetou I." Schwierigkeiten beim May-Verfilmen. Zwangloses Drehpausen-Gespräch mit Dr. Harald Reinl, dem "Winnetou I"-Regisseur. Microfilm, Archiv des Deutschen Filminstituts/Deutschen Filmmuseums, Frankfurt.
46. "Fragen an Lex Barker." Microfilm. Archiv des Deutschen Filminstituts/ Deutschen Filmmuseums, Frankfurt.
47. Richard Cracroft. "The American West of Karl May." In *American Quarterly*, Vol. 19, No. 2, Part 1 (Summer, 1967), 254.
48. "Ein Freundespaar: Winnetou und Old Shatterhand." Constantin Verleih, Microfilm. Textarchiv des Deutschen Filminstituts, Frankfurt.
49. Liselotte Henckel. "Der Schatz im Silbersee: Wo Frauen zu Helden warden." Constantin Verleih, Microfilm. Textarchiv des Deutschen Filminstituts, Frankfurt.
50. Schneider. "Finding a New Heimat in the Wild West," 56–57.
51. Cracroft. "The American West of Karl May," 253.
52. Lutz. *"Indianer" und "Native Americans,"* 333.
53. "Winnetou II." In *Ruhrwacht*, Oberhausen, November 7, 1964. Constantin Verleih, Textarchiv des Deutschen Filminstituts, Frankfurt.
54. Marie Versini. *Ich war Winnetous Schwester*. Bamberg: Karl May Verlag, 2003, 36.
55. Meredith McClain. Personal correspondence.
56. BArch, FilmSG1/12515 *Osceola*. "'Osceloa': Diesmal der Kampf der Seminolen." *National Zeitung*, Berlin, June 25, 1961, "Gesunde Spannung: 'Osceola' mit Profil – Realistisches DEFA-Abenteuer." *Der Neue Weg*, Halle,

July 23, 1971, "Unsere Filmrezension 'Osceola.'" *Freiheit*, Halle, August 13, 1971.

57. Jeffrey L. Sammons. *Ideology, Mimesis, Fantasy: Charles Sealsfield, Friedrich Gerstaecker, Karl May, and Other German Novelists of America*. Chapel Hill: University of North Carolina Press, 1998, 105–109 and 239. Ray Allen Billington. *Land of Savagery, Land of Promise: The European Image of the American Frontier in the Nineteenth Century*. New York: W.W. Norton & Company, 1981, 286.

58. Maria Höhn and Martin Klimke. *A Breath of Freedom: The Civil Rights Struggle, African American GIs, and Germany*. New York: Palgrave Macmillan, 2010, 139–141.

59. Mary Nolan. "American in the German Imagination." In *Transactions, Transgressions, Transformations: American Culture in Western Europe and Japan*. Heide Fehrenbach and Uta G. Poiger, eds. New York: Berghahn Books, 2000, 11–12.

60. Schneider. "Finding a New Heimat in the Wild West," 52–53.

61. Cracroft. "The American West of Karl May," 255.

62. Lutz. *"Indianer" und "Native Americans,"* 351.

63. Gemünden. "Between Karl May and Karl Marx," 26–28.

64. BArch, DR1-Z/2315 *Chingachgook, die große Schlange*. Bereich Filmpolitik, Berlin, den 2.5.1967, Stellungnahme zur Abnahme des Films "Chingachgook – die Große Schlange." Babelsberg, den April 17, 1967.

65. Gojko Mitic interview. In *The Apaches*, special features.

66. J. Boyd Morning Storm. *The American Indian Warrior: Native Americans in Modern U.S. Warfare*. Manhattan: Sunflower University Press, 2004, xi–xii.

67. Gemünden, "Between Karl May and Karl Marx," 31.

68. "Lokomotive rammt Saloon: Winnetou und die Apatschen entscheiden die Schlacht um Roswell." Constantin Film Studio. Dokumentation. Microfilm. Archiv des Deutschen Filminstituts/Deutschen Filmmuseums. Frankfurt.

69. "Winnetou I: Schwierigkeiten beim May-Verfilmen. Zwangloses Drehpausen-Gespräch mit Dr. Harald Reinl, dem 'Winnetou I'-Regisseur." Constantin Film Studio. Dokumentation. Microfilm. Archiv des Deutschen Filminstituts/Deutschen Filmmuseums. Frankfurt.

70. As quoted in Versini. *Ich war Winnetous Schwester*, 23–31.

71. "Winnetou I: Halsbrecherischer 'Winnetou.' Bericht von den Dreharbeiten der neuen Karl-May-Verfilmung." Constantin Film Studio. Dokumentation. Microfilm. Archiv des Deutschen Filminstituts/Deutschen Filmmuseums. Frankfurt.

72. "Old Shatterhand in Zahlen: Drehbuchautor Karl May rettet den deutschen Film." In *Kölnische Rundschau*, April 4, 1964. "Winnetou-Impressionen." Ringpress. Dokumentation. Microfilm. Archiv des Deutschen Filminstituts/Deutschen Filmmuseums. Frankfurt.

73. "Lex Barker: Lollo konnte seine Karierre nicht aufhalten." Ringpress. Dokumentation. Microfilm. Archiv des Deutschen Filminstituts/Deutschen Filmmuseums. Frankfurt.

74. "Winnetou – 3. Teil: 'Ich liebe das Abenteuer.'" Constantin Film Studio. Dokumentation. Microfilm. Archiv des Deutschen Filminstituts/Deutschen Filmmuseums. Frankfurt.

75. Wolf Schoen. "Wildwest auf deutsch: Ufa-Palast: 'Der Schatz im Silbersee.'" In *Kölnische Rundschau*, January 5, 1963. "Die May-Welle des deutschen

Films." In *Süddeutsche Zeitung*, December 18, 1962. Archiv des Deutschen Filminstituts/Deutschen Filmmuseums. Frankfurt.

76. "Die May-Welle des deutschen Films." In *Süddeutsche Zeitung*, December 18, 1962. Archiv des Deutschen Filminstituts/Deutschen Filmmuseums. Frankfurt. Klaus Hebecker. "Wildwest aus deutscher Hand: Zu Beginn einer Karl-May-Welle: 'Der Schatz im Silbersee.'" In *Hamburger Echo*, February 2, 1963. Archiv des Deutschen Filminstituts/Deutschen Filmmuseums. Frankfurt.

77. "Wildwest – made in Germany: Palast-Theater zeigt: 'Der Schatz im Silbersee.'" In *Mühlheimer Zeitung*, December 12, 1962 and "Der Schatz im Silbersee." In *Westfälische Rundschau*, December 22, 1962. Archiv des Deutschen Filminstituts/Deutschen Filmmuseums. Frankfurt.

78. "Old Shatterhands fröhliche Urständ: 'Der Schatz im Silbersee' im Rivoli am Steintor." In *Hannover Presse*, December 15–16, 1962. Archiv des Deutschen Filminstituts/Deutschen Filmmuseums. Frankfurt.

79. ABBAW, Folder 121.

4 German Indian Heroes and Intercultural Transfer

1. Richard Cracroft. "The American West of Karl May." In *American Quarterly*, Vol. 19, No. 2, Part 1 (Summer, 1967), 256.

2. Christian Schröder. "Zieh' dich aus, Tarzan!" In *Der Tagesspiegel*. Berlin, May 18, 2003. Archiv des Deutschen Filminstituts/Deutschen Filmmuseums. Frankfurt.

3. Gerd Gemünden. "Between Karl May and Karl Marx: The DEFA Indianerfilme (1965–1983)." In *New German Critique*, No. 82, East German Film (Winter, 2001), 34–35.

4. Cracroft. "The American West of Karl May," 250–251.

5. Colleen Cook. "Germany's Wild West Author: A Researcher's Guide to Karl May." In *German Studies Review*, Vol. 5, No. 1, February 1982, 72.

6. Christopher Frayling. *Spaghetti Westerns: Cowboys and Europeans from Karl May to Sergio Leone*. New York: I.B. Tauris, 2006, 112.

7. His-Huey Liang, in a letter to *New York Times* titled "May's Nationalism," October 25, 1990.

8. ABBAW, Folder 179.

9. Cracroft. "The American West of Karl May," 255.

10. Frayling. *Spaghetti Westerns*, 103.

11. Cracroft. "The American West of Karl May," 254.

12. Mitic interview in *The Sons of Great Mother Bear*, special features. DEFA Film Studios, 1965. ICESTORM Entertainment GmbH, Berlin, 2006.

13. Cracroft. "The American West of Karl May," 256–257.

14. ABBAW, Folder 147.

15. Gemünden. "Between Karl May and Karl Marx," 26–28.

16. Ibid., 37.

17. Matthias Peipp and Bernhard Springer. *Edle Wilde Rote Teufel: Indianer im Film*. München: Wilhelm Heyne Verlag, 1997, 160.

18. Bundesarchiv, DR1-Z/766. Stellungnahme zum Film "Apachen," January 24, 1973.

19. Oliver Baumgarten. "Euro-Gunfighter: Karl May und die deutsche Eurowestern-Erfolgswell (1962–1968)." In *Um Sie weht der Hauch des Todes. Der Italo-Western – die Geschichte eines Genres.* Georg Seesslen, Schifferle Hans and Hans-Christoph Blumenberg, eds. Koeln: Schnitt Verlag, 1998, 15. Michael Petzel. "Deutsche Helden: Karl May im Film." In *Karl May im Film: eine Bilddokumentation.* Christian Unucka, ed. Dachau: Vereinigte Verlagsgesellschaften, 1980, 15. Marie Versini. *Ich war Winnetous Schwester.* Bamberg: Karl May Verlag, 2003, 23. "Der Schatz im Silbersee." In *Frankfurter Allgemeine Zeitung,* January 26, 1963. Archiv des Deutschen Filminstituts/ Deutschen Filmmuseums. Frankfurt.

20. Hans Höhn. "Karl May oder nicht Karl May…das ist die Frage bein den Dreharbeiten zum zweiten 'Winnetou'-Film." In *Bonner Rundschau,* August 1, 1964. "Winnetou 2. Teil: Drehbuchautor H.G. Peterson: Winnetou war der Held meiner Jugend." Constantin Film Studio. Dokumentation. Microfilm. Archiv des Deutschen Filminstituts/Deutschen Filmmuseums. Frankfurt.

21. Thomas Adam. *Intercultural Transfers and the Making of the Modern World: Sources and Contexts.* New York: Palgrave Macmillan, 2012, 3–6.

22. Thaddeus Russell. *A Renegade History of the United States.* New York: Free Press, 2010, 285–294.

23. Ibid.

24. Gemünden. "Between Karl May and Karl Marx," 35.

25. Versini. *Ich war Winnetous Schwester,* 48 and 136.

26. Cracroft. "The American West of Karl May," 255.

27. Ibid., 253.

28. Tassilo Schneider. "Finding a New Heimat in the Wild West: Karl May and the German Western of the 1960s." In *Journal of Film and Video,* 47, 1–3 (Spring–Fall 1995), 58–59.

29. Thomas Adam. *Buying Respectability: Philanthropy and Urban Society in Transnational Perspective, 1840s to 1930s.* Bloomington: Indiana University Press, 2009, 3–6.

30. "Lex Barker: Lollo konnte seine Karierre nicht aufhalten." Ringpress. Dokumentation. Microfilm. Archiv des Deutschen Filminstituts/Deutschen Filmmuseums. Frankfurt.

31. Gemünden. "Between Karl May and Karl Marx," 35.

32. "Ein Stück deutsch-deutsche Geschichte: eine Sonderausstellung widmet sich den Indianerfilmen in Ost und West." *Karl May & Co.,* Nr. 92, 26–27. Archiv des Deutschen Filminstituts/Deutschen Filmmuseums. Frankfurt.

33. Hans J. Hillerbrand. "The Spread of the Protestant Reformation of the Sixteenth Century." In *The Transfer of Ideas: Historical Essays.* C.D.W. Goodwin and I.B. Holley, Jr., eds. Durham: The South Atlantic Quarterly, 1968, 67–68.

34. Stephen McVeigh. *The American Western.* Edinburgh: Edinburgh University Press, 2007, 13.

35. Laura A. Belmonte. "A Family Affair? Gender, the U.S. Information Agency, and Cold War Ideology, 1945–1960." In *Culture and International History.* Jessica C.E. Gienow-Hecht and Frank Schumacher, eds. New York: Berghahn Books, 2003, 80.

36. Jan Bakker. "The Popular Western: Window to the American Spirit." In *The American West.* Rob Kroes, ed. Amsterdam: Free University Press, 1989, 237.

John H. Lenihan. *Showdown: Confronting Modern America in the Western Film.* Urbana: University of Illinois Press, 1980, 4. John Belton. *American Cinema/ American Culture.* New York: McGrawHill, 2005, 260. Kevin Mulroy, ed., *Western Amerykanski: Polish Poster Art & the Western.* Seattle: University of Washington Press, 1999, 21, 63–64. Belmonte. "A Family Affair?," 80. Stanley Corkin. *Cowboys as Cold Warriors: The Western and U.S. History.* Philadelphia: Temple University Press, 2004, 6. Loy R. Philip. *Westerns in a Changing America, 1955–2000.* Jefferson, North Carolina: McFarland & Company, Inc., Publishers, 2004, 7. George N. Fenin and William K. Everson. *The Western: From Silents to the Seventies.* New York: Grossman Publishers, 1973, 45.

37. Michael Munn. *John Wayne: The Man behind the Myth.* New York: New American Library, 2003, 5 and 194–195.

38. Bill Niven. "The GDR and the Memory of the Bombing of Dresden." In *Germans as Victims: Remembering the Past in Contemporary Germany.* Bill Niven, ed. New York: Palgrave Macmillan, 2006, 109–120.

39. Peter Steinbach. "Widerstandsforschung im politischen Spannungsfeld." In *Widerstand gegen den Nationalsozialismus.* Peter Steinbach and Johannes Tuchel, eds. Berlin: Akademie Verlag, 1994, 597–622.

40. Lenihan. *Showdown,* 9–10. Heide Fehrenbach. *Cinema in Democratizing Germany: Reconstructing National Identity after Hitler.* Chapel Hill: The University of North Carolina Press, 1995, 11. Alexander Stephen. "Cold War Alliances and the Emergence of Transatlantic Competition: An Introduction." In *The Americanization of Europe: Culture, Diplomacy, and Anti-Americanism after 1945.* Alexander Stephan, ed. New York: Berghahn Books, 2006, 2–3.

41. Christina Haase. *When Heimat Meets Hollywood: German Filmmakers and America, 1985–2005.* Rochester: Camden House, 2007, 1.

42. Ian Tyrrell. *Transnational Nation: United States History in Global Perspective since 1789.* New York: Palgrave Macmillan, 2007, 3.

43. Adam. *Intercultural Transfers and the Making of the Modern World, 1800–2000,* 2012, 3.

44. Kirsten Belgum. "Reading Alexander von Humboldt: Cosmopolitan Naturalist with an American Spirit." In *German Culture in Nineteenth-Century America: Reception, Adaptation, Transformation.* Lynne Tatlock and Matt Erlin, eds. New York: Camden House, 2005, 107.

45. Ibid., 108.

46. Knud Krakau. "Einführende überlegungen zur Entstehung und Wirkung von Bildern, die sich Nationen von sich und anderen machen." In *Deutschland und Amerika: Perzepzion und historische Realitaet.* Berlin: Colloquium Verlag, 1985, 11–12.

47. Mary Nolan. "American in the German Imagination." In *Transactions, Transgressions, Transformations: American Culture in Western Europe and Japan.* Heide Fehrenbach and Uta G. Poiger, eds. New York: Berghahn Books, 2000, 7–8.

48. Matthias Middell. "Kulturtransfer und Historische Komparatistik- Thesen zu ihrem Verhältnis." In *Kulturtransfer und Vergleich.* Matthias Midell, ed. Leipzig: Leipziger Universitätsverlag, 2000, 18.

49. Richard Pells. "American Culture Abroad: The European Experience Since 1945." In *Cultural Transmissions and Receptions: American Mass Culture in*

Europe. R. Kroes, Robert W. Rydell and D.F.J. Bosscher, eds. Amsterdam: VU University Press, 1993, 67.

50. Rob Kroes. "Americanisation: What Are We Talking About?" In *Cultural Transmissions and Receptions: American Mass Culture in Europe*. R. Kroes, Robert W. Rydell, and D.F.J. Bosscher, eds. Amsterdam: VU University Press, 1993, 303–304.

51. Michel Espagne. "Kulturtransfer und Fachgeschichte der Geisteswissenschaften." In *Kulturtransfer und Vergleich*. Matthias Midell, ed. Leipzig: Leipziger Universitaetsverlag, 2000, 44.

52. Tyrrell. *Transnational Nation*, 3.

53. Adam. *Intercultural Transfers and the Making of the Modern World*, 1.

54. Uta G. Poiger. "A New, 'Western' Hero? Reconstructing German Masculinity in the 1950s." In *The Miracle Years: A Cultural History of West Germany, 1949– 1968*. Hanna Schissler, ed. Princeton: Princeton University Press, 2001, 416.

5 The Quest for National Identity

1. "Erfolgreichster Film: Bully schlaegt Otto." *Spiegel Online*, October 23, 2001. http://www.spiegel.de/kultur/kino/0,1518,163968,00.html.

2. *Manitou's Shoe*. http://www.imdb.com/title/tt0248408/.

3. "A German New Wave of Unvarnished Reality." Karen Durbin. *New York Times*, November 10, 2002. http://www.nytimes.com/2002/11/10/movies/ film-a-german-new-wave-of-unvarnished-reality.html.

4. "Karl May, Fantast und Superstar." Deutschlandradio Kultur, February 25, 2012. http://www.dradio.de/dkultur/sendungen/imgespraech/1685163/.

5. Kevin Mulroy, ed. *Western Amerykanski: Polish Poster Art & the Western*. Seattle: University of Washington Press, 1999, 21.

6. Dirk Hoerder. "From Euro- and Afro-Atlantic to Pacific Migration System: A Comparative Migration Approach to North American History." In *Rethinking American History in a Global Age*. Thomas Bender, ed. Raleigh: University of North Carolina Press, 2002, 197.

7. Thomas White. "Pennsylvania." In *Germany and the Americas: Culture, Politics, and History. A Multidisciplinary Encyclopedia*. Thomas Adam, ed. Santa Barbara: ABC-CLIO, 2005, 872–876.

8. Robert A. Calvert, Arnoldo De Leon, Greg Cantrell. *History of Texas*. Wheeling: Harlan Davidson, Inc., 2007, 198.

9. Carl Hammer Jr. "A Glance at Three Centuries of German-American Writing." In *Ethnic Literatures Since 1776: The Many Voices of America*. Wolodymyr T. Zyla and Wendell M. Aycock, eds. Lubbock: Texas Tech Press, 1978, 218. Colin G. Calloway. "Historical Encounters across Five Centuries." In *Germans and Indians: Fantasies, Encounters, Projections*. Colin G. Calloway, Gerd Gemünden, and Suzanne Zantop, eds. Lincoln: University of Nebraska Press, 2002, 47–49. Russell A. Kazal. *Becoming Old Stock: The Paradox of German-American Identity*. Princeton: Princeton University Press, 2004, 1.

10. Calloway. "Historical Encounters across Five Centuries," 77.

11. Hartmut Lutz. "German Indianthusiasm: A Socially Constructed German National(ist) Myth." In *Germans and Indians: Fantasies, Encounters,*

Projections. Colin G. Calloway, Gerd Gemünden, and Suzanne Zantop, eds. Lincoln: University of Nebraska Press, 2002, 169–170.

12. Ibid., 171–175.

13. Jörg Meindl. "Adelung, Johann Christoph." In *Germany and the Americas: Culture, Politics, and History. A Multidisciplinary Encyclopedia.* Thomas Adam, ed. Santa Barbara: ABC-CLIO, 2005, 43–44.

14. Philip Otterness. *Becoming German: The 1709 Palatinate Migration to New York.* Ithaca: Cornell University Press, 2004, 56–156.

15. Christian F. Feest. "Germany's Indians in a European Perspective." In *Germans and Indians: Fantasies, Encounters, Projections.* Colin G. Calloway, Gerd Gemünden, and Suzanne Zantop, eds. Lincoln: University of Nebraska Press, 2002, 29.

16. Ibid.

17. Hans Rudolf Rieder. "Zur Einfuehrung." In *Langspeer: Eine Selbstdarstellung des letzten Indianers. Häuptling Bueffelkind Langspeer.* Leipzig: Paul List Verlag, 1929, 1. Translated by Rudolf Conrad. "Mutual Fascination: Indians in Dresden and Leipzig." In *Indians and Europe: An Interdisciplinary Collection of Essays.* Christian F. Feest, ed. Lincoln: University of Nebraska Press, 1999, 459.

18. Suzanne Zantop. "Close Encounters: Deutsche and Indianer." In *Germans and Indians: Fantasies, Encounters, Projections.* Colin G. Calloway, Gemünden, and Suzanne Zantop, eds. Lincoln: University of Nebraska Press, 2002, 4.

19. Hartmut Lutz. *Approaches: Essays in Native North American Studies and Literature.* Augsburg: Wissner, 2002, 13–16.

20. Daniele Fiorentino. "Those Red-Brick Faces: European Press Reactions to the Indians of Buffalo Bill's Wild West Show." In *Indians and Europe: An Interdisciplinary Collection of Essays.* Christian F. Feest, ed. Lincoln: University of Nebraska Press, 1999, 403–404.

21. *Lokal-Anzeiger* (Berlin), July 24, 1890. As quoted in Eric Ames. "Seeing the Imaginary: On the Popular Reception of Wild West Shows in Germany, 1885–1910." In *I Like America: Fictions of the Wild West.* Pamela Kort and Max Hollein, eds. New York: Prestel, 2007, 213.

22. John F. Sears. "Bierstadt, Buffalo Bill, and the Wild West in Europe." In *Cultural Transmissions and Receptions: American Mass Culture in Europe.* R. Kroes, Robert W. Rydell, and D.F.J. Bosscher, eds. Amsterdam: VU University Press, 1993, 5–14.

23. Gregory P. Shealy, Jr. "Buffalo Bill in Germany: Gender, Heroism, and the American West in Imperial Germany." Master's thesis, University of Wisconsin-Madison, 2003, 2–3.

24. Charles Eldridge Griffin. *Four Years in Europe with Buffalo Bill.* Albia: Stage Publishing Co., 1908, 79–82.

25. Katinka Kocks. *Indianer im Kaiserreich: Voelkerschauen und Wild West Shows zwischen 1880 und 1914.* Gerolzhofen: Spiegel & Co., 2004, 57–59 and 86–89.

26. Ray Allen Billington. *Land of Savagery Land of Promise: The European Image of the American Frontier in the Nineteenth Century.* New York: W.W. Norton & Company, 1981, 30–32. James K. Folsom. "Precursors of the Western Novel." In *A Literary History of the American West.* Fort Worth: Texas

Christian University Press, 1987, 147. Klaus Lubbers. " 'So Motley a Dramatis Personae': Transatlantic Encounters in James Fenimore Cooper's *The Pioneers.*" In *Transatlantic Encounters: Studies in European-American Relations.* Udo J. Hebel and Karl Ortseifen, eds. Trier: Wissenschaftlicher Verlag, 1995, 136–137.

27. H. Glenn Penny. "Illustrating America: Images of the North American West in German Periodicals, 1825–1890." In *I Like America: Fictions of the Wild West.* New York: Prestel, 2007, 141. Karsten Fitz. "Screen Indians in the EFL-Classroom: Transnational Perspectives." In *American Studies Journal*, Nr. 51 (2008), 3.

28. As translated by Jeffrey L. Sammons. "Nineteenth-Century German Representations of Indians from Experience." In *Germans and Indians: Fantasies, Encounters, Projections.* Colin G. Calloway, Gerd Gemünden, and Suzanne Zantop, eds. Lincoln: University of Nebraska Press, 2002, 186.

29. Kocks. *Indianer im Kaiserreich*, 18–19. Billington. *Land of Savagery Land of Promise*, 39. Richard Cracroft. "The American West of Karl May." In *American Quarterly*, Vol. 19, No. 2, Part 1 (Summer, 1967), 162–163. Lutz. *Approaches*, 15–16. Sammons. "Nineteenth-Century German Representations of Indians from Experience," 186–190.

30. Karl May. *Winnetou III.* Guetersloh: Bertelsmann, 1964, kindle edition, 17691–17696. Cracroft. "The American West of Karl May," 256.

31. Cracroft. "The American West of Karl May," 256.

32. Jeffrey L. Sammons. *Ideology, Mimesis, Fantasy: Charles Sealsfield, Friedrich Gerstaecker, Karl May, and Other German Novelists of America.* Chapel Hill: The University of North Carolina Press, 1998, 230. Frederik Hetmann. *Old Shatterhand, das bin ich: Die Lebensgeschichte des Karl May.* Weinheim: Beltz & Gelberg, 2001, 151.

33. Karl May. *Winnetou I.* Guetersloh: Bertelsmann, 1964, kindle edition. Hetmann. *Old Shatterhand, das bin ich*, 141.

34. Sammons. *Ideology, Mimesis, Fantasy*, 96. Jerry Schuchalter. *Narratives of America and the Frontier in Nineteenth-Century German Literature.* New York: Peter Lang, 2000, 57–58.

35. Annette Bühler-Dietrich. "Strubberg, Friedrich August." In *Germany and the Americas: Culture, Politics, and History.* Thomas Adam, ed. Santa Barbara: ABC-CLIO, 2005, 1017–1018.

36. Sammons. *Ideology, Mimesis, Fantasy.*

37. Ibid., 139–149 and 229–244. Schuchalter. *Narratives of America and the Frontier in Nineteenth-Century German Literature*, 24–25 and 71. Billington. *Land of Savagery Land of Promise*, 74–275. Norbert Honsza and Wojciech Kunicki. *Karl May-Anatomia Sukcesu: Zycie-Tworczosc-Recepcja.* Katowice: Wydawnictwo Slask, 1986, 66–97.

38. Colleen Cook. "Germany's Wild West Author: A Researcher's Guide to Karl May." In *German Studies Review*, Vol. 5, No. 1, February 1982, 70.

39. "Ich bin ein Cowboy: Modern Germany's Favorite Author Will Come as a Surprise." *The Economist*, May 24, 2001.

40. Jörg Kastner. *Das große Karl May Buch: Sein Leben-Seine Bücher -Die Filme.* Bergisch Glasbach: Bastei Verlag, 1992, 22. Hetmann. *Old Shatterhand, das bin ich*, 18–24. Honsza and Kunicki, *Karl May-Anatomia Sukcesu*, 13.

41. Helmut Fritz. *Roter Bruder Winnetou: Karl May als Erzieher. Eine Sendung zum 150. Geburtstag des Dichters.* Siegen, 1992, 2.
42. Kastner. *Das große Karl May Buch,* 25. Hetmann. *Old Shatterhand, das bin ich,* 38–39 and 139.
43. Danica Tutush. "The Strange Life and Legacy of Karl May." In *Cowboys & Indians,* September 1999, 150. Kastner. *Das große Karl May Buch,* 25–27. Katja Wuestenbecker. "Karl May." In *Germany and the Americas.* Thomas Adam, ed. Santa Barbara: ABC-CLIO, 2005, 724.
44. As quoted in Hetmann. *Old Shatterhand, das bin ich,* 218–233.
45. Kastner. *Das große Karl May Buch,* 53.
46. Cook. "Germany's Wild West Author." 72. Wuestenbecker. "Karl May," 725–726.
47. Christopher Frayling. *Spaghetti Westerns: Cowboys and Europeans from Karl May to Sergio Leone.* New York: I.B. Tauris, 2006, 104. Kastner. *Das große Karl May Buch,* 44.
48. Walter Laqueur. "Cowboys for the Kaiser: Cowboys." In *New York Times,* January 29, 1978.
49. Cracroft. "The American West of Karl May." 257.
50. N. Richter. "Karl May:...sogar Literatur. Späte Anerkennung für den phantasievollen Sachsen/"Der Schatz im Silbersee," ein deutscher Großfilm. Constantin-Verleih, Microfilm. Textarchiv des Deutschen Filminstituts, Frankfurt.
51. "Reite ihn, Cowboy: Concerning Marlene Dietrich and Germanic Writer of 'Westerns.'" *New York Times,* December 3, 1939.
52. Rolf Bernhard Essig and Gudrun Schury. *Alles über Karl May.* Berlin: Aufbau Verlagsgruppe GmbH, 2007, 68–69. Hetmann. *Old Shatterhand, das bin ich,* 277–278. Cracroft. "The American West of Karl May." 251.
53. "Der Schatz im Silbersee: mehr als ein Drehbuch!" Microfilm. Archiven des Deutschen Filminstituts/Deutschen Filmmuseums.
54. Reinhard Weber. *Artur Brauners Old Shatterhand.* Landshut: Fachverlag für Filmliteratur, 2002, 50.
55. Ibid., 57–60.
56. Tassilo Schneider. "Finding a New Heimat in the Wild West: Karl May and the German Western of the 1960s." In *Journal of Film and Video,* Vol. 47, No. 1–3 (Spring–Fall, 1995), 60.
57. Weber. *Artur Brauners Old Shatterhand,* 51.
58. Reiner Boller and Christina Boehme. *Lex Barker: Die Biographie.* Berlin: Schwarzkopf & Schwarzkopf, 2008, 303–308.
59. Weber. *Artur Brauners Old Shatterhand,* 75.
60. Weber. *Artur Brauners Old Shatterhand,* 19. Manfred Barthel. *So war es wirklich: Der deutsche Nachkriegsfilm.* München: Herbig Verlag, 1989, 161–163.
61. Weber. *Artur Brauners Old Shatterhand,* 51.
62. Schneider. "Finding a New Heimat in the Wild West." 50–51.
63. Boller and Boehme. *Lex Barker,* 310. Kastner. *Das grosse Karl May Buch,* 146.
64. As quoted in Kastner. *Das große Karl May Buch,* 148.
65. F.-B. Habel. *Das Große Lexikon der DEFA-Spielfilme.* Berlin: Schwarzkopf & Schwarzkopf, 2000, 555–556.

66. Frank-Burhard Habel. *Gojko Mitic, Mustangs, Marterpfähle: Die Indianerfilme. Das große Buch für Fans.* Berlin: Schwarzkopf & Schwarzkopf, 1997, 6–12.
67. Ibid.
68. Klaus Wischnewski. "Träumer und Gewohnliche Leute 1966 bis 1979." In *Das zweite Leben der Filmstadt Babelsberg: DEFA-Spielfilme 1946–1992.* Ralf Schenk, ed. Berlin: Filmmuseum Potsdam, 1994, 220–221.
69. Gerd Gemünden. "Between Karl May and Karl Marx: The DEFA Indianerfilme." In *Germans & Indians: Fantasies, Encounters, and Projections.* Colin G. Calloway, Gerd Gemünden and Suzanne Zantop, eds. Lincoln: University of Nebraska Press, 2002, 29.
70. Lutz. *Approaches,* 17.
71. Horst Haase, Hans Jürgen Geerdts, Erich Kuehne, and Walter Pallus. *Geschichte der Literatur der Deutschen Demokratischen Republik.* Berlin: Volk und Wissen Volkseigener Verlag, 1976, 242–243, 312.
72. Erik Lorenz. *Liselotte Welskopf-Henrich und die Indianer: Eine Biographie.* Chemnitz: Palisander, 2009, 15–23. Elsa Christina Muller. "A Cultural Study of the Sioux Novels of Liselotte Welskopf-Henrich." PhD diss., 1995, 102.
73. Muller. "A Cultural Study of the Sioux Novels of Liselotte Welskopf-Henrich," 106–108.
74. Gemünden. "Between Karl May and Karl Marx." 251.
75. H. Glenn Penny. "Red Power: Liselotte Welskopf-Henrich and Indian Activist Networks in East and West Germany." *Central European History* (2008), 450.
76. Ibid.
77. ABBAW, Folder 86. Muller. "A Cultural Study of the Sioux Novels of Liselotte Welskopf-Henrich," 111.
78. ABBAW, Folder 180.
79. Mueller. "A Cultural Study of the Sioux Novels of Liselotte Welskopf-Henrich," 343–371.
80. ABBAW, Folder 15.
81. ABBAW, Folder 179. James S. Olson, ed. *Encyclopedia of American Indian Civil Rights.* Westport: Greenwood Press, 1997, 385–386. Harvey Markowitz, ed. *American Indian Biographies.* Pasadena: Salem Press, Inc., 1999, 215.
82. ABBAW, Folder 180.
83. ABBAW, Folder 179.
84. ABBAW, Folder 179.
85. Jonathan R. Zatlin. *The Currency of Socialism: Money and Political Culture in East Germany.* Cambridge: Cambridge University Press, 2007, 172–174. Hetmann. *Old Shatterhand, das bin ich,* 11–12.
86. ABBAW, Folder 179.
87. Zatlin. *The Currency of Socialism,* 255–256.
88. ABBAW, Folder 179.
89. Penny. "Red Power," 451–452.
90. Maria Höhn and Martin Klimke. "The Civil Rights Struggle, African-American GIs, and Germany." HCA. Heildelberg Center for American Studies. http://www.hca.uni-heidelberg.de/.
91. ABBAW, Folder 179.
92. ABBAW, Folder 180.
93. ABBAW, Folder 180.

94. ABBAW, Folder 180.
95. Muller. "A Cultural Study of the Sioux Novels of Liselotte Welskopf-Henrich," 456–459.
96. Uli Otto and Till Otto. *Auf den Spuren der Söhne der großen Bärin.* Regensburg: Kern Verlag, 2001, 14–32.
97. ABBAW, Folder 179.
98. Mueller. "A Cultural Study of the Sioux Novels of Liselotte Welskopf-Henrich," 513. ABBAW, Folder 179.
99. ABBAW, Folder 121.
100. ABBAW, Folder 15.
101. ABBAW, Folder 15.
102. Penny. "Red Power," 458. Gemünden. "Karl May and Karl Marx," 27–28.

Conclusion

1. Ruth Ellen Gruber. "Deep in the Heart of … Bavaria." In *The New York Times,* April 11, 2004.
2. Michael David-Fox. "Transnational History and the East-West Divide." In *Imagining the West in Eastern Europe and the Soviet Union.* Gyorgy Peteri, ed. Pittsburgh: University of Pittsburgh Press, 2010, 262–267.
3. Hans Ake-Persson. " 'Soweit die deutsche Zunge klingt': State and Identity in German History." In *Europe: The Return of History.* Sven Tagil, ed. Lund: Nordic Academic Press, 2001, 285–287.
4. David F. Crew. "Consuming Germany in the Cold War." In *Consuming Germany in the Cold War.* David F. Crew, ed. New York: Berge, 2003, 1–2.
5. Rydell and Rob Kroes. *Buffalo Bill in Bologna: The Americanization of the World, 1869–1922.* Chicago: The University of Chicago Press, 2005, 9–10.
6. Ibid., 174.
7. Laszlo Kurti and Juliet Langman. "Introduction: Searching for Identities in the New East Central Europe." In *Beyond Borders: Remaking Cultural Identities in the New East and Central Europe.* Laszlo Kurti and Juliet Langman, eds. Boulder: Westview Press, 1997, 3.
8. Gerd-Rainer Horn and Padraic Kenney. "Introduction: Approaches to the Transnational." *Transnational Moments of Change.* Gerd-Rainer Horn and Padraic Kenney, eds. Lanham: Rowman & Littlefield Publishers, Inc., 2004, xiii.
9. Thomas Lindenberger. "Divided but Not Disconnected: Germany as a Border Region of the Cold War." In *Divided but Not Disconnected: German Experiences of the Cold War.* Tobias Hochscherf, Christoph Laucht, and Andrew Plowman, eds. New York: Berghahn Books, 2010, 13–14.
10. "Winnetou-Darsteller Mitic: Apache in der Patsche." *Der Spiegel,* July 6, 2006. http://www.spiegel.de/kultur/gesellschaft/0,1518,425029,00.html.
11. Friedrich von Borries, Jens-Uwe Fischer. *Sozialistische Cowboys: Der Wilde Westen Ostdeutschlands.* Frankfurt am Main: Suhrkamp, 2008, 7–8.

Bibliography

Archival collections, Germany

Archiv der Berlin-Brandenburgischen Akademie der Wissenschaften (ABBAW).
Bundesarchiv, Berlin (BArch).
Textarchiv des Deutschen Filminstituts/Deutschen Filmmuseums, Frankfurt.

Films

Apachen (*Apache Indians*), 1973. Deutsche Film (DEFA). Gottfried Kolditz, director.
Blutsbrüder (*Blood Brothers*), 1975. Deutsche Film (DEFA), Werner W. Wallroth, director.
Chingachgook, die große Schlange (*Chingachgook, the Great Snake*), 1967. Deutsche Film (DEFA). Richard Grosschopp, director.
Der Schatz im Silbersee (*The Treasure of Silverlake*), 1962. Rialtofilm Preben Philipsen/Jadran-Film. Dr. Harald Reinl, director.
Der Schuh des Manitu (*Manitou's Shoe*), 2001. HerbX film gmbh. Michael Herbig, director.
Die Söhne der großen Bärin (*The Sons of Great Mother Bear*), 1966. Deutsche Film (DEFA). Josef Mach, director.
Limonádový Joe aneb Konská opera (*Lemonade Joe*), 1964. Filmove Studio Barrandov. Oldrich Lipsky, director.
Old Shatterhand, 1964. CCC Filmproduktion GmbH. Hugo Fregonese, director.
Osceola, 1971. DEFA-Studio, Kinozentrum Sofia, ICAIC Havana. Konrad Petzold, director.
Tödlicher Irrtum (*Fatal Error*), 1970. Deutsche Studio (DEFA). Konrad Petzold, director.
Unter Geiern (*Among Vultures*), 1964. Rialtofilm Preben Philipsen/Jadran-Film/Societe Nouvelle de Cinematographie. Dr. Harald Reinl, director.
Weiße Wölfe (*White Wolves*), 1969. Deutsche Studio (DEFA). Konrad Petzold, director.
Wilcze Echa (*The Wolves' Echoes*), 1967. Zespol Filmowy "Rytm." Aleksander Scibor-Rylski, director.
Winnetou 1, 1963. Rialtofilm Preben Philipsen/Jadran-Film. Harald Reinl, director.
Winnetou II, 1964. Rialtofilm Preben Philipsen/Jadran-Film. Harald Reinl, director.
Winnetou III, 1965. Rialtofilm Preben Philipsen/Jadran-Film. Harald Reinl, director.

Winnetou und das Halbblut Apanatschi (*Half-Breed*), 1966. Rialtofilm Preben Philipsen/Jadran-Film. Harald Philipp, director.

Newspapers and periodicals

Berliner Zeitung
Bonner Rundschau
Darmstaedter Echo
Der Spiegel
Der Tagesspiegel, Berlin
Deutsche Zeitung, Stuttgart/Koeln
Düsseldorfer Nachrichten
Film Beobachter
Film Dienst
Frankfurter Allgemeine Zeitung
Frankfurter Rundschau
Freiheit, Halle
Hamburger Echo
Hannover Presse
Kölnische Rundschau
Maerkische Volksstimme, Potsdam
Mühlheimer Zeitung
Nationalzeitung Berlin
Neue Weg, Halle
Süddeutsche Zeitung
The New York Times
Welt
Westdeutsche Allgemeine, Essen
Westfälische Rundschau

Books

Primary sources

Adam, Thomas. *Buying Respectability*. Bloomington: Indiana University Press, 2009.

Adam, Thomas. *Intercultural Transfers and the Making of the Modern World, 1800–2000: Sources and Context*. New York: Palgrave Macmillan, 2012.

Belgun, Kirsten. "Reading Alexander von Humboldt: Cosmopolitan Naturalist with an American Spirit." In *German Culture in Nineteenth-Century America: Reception, Adaptation, Transformation*. Lynne Tatlock and Matt Erlin, eds. New York: Camden House, 2005.

Brandt, Willy. *My Life in Politics*. New York: Viking, 1992.

Brice, Pierre. *Mein wahres Leben*. Bergisch Gladbach: Gustav Luebbe Verlag, 2004.

Dietrich, Otto. *The Hitler I Knew: The Memoirs of the Third Reich's Press Chief.* New York: Skyhorse Publishing, 2010.

Espagne, Michel. "Kulturtransfer und Fachgeschichte der Geisteswissenschaften." In *Kulturtransfer und Vergleich*. Matthias Midell, ed. Leipzig: Leipziger Universitaetsverlag, 2000.

Hochhuth, Rolf. *The Deputy*. New York: Grove Press, Inc., 1964.

Midell, Matthias, ed. *Kulturtransfer und Vergleich*. Leipzig: Leipziger Universitätsverlag, 2000.

Nolte, Ernst. *Deutschland und der kalte Krieg*. München: R. Piper & Co. Vorlag, 1974.

Olson, James S., ed. *Encyclopedia of American Indian Civil Rights*. Westport: Greenwood Press, 1997.

Speer, Albert. *Spandau: The Secret Diaries*. New York: Macmillan Publishing Co., Inc., 1976.

Stückrath, Fritz and Schottmayer, Georg. *Fernsehen und Grossstadtjugend*. Braunschweig: Georg Westermann Verlag, 1967.

Tyrrell, Ian. *Transnational Nation: United States History in Global Perspective since 1789*. New York: Palgrave Macmillan, 2007.

Versini, Marie. *Ich war Winnetous Schwester*. Bamberg: Karl May Verlag, 2003.

Secondary sources

Adam, Thomas, ed. *Germany and the Americas: Culture, Politics, and History. A Multidisciplinary Encyclopedia*. Santa Barbara: ABC-CLIO, 2005.

Ake-Persson, Hans. "Soweit die deutsche Zunge klingt": State and Identity in German History. In *Europe: The Return of History*. Sven Tagil, ed. Lund: Nordic Academic Press, 2001.

Allan, Sean and Sandford, John, eds. *DEFA: East German Cinema, 1946–1992*. New York: Berghahn Books, 1999.

Ames, Eric. "Seeing the Imaginary: On the Popular Reception of Wild West Shows in Germany, 1885–1910." In *I Like America: Fictions of the Wild West*. Pamela Kort and Max Hollein, eds. New York: Prestel, 2007.

Arendt, Hannah. *Responsibility and Judgment*. New York: Schocken Books, 2003.

Bakker, Jan. *The Popular Western: Window to the American Spirit*. In *The American West*. Rob Kroes, ed. Amsterdam: Free University Press, 1989.

Balfour, Michael. *West Germany: A Contemporary History*. New York: St. Martin's Press, 1982.

Barthel, Manfred. *So war es wirklich: Der deutsche Nachkriegsfilm*. München: Herbig Verlag, 1989.

Baumgarten, Oliver. "Euro-Gunfighter: Karl May und die deutsche Eurowestern-Erfolgswelle (1962–1968)." In *Um Sie weht der Hauch des Todes. Der Italo-Western – die Geschichte eines Genres*. Georg Seesslen, Hans Schifferle, and Hans-Christoph Blumenberg, eds. Koeln: Schnitt Verlag, 1998.

Beattie, Andrew H. "The Victims of Totalitarianism and Centrality of Nazi Genocide: Continuity and Change in German Commemorative Politics." In *Germans as Victims: Remembering the Past in Contemporary Germany*. Bill Niven, ed. Houndmills, Basingstoke: Palgrave Macmillan, 2006.

Behrenbeck, Sabine. "The Transformation of Sacrifice: German Identity between Heroic Narrative and Economic Success." In *Pain and Prosperity: Reconsidering Twentieth-Century German History.* Paul Betts and Greg Eghigian, eds. Stanford: Stanford University Press, 2003.

Belmonte, Laura A. "A Family Affair? Gender, the U.S. Information Agency, and Cold War Ideology, 1945–1960." In *Culture and International History.* Jessica C.E. Gienow-Hecht and Frank Schumacher, eds. New York: Berghahn Books.

Belton, John. *American Cinema/American Culture.* New York: McGrawHill, 2005.

Bender, Thomas. "Introduction: Historians, the Nation, and the Plenitude of Narratives." In *Rethinking American History in a Global Age.* Thomas Bender, ed. Raleigh: University of North Carolina Press, 2002.

Bergfelder, Tim. *International Adventures: German Popular Cinema and European Co-Productions in the 1960s.* New York: Berghahn Books, 2005.

Betts, Paul and Eghigian, Greg, eds. *Pain and Prosperity: Reconsidering Twentieth-Century German History.* Stanford: Stanford University Press, 2003.

Billington, Ray Allen. *Land of Savagery Land of Promise: The European Image of the American Frontier in the Nineteenth Century.* New York: W.W. Norton & Company, 1981.

Boller, Reiner and Boehme, Christina. *Lex Barker: Die Biographie.* Berlin: Schwarzkopf and Schwarzkopf, 2008.

Borries, Friedrich von and Fischer, Jens-Uwe. *Sozialistische Cowboys: Der Wilde Westen Ostdeutschlands.* Frankfurt am Main: Suhrkamp, 2008.

Browning, Christopher. *Ordinary Men: Reserve Police Battalion 101 and the Final Solution in Poland.* New York: Harper Perennial, 1998.

Burleigh, Michael. *The Third Reich: A New History.* New York: Hill and Wang, 2000.

Byg, Barton. "DEFA Traditions of International Cinema." In *DEFA: East German Cinema, 1946–1992.* Sean Allan and John Sandford, eds. New York: Berghahn Books, 1999.

Calloway, Colin G., Gemünden, Gerd, and Zantop, Suzanne, eds. *Germans and Indians: Fantasies, Encounters, Projections.* Lincoln: University of Nebraska Press, 2002.

Calvert, Robert A., De Leon, Arnoldo, and Cantrell, Greg. *History of Texas.* Wheeling: Harlan Davidson, Inc., 2007.

Childs, David, ed. *Honecker's Germany.* Boston: Allen & Unwin, 1985.

Christopher, Inge. "The Written Constitution: The Basic Law of a Socialist State?" In *Honecker's Germany.* David Childs, ed. Boston: Allen & Unwin, 1985.

Confino, Alon. *Germany as a Culture of Remembrance: Promises and Limits of Writing History.* Chapel Hill: The University of North Carolina Press, 2006.

Corkin, Stanley. *Cowboys as Cold Warriors: The Western and U.S. History.* Philadelphia: Temple University Press, 2004.

Crew, David F. "Consuming Germany in the Cold War: Consumption and National Identity in East and West Germany, 1949–1989." In *Consuming Germany in the Cold War.* David F. Crew, ed. New York: Berge, 2003.

David-Fox, Michael. "Transnational History and the East-West Divide." In *Imagining the West in Eastern Europe and the Soviet Union.* Gyorgy Peteri, ed. Pittsburgh: University of Pittsburgh Press, 2010.

Demshuk, Andrew. *The Lost German East: Forced Migration and the Politics of Memory, 1945–1970.* New York: Cambridge University Press, 2012.

Dennis, Mike. *The Rise and Fall of the German Democratic Republic 1945–1990.* Harlow: Longman, 2000.

Diefendorf, Jeffry M., Frohn, Axel, and Rupieper, Hermann-Josef, eds. *American Policy and the Reconstruction of West Germany, 1945–1955.* New York: Cambridge University Press, 1993.

Diner, Dan. *America in the Eyes of the Germans: An Essay on Anti-Americanism.* Princeton: Markus Wiener Publishers, 1996.

Dirke, Sabine von. *"All Power to the Imagination." The West German Counterculture from the Student Movement to the Greens.* Lincoln: University of Nebraska Press, 1997.

Distelmeyer, Jan. "Mister Dynamit – Morgen küsst euch der Tod (1967)." In *Fredy Bockbein trifft Mister Dynamit: Filme auf den zweiten Blick.* Christoph Fuchs und Michael Toeteberg, eds. München: Edition text + kritik, 2007.

Duerr, Volker. "Introduction." In *Coping with the Past: Germany and Austria after 1945.* Kathy Harms, Lutz R. Reuter, and Volker Duerr, eds. Madison: The University of Wisconsin Press, 2005.

Essig, Rolf Bernhard and Schury, Gudrun. *Alles über Karl May: Ein Sammelsurium von A bis Z.* Berlin: Aufbau Verlagsgruppe, 2007.

Feest, Christian F. "Germany's Indians in a European Perspective." In *Germans and Indians: Fantasies, Encounters, Projections.* Colin G. Calloway, Gerd Gemünden, and Suzanne Zantop, eds. Lincoln: University of Nebraska Press, 2002.

Feest, Christian F., ed. *Indians and Europe: An Interdisciplinary Collection of Essays.* Lincoln: University of Nebraska Press, 1999.

Fehrenbach, Heide. *Cinema in Democratizing Germany: Reconstructing National Identity after Hitler.* Chapel Hill: The University of North Carolina Press, 1995.

Fehrenbach, Heide and Poiger, Uta G., eds. *Transactions, Transgressions, Transformations: American Culture in Western Europe and Japan.* New York: Berghahn Books, 2000.

Fenin, George N. and Everson, William K. *The Western: From Silents to the Seventies.* New York: Grossman Publishers, 1973.

Fiorentino, Daniele. "Those Red-Brick Faces: European Press Reactions to the Indians of Buffalo Bill's Wild West Show." In *Indians and Europe: An Interdisciplinary Collection of Essays.* Christian F. Feest, ed. Lincoln: University of Nebraska Press, 1999.

Folsom, James K. "Precursors of the Western Novel." In *A Literary History of the American West.* Fort Worth: Texas Christian University Press, 1987.

Frayling, Christopher. *Spaghetti Westerns: Cowboys and Europeans from Karl May to Sergio Leone.* New York: I.B. Tauris, 2006.

Friedrichsmeyer, Sara, Lennox, Sara, and Zantop, Susanne, eds. *The Imperialist Imagination: German Colonialism and Its Legacy.* Ann Arbor: The University of Michigan Press, 1998.

Fritz, Helmut. *Roter Bruder Winnetou: Karl May als Erzieher. Eine Sendung zum 150. Geburtstag des Dichters.* Siegen, 1992.

Fuchs, Christopher und Toeteberg, Michael, eds. *Fredy Bockbein trifft Mister Dynamit: Filme auf den zweiten Blick.* München: Edition text + kritik, 2007.

Fulbrook, Mary. *A Concise History of Germany.* New York: Cambridge University Press, 1991.

Fulbrook, Mary, ed. *German History since 1800.* New York: Arnold, 1997.

Fulbrook, Mary and Swales, Martin, eds. *Representing the German Nation: History and Identity in Twentieth-Century Germany.* New York: Manchester University Press, 2000.

Gemünden, Gerd. "Between Karl May and Karl Marx: The DEFA Indianerfilme." In *Germans & Indians: Fantasies, Encounters, and Projections.* Colin G. Calloway, Gerd Gemünden, and Suzanne Zantop, eds. Lincoln: University of Nebraska Press, 2002.

Geyer, Michael and Hansen, Miriam. "German-Jewish Memory and National Consciousness." In *Holocaust Remembrance: The Shapes of Memory.* Geoffrey H. Hartman, ed. Cambridge: Blackwell, 1994.

Gienow-Hecht, Jessica, C.E. and Schumacher, Frank, eds. *Culture and International History.* New York: Berghahn Books, 2003.

Glaser, Hermann. *Deutsche Kultur 1945–2000.* München: Carl Hansen Verlag, 1997.

Goodwin, C.D.W. and Holley Jr., I.B., eds. Durham: The South Atlantic Quarterly, 1968.

Griffin, Charles Eldridge. *Four Years in Europe with Buffalo Bill.* Albia: Stage Publishing Co., 1908.

Guback, Thomas H. *The International Film Industry, Western Europe and America since 1945.* Bloomington: Indiana University Press, 1969.

Haase, Christina. *When Heimat Meets Hollywood: German Filmmakers and America, 1985–2005.* Rochester: Camden House, 2007.

Haase, Horst, Geerdts, Hans Jürgen, Kuehne, Erich, and Pallus, Walter. *Geschichte der Literatur der Deutschen Demokratischen Republik.* Berlin: Volk und Wissen Volkseigener Verlag, 1976.

Habel, F.-B. *Das Grosse Lexikon der DEFA-Spielfilme.* Berlin: Schwarzkopf & Schwarzkopf, 2000.

Habel, Frank-Burhard. *Gojko Mitic, Mustangs, Marterpfähle: Die Indianerfilme. Das große Buch für Fans.* Berlin: Schwarzkopf & Schwarzkopf, 1997.

Hagemann, Karen and Schuler-Springorum, Stefanie, eds. *Home/Front: The Military, War and Gender in Twentieth-Century Germany.* New York: Berg, 2002.

Hake, Sabine. *German National Cinema.* New York: Routledge, 2002.

Halle, Randal and McCarthy, Margaret, eds. *Light Motives: German Popular Film in Perspective.* Detroit: Wayne State University Press, 2003.

Hammer, Carl Jr. "A Glance at Three Centuries of German-American Writing." In *Ethnic Literatures since 1776: The Many Voices of America.* Wolodymyr T. Zyla and Wendell M. Aycock, eds. Lubbock: Texas Tech Press, 1978.

Harap, Louis. *The Image of the Jew in American Literature: From Early Republic to Mass Immigration.* Philadelphia: The Jewish Publication Society of America, 1974.

Hartman, Geoffrey H., ed. *Holocaust Remembrance: The Shapes of Memory.* Cambridge: Blackwell, 1994.

Hebel, Udo J. and Ortseifen, Karl. *Transatlantic Encounters: Studies in European-American Relations.* Trier: Wissenschaftlicher Verlag, 1995.

Hermand, Jost. *Kultur im Wiederaufbau: Die Bundesrepublik Deutschland 1945–1965.* Muenchen: Nymphenburger, 1986

Hetmann, Frederik. *Old Shatterhand, das bin ich: Die Lebensgeschichte des Karl May.* Weinheim: Beltz & Gelberg, 2001.

Higson, Andrew and Maltby, Richard, eds. *"Film Europe" and "Film America": Cinema, Commerce and Cultural Exchange 1920–1939*. Exeter: University of Exeter Press, 1999.

Hillerbrand, Hans J. "The Spread of the Protestant Reformation of the Sixteenth Century." In *The Transfer of Ideas: Historical Essays*. C.D.W. Goodwin and I.B. Holley, Jr., eds. Durham: The South Atlantic Quarterly, 1968.

Hoerder, Dirk. "From Euro- and Afro-Atlantic to Pacific Migration System: A Comparative Migration Approach to North American History." In *Rethinking American History in a Global Age*. Thomas Bender, ed. Raleigh: University of North Carolina Press, 2002.

Höhn, Maria. *"Heimat* in Turmoil: African-American GIs in 1950s West Germany." In *The Miracle Years: A Cultural History of West Germany, 1949–1968*. Hanna Schissler, ed. Princeton: Princeton University Press, 2001.

Höhn, Maria and Klimke, Martin. *A Breath of Freedom: The Civil Rights Struggle, African American GIs, and Germany*. New York: Palgrave Macmillan, 2010.

Honsza, Norbert and Kunicki, Wojciech. *Karl May-Anatomia Sukcesu: Zycie-Tworczosc-Recepcja*. Katowice: Wydawnictwo Slask, 1986.

Horn, Gerd-Rainer and Kenney, Padraic. "Introduction: Approaches to the Transnational." *Transnational Moments of Change*. Gerd-Rainer Horn and Padraic Kenney, eds. Lanham: Rowman & Littlefield Publishers, Inc., 2004.

Hughes, Howard. *Once upon a Time in the Italian West: The Filmgoers' Guide to Spaghetti Westerns*. New York: I.B. Tauris, 2004.

Jadran in Profile. Zagreb: Publicity Dept. Jadran Film, 1986, 2.

James, Peter, ed. *Modern Germany: Politics, Society and Culture*. New York: Routledge, 1998.

Jarausch, Konrad H. *After Hitler: Recivilizing Germans, 1945–1995*. New York: Oxford University Press, 2006.

Jarausch, Konrad H., ed. *After Unity: Reconfiguring German Identities*. Providence: Berghahn Books, 1997.

Jeier, Thomas. *Der Western-Film*. München: Wilhelm Verlag, 1995.

Jochmann, Werner, ed. *Adolf Hitler Monologe im FuehrerHauptquartier 1941–1944: Die Aufzeichnungen Heinrich Heims*. Hamburg: Albrecht Knaus Verlag, 1980.

Jordan, Lothar and Kortlaender, Bernd, eds. *Nationale Grenzen und Internationaler Austausch: Studien zum Kultur- und Wissenschaftstransfer in Europa*. Tübingen: Niemeyer, 1995.

Kansteiner, Wulf. *In Pursuit of German Memory: History, Television, and Politics after Auschwitz*. Athens: Ohio University Press, 2006.

Kastner, Jörg. *Das große Karl May Buch: Sein Leben-Seine Bücher-Die Filme*. Bergisch Glasbach: Bastei Verlag, 1992.

Kaufman, David. "The Nazi Legacy: Coming to Terms with the Past." In *Modern Germany: Politics, Society and Culture*. Peter James, ed. New York: Routledge, 1998.

Kazal, Russell A. *Becoming Old Stock: The Paradox of German-American Identity*. Princeton: Princeton University Press, 2004.

Kershaw, Ian. *Hitler: A Biography*. New York: W.W. Norton & Company, 2008.

Klessmann, Christoph. *Zwei Staaten, eine Nation: Deutsche Geschichte 1955–1970*. Goettingen: Vandenhoeck & Ruprecht, 1988.

Kocks, Katinka. *Indianer im Kaiserreich: Völkerschauen und Wild West Shows zwischen 1880 und 1914*. Gerolzhofen: Spiegel & Co., 2004.

Kort, Pamela and Hollein, Max, eds. *I Like America: Fictions of the Wild West*. New York: Prestel, 2007.

Krakau, Knud. "Einführende überlegungen zur Entstehung und Wirkung von Bildern, die sich Nationen von sich und anderen machen." In *Deutschland und Amerika: Perzepzion und historische Realität*. Berlin: Colloquium Verlag, 1985.

Kreis, Karl Markus. "German Wild West: Karl May's Invention of the Definitive Indian." In *I Like America: Fictions of the Wild West*. Pamela Kort and Max Hollein, eds. New York: Prestel, 2007.

Kroes, Rob. "American Empire and Cultural Imperialism: A View from the Receiving End." In *Rethinking American History in a Global Age*. Thomas Bender, ed. Raleigh: University of North Carolina Press, 2002.

Kroes, R., Rydell, Robert W., and Bosscher, D.F.J., eds. *Cultural Transmissions and Receptions: American Mass Culture in Europe*. Amsterdam: VU University Press, 1993.

Kroes, Rob, ed. *The American West*. Amsterdam: Free University Press, 1989.

Kroes, Rob. "Americanisation: What Are We Talking About?" In *Cultural Transmissions and Receptions: American Mass Culture in Europe*. R. Kroes, Robert W. Rydell, and D.F.J. Bosscher, eds. Amsterdam: VU University Press, 1993.

Kundnani, Hans. *Utopia or Auschwitz: Germany's 1968 Generation and the Holocaust*. New York: Columbia University Press, 2009.

Kurti, Laszlo and Langman, Juliet. "Introduction: Searching for Identities in the New East Central Europe." In *Beyond Borders: Remaking Cultural Identities in the New East and Central Europe*. Laszlo Kurti and Juliet Langman, eds. Boulder: Westview Press, 1997.

LaCapra, Dominick. *History and Memory after Auschwitz*. Ithaca: Cornell University Press, 1998.

Laszewski, Chuck. *Rock 'n' Roll Radical: The Life and Mysterious Death of Dean Reed*. Edina: Beaver's Pond Press, Inc., 2005, 106.

Lenihan, John H. *Showdown: Confronting Modern America in the Western Film*. Urbana: University of Illinois Press, 1980.

Lindenberger, Thomas. "Divided but Not Disconnected: Germany as a Border Region of the Cold War." In *Divided but Not Disconnected: German Experiences of the Cold War*. Tobias Hochscherf, Christoph Laucht, and Andrew Plowman, eds. New York: Berghahn Books, 2010.

Linkemeyer, Gerhard. *Was hat Hitler mit Karl May zu tun?* Ubstadt: KMG-Presse, 1987.

Lorenz, Erik. *Liselotte Welskopf-Henrich und die Indianer: Eine Biographie*. Chemnitz: Palisander, 2009.

Loy, R. Philip. *Westerns in a Changing America, 1955–2000*. Jefferson, North Carolina: McFarland & Company, Inc., Publishers, 2004.

Lubbers, Klaus. "'So Motley a Dramatis Personae': Transatlantic Encounters in James Fenimore Cooper's *The Pioneers*." In *Transatlantic Encounters: Studies in European-American Relations*. Udo J. Hebel and Karl Ortseifen, eds. Trier: Wissenschaftlicher Verlag, 1995.

Lutz, Hartmut. *Approaches: Essays in Native North American Studies and Literature*. Augsburg: Wissner, 2002.

Lutz, Hartmut. "German Indianthusiasm: A Socially Constructed German National(ist) Myth." In *Germans and Indians: Fantasies, Encounters, Projections*.

Colin G. Calloway, Gerd Gemünden, and Suzanne Zantop, eds. Lincoln: University of Nebraska Press, 2002.

Lutz, Hartmut. *"Indianer" und "Native Americans." Zur social- und literarhistorischen Vermittlung eines Stereotyps.* New York: Georg Olms Verlag, 1985.

Maase, Kaspar. *Bravo Amerika: Erkundungen zur Jugendkultur der Bundesrepublik in den fünfziger Jahren.* Hamburg: Junius, 1992.

Major, Patrick and Osmond, Jonathan, eds. *The Workers' and Peasants' State: Communism and Society in East Germany under Ulbricht 1945–1971.* New York: Manchester University Press, 2002.

Maltby, Richard and Vasey, Ruth. " 'Temporary American Citizens': Cultural Anxieties and Industrial Strategies in the Americanization of European Cinema." In *"Film Europe" and "Film America": Cinema, Commerce and Cultural Exchange 1920–1939.* Andrew Higson and Richard Maltby, eds. Exeter: University of Exeter Press, 1999.

Manvell, Roger and Fraenkel, Heinrich. *The German Cinema.* New York: Praeger Publishers, 1971.

Markowitz, Harvey, ed. *American Indian Biographies.* Pasadena: Salem Press, Inc., 1999.

May, Karl. *Winnetou I–III.* Gütersloh: Bertelsmann, 1964, kindle edition.

McCormick, Richard. "Memory and Commerce, Gender and Restoration: Woflgang Staudte's Roses for the State Prosecutor (1959) and West German Film in the 1950s." In *The Miracle Years: A Cultural History of West Germany, 1949–1968.* Hanna Schissler, ed. Princeton: Princeton University Press, 2001.

McVeigh, Stephen. *The American Western.* Edinburgh: Edinburgh University Press, 2007.

Michalski, Czeslaw. *Western I jego bohaterowie.* Warszawa: Wydawnictwa Artystyczne I Filmowe, 1972.

Misch, Juergen. *Der letzte Kriegspfad: Der Schicksalskampf der Sioux und Apachen.* Stuttgart: Union Verlag Stuttgart, 1970.

Miskolczy, Ambrus. *Hitler's Library.* New York: Central European University Press Budapest, 2003.

Moeller, Robert G. "The Politics of the Past in the 1950s: Rhetorics of Victimization in East and West Germany." In *Germans as Victims: Remembering the Past in Contemporary Germany.* Bill Niven, ed. New York: Palgrave Macmillan, 2006.

Moltke, Johannes von. *No Place Like Home: Locations of Heimat in German Cinema.* Ann Arbor: University of Michigan Press, 2010.

Mommsen, Wolfgang J. "The Germans and Their Past: History and Political Consciousness in the Federal Republic of Germany." In *"German History after 1945."* In *Coping with the Past: Germany and Austria after 1945.* Kathy Harms, Lutz R. Reuter, and Volker Duerr, eds. Madison: The University of Wisconsin Press, 2005.

Morning Storm, J. Boyd. *The American Indian Warrior: Native Americans in Modern U.S. Warfare.* Manhattan: Sunflower University Press, 2004.

Mulroy, Kevin, ed. *Western Amerykanski: Polish Poster Art & the Western.* Seattle: University of Washington Press, 1999.

Munn, Michael. *John Wayne: The Man behind the Myth.* New York: New American Library, 2003.

Naughton, Leonie. *That Was the Wild East: Film, Culture, Unification, and the "New" Germany.* Ann Arbor: The University of Michigan Press, 2002.

Niven, Bill, ed. *Germans as Victims: Remembering the Past in Contemporary Germany.* New York: Palgrave Macmillan, 2006.

Nolan, Mary. "American in the German Imagination." In *Transactions, Transgressions, Transformations: American Culture in Western Europe and Japan.* Heide Fehrenbach and Uta G. Poiger, eds. New York: Berghahn Books, 2000.

Nolte, Ernst. "Between Historical Legend and Revisionism? The Third Reich in Perspective of 1980." In *Forever in the Shadow of Hitler? Original Documents of the Historikerstreit. The Controversy Concerning the Singularity of the Holocaust.* James Knowlton, ed. Atlantic Highlands: Humanities Press, 1993.

Otterness, Philip. *Becoming German: The 1709 Palatine Migration to New York.* Ithaca: Cornell University Press, 2004.

Otto, Uli and Otto, Till. *Auf den Spuren der Söhne der großen Bärin.* Regensburg: Kern Verlag, 2001.

Peipp, Matthias and Springer, Bernhard. *Edle Wilde Rote Teufel: Indianer im Film.* München: Wilhelm Heyne Verlag, 1997.

Pells, Richard. "American Culture Abroad: The European Experience since 1945." In *Cultural Transmissions and Receptions: American Mass Culture in Europe.* R. Kroes, Robert W., and D.F.J. Bosscher, eds. Amsterdam: VU University Press, 1993.

Penny, H. Glenn. "Illustrating America: Images of the North American West in German Periodicals, 1825–1890." In *I Like America: Fictions of the Wild West.* New York: Prestel, 2007.

Petzel, Michael. "Deutsche Helden: Karl May im Film." In *Karl May im Film: eine Bilddokumentation.* Christian Unucka, ed. Dachau: Vereinigte Verlagsgesellschaften, 1980.

Petzel, Michael. *Karl May. Old Shatterhand: Film-Bildbuch.* Karl-May-Verlag, 2003.

Philip, Loy R. *Westerns in a Changing America, 1955–2000.* Jefferson, North Carolina: McFarland & Company, Inc., Publishers, 2004.

Pinson, Koppel S. *Modern Germany: Its History and Civilization.* New York: The Macmillan Company, 1964.

Poiger, Uta. "A New, 'Western' Hero? Reconstructing German Masculinity in the 1950s." In *The Miracle Years: A Cultural History of West Germany, 1949–1968.* Hanna Schissler, ed. Princeton: Princeton University Press, 2001.

Poiger, Uta. "Fear and Fascination: American Popular Culture in a Divided Germany, 1945–1968." In *Kazaaam! Splat! Ploof! The American Impact on European Popular Culture since 1945.* Sabrina P. Ramet and Gordana O. Crnkovic, eds. Boston: Rowman & Littlefield Publishers, Inc., 2003.

Pommerin, Reiner. "Some Remarks on the Cultural History of the Federal Republic of Germany." In *Culture in the Federal Republic of Germany, 1945–1995.* Reiner Pommerin, ed. Herndon: Berg, 1996.

Postone, Moishe. "After the Holocaust: History and Identity in West Germany." In "German History after 1945." In *Coping with the Past: Germany and Austria after 1945.* Kathy Harms, Lutz R. Reuter, and Volker Duerr, eds. Madison: The University of Wisconsin Press, 2005.

Prowe, Diethelm. "German Democratization as Conservative Restabilization: The Impact of American Policy." In *American Policy and the Reconstruction of West*

Germany, 1945–1955. Jeffry M. Diefendorf, Axel Frohn, and Hermann-Josef Rupieper, eds. New York: Cambridge University Press, 1993.

Ramet, Sabrina P. and Crnkovic, Gordana P., eds. *Kazaaam! Splat! Ploof! The American Impact on European Popular Culture since 1945.* Boston: Rowman & Littlefield Publishers, Inc., 2003.

Rieder, Hans Rudolf. *Langspeer: Eine Selbstdarstellung des letzten Indianers. Haeuptling Bueffelkind Langspeer.* Leipzig: Paul List Verlag, 1929.

Roseman, Mark. "Division and Stability: The Federal Republic of Germany, 1949–1989." In *German History since 1800.* Mary Fulbrook, ed. New York: Arnold, 1997.

Rosenstone, Robert A. *History on Film/Film on History.* Harlow: Pearson Longman, 2006.

Russell, Thaddeus. *A Renegade History of the United States.* New York: Free Press, 2010.

Sammons, Jeffrey L. *Ideology, Mimesis, Fantasy: Charles Sealsfield, Friedrich Gerstäcker, Karl May, and Other German Novelists of America.* Chapel Hill: The University of North Carolina Press, 1998.

Sammons, Jeffrey L. "Nineteenth-Century German Representations of Indians from Experience." In *Germans and Indians: Fantasies, Encounters, Projections.* Colin G. Calloway, Gerd Gemuenden, and Suzanne Zantop, eds. Lincoln: University of Nebraska Press, 2002.

Schenk, Ralf, ed. *Das zweite Leben der Filmstadt Babelsberg: DEFA-Spielfilme 1946–1992.* Berlin: Filmmuseum Potsdam, 1994.

Schissler, Hanna, ed. *The Miracle Years: A Cultural History of West Germany, 1949–1968.* Princeton: Princeton University Press, 2001.

Schroeder, Aribert. "They Lived Together with Their Dogs and Horses: 'Indian Copy' in West German Newspapers 1968–1982." In *Indians and Europe: An Interdisciplinary Collection of Essays.* Christian F. Feest, ed. Lincoln: University of Nebraska Press, 1999.

Schuchalter, Jerry. *Narratives of America and the Frontier in Nineteenth-Century German Literature.* New York: Peter Lang, 2000.

Sears, John F. "Bierstadt, Buffalo Bill, and the Wild West in Europe." In *Cultural Transmissions and Receptions: American Mass Culture in Europe.* R. Kroes, Robert W. Rydell, and D.F.J. Bosscher, eds. Amsterdam: VU University Press, 1993.

Seesslen, Georg, Schifferle, Hans, and Blumenberg, Hans-Christoph, eds. *Um Sie Weht Der Hauch Des Todes: Der Italowestern – die Geschichte eines Genres.* Koeln: Schnitt Verlag, 1999.

Shandley, Robert R. *Rubble Film: German Cinema in the Shadow of the Third Reich.* Philadelphia: Temple University Press, 2001.

Shaw, Tony. *Hollywood's Cold War.* Amherst: University of Massachusetts Press, 2007.

Shiach, Don. *Stewart Granger: The Last of the Swashbucklers.* London: Aurum, 2005.

Sieg, Katrin. "Ethnic Drag and National Identity: Multicultural Crises, Crossings, and Interventions." In *The Imperialist Imagination: German Colonialism and Its Legacy.* Sara Friedrichsmeyer, Sara Lennox, and Susanne Zantop, eds. Ann Arbor: The University of Michigan Press, 1998.

Slotkin, Richard. *Gunfighter Nation: Myth of the Frontier in Twentieth-Century America.* Norman: University of Oklahoma Press, 1998.

Stackelberg, Roderick. *Hitler's Germany.* New York: Routledge, 1999.

Stark, Isolde, ed. *Elisabeth Charlotte Welskopf und die alte Geschichte in der DDR.* Stuttgart: Franz Steiner Verlag, 2005.

Steinbach, Peter. "Widerstandsforschung im politischen Spannungsfeld." In *Widerstand gegen den Nationalsozialismus.* Peter Steinbach and Johannes Tuchel, eds. Berlin: Akademie Verlag, 1994.

Stephan, Alexander, ed. *The Americanization of Europe: Culture, Diplomacy, and Anti-Americanism after 1945.* New York: Berghahn Books, 2006.

Stern, Frank. "Film in the 1950s: Passing Images of Guilt and Responsibility." In *The Miracle Years: A Cultural History of West Germany, 1949–1968.* Hanna Schissler, ed. Princeton: Princeton University Press, 2001.

Stückrath, Fritz and Schottmayer, Georg. *Fernsehen und Grossstadtjugend.* Braunschweig: Georg Westermann Verlag, 1967.

Tatlock, Lynne and Erlin, Matt, eds. *German Culture in Nineteenth-Century America: Reception, Adaptation, Transformation.* New York: Camden House, 2005.

Thomas, Nigel. "Germany and Europe." In *Modern Germany: Politics, Society and Culture.* Peter James, ed. New York: Routledge, 1998.

Toland, John. *Adolf Hitler.* Garden City: Doubleday & Company, Inc., 1976.

Tyrrell, Ian. *Transnational Nation: United States History in Global Perspective since 1789.* New York: Palgrave Macmillan, 2007.

Unucka, Christine, ed. *Karl May im Film: Eine Bilde Dokumentation.* Dachau: Vereinigte Verlagsgesellschaften, 1980.

Versini, Marie. *Ich war Winnetous Schwester.* Bamberg: Karl May Verlag, 2003.

Waite, Robert G.L. *The Psychopathic God: Adolf Hitler.* New York: Basic Books, Inc., Publishers, 1977.

Weber, Reinhard. *Artur Brauners Old Shatterhand.* Landshut: Fachverlag für Filmliteratur, 2002.

Wegnleitner, Reinhold and May, Elaine. *Here, There, and Everywhere: The Foreign Politics of American Popular Culture.* Hanover: University Press of New England, 2000.

Whaley, Joachim. "The German Lands before 1815." In *German History since 1800.* Mary Fulbrook, ed. New York: Arnold, 1997.

Whitfield, Stephen J. *The Culture of the Cold War.* Baltimore: The Johns Hopkins University Press, 1996.

Wierling, Dorothee. "Mission to Happiness: The Cohort of 1949 and the Making of East and West Germans." In *The Miracle Years: A Cultural History of West Germany, 1949–1968.* Hanna Schissler, ed. Princeton: Princeton University Press, 2001.

Wischnewski, Klaus. "Träumer und Gewohnliche Leute 1966 bis 1979." In *Das zweite Leben der Filmstadt Babelsberg: DEFA-Spielfilme 1946–1992.* Ralf Schenk, ed. Berlin: Filmmuseum Potsdam, 1994.

Wittlinger, Ruth. *German National Identity in the Twenty-First Century: A Different Republic after All?* New York: Palgrave Macmillan, 2010.

Wittlinger, Ruth. "Taboo or Tradition? The 'German as Victims' Theme in the federal Republic until the mid-1990s." In *Germans as Victims: Remembering the Past in Contemporary Germany.* Bill Niven, ed. New York: Palgrave Macmillan, 2006.

Zantop, Suzanne. "Close Encounters: Deutsche and Indianer." In *Germans and Indians: Fantasies, Encounters, Projections.* Colin G. Calloway, Gerd Gemünden, and Suzanne Zantop, eds. Lincoln: University of Nebraska Press, 2002.

Zatlin, Jonathan R. *The Currency of Socialism: Money and Political Culture in East Germany.* Cambridge: Cambridge University Press, 2007.

Zyla, Wolodymyr T. and Aycock, Wendell M., eds. *Ethnic Literatures since 1776: The Many Voices of America.* Lubbock: Texas Tech Press, 1978.

A Literary History of the American West. Fort Worth: Texas Christian University Press, 1987.

Articles

Cook, Colleen. "Germany's Wild West Author: A Researcher's Guide to Karl May." In *German Studies Review*, Vol. 5, No. 1 (February 1982).

Cracroft, Richard. "The American West of Karl May." In *American Quarterly*, Vol. 19, No. 2, Part 1 (Summer, 1967).

Dernen, Rolf. "Grün-goldene Erfolgsgeschichte – 90 Jahre Karl-May-Verlag." *Karl May & Co.*, Nr. 92 (June, 2003).

Fitz, Karsten. "Screen Indians in the EFL-Classroom: Transnational Perspectives." In *American Studies Journal*, Nr. 51 (2008).

Gerd Gemünden. "Between Karl May and Karl Marx: The DEFA Indianerfilme (1965–1983)." In *New German Critique*, No. 82, East German Film (Winter, 2001).

Harner, Ariana. "Values in Conflict: The Singing Marxist." In *Colorado Heritage* (Winter 1999).

Herb, Guntram H. "Double Vision: Territorial Strategies in the Construction of National Identities in Germany, 1949–1979." In *Annals of the Association of American Geographers*, Vol. 94, No. 1 (March 2004).

Mann, Klaus. "Cowboy Mentor of the Führer." In *The Living Age* (November 1940).

Penny, H. Glenn. "Red Power: Liselotte Welskopf-Henrich and Indian Activist Networks in East and West Germany." *Central European History* (2008).

Schneider, Tassilo. "Finding a New Heimat in the Wild West: Karl May and the German Western of the 1960s." In *Journal of Film and Video*, Vol. 47, No. 1–3 (Spring–Fall 1995).

Tutush, Danica. "The Strange Life and Legacy of Karl May." In *Cowboys & Indians*, (September 1999).

"Ein Stück deutsch-deutsche Geschichte: eine Sonderausstellung widmet sich den Indianerfilmen in Ost und West." *Karl May & Co.*, Nr. 92, 26–27.

"Ich bin ein Cowboy: Modern Germany's Favorite Author Will Come as a Surprise." *The Economist* (May 24, 2001).

"Vom Filme über die Bühne zum Hörspiel: Interview mit Chris Howland." *Karl May & Co.*, Nr. 92.

"Zu unserem Titelbild: 'von der Barker-Familie autorisiert.'" *Karl May & Co.*, Nr. 92 (June 2003).

Unpublished works

Muller, Elsa Christina. "A Cultural Study of the Sioux Novels of Liselotte Welskopf-Henrich." PhD diss., 1995.

Shealy Jr., Gregory P. "Buffalo Bill in Germany: Gender, Heroism, and the American West in Imperial Germany." Master's thesis, University of Wisconsin-Madison, 2003.

Electronic resources

www.beltz.de
www.britannica.com
www.documentarchiv.de
www.dradio.de
www.hca.uni-heidelberg.de
www.heritage.org
www.heroldmusic.com
www.imdb.com
www.jewishvirtuallibrary.org
www.karl-may-magazin.de
www.movieposterdb.com

Index